THE U2 READER

A Quarter Century of Commentary, Criticism, and Reviews

Compiled and Edited by
HANK BORDOWITZ

Foreword by
John Swenson

Published by Hal Leonard Corporation
7777 West Bluemound Road
P.O. Box 13819
Milwaukee, WI 53213, USA

Trade Book Division Editorial Offices:
151 West 46th Street, 8th Floor
New York, NY 10036

Visit Hal Leonard online at www.halleonard.com

Library of Congress Cataloging-in-Publication Data

The U2 reader : a quarter century of commentary, criticism, and reviews / compiled and edited by Hank Bordowitz ; foreword by John Swenson.-- 1st ed.
p. cm.

Includes index.

ISBN 0-634-03832-X

1. U2 (Musical group) 2. Rock groups--Ireland--Biography.
I. Bordowitz, Hank.
ML421.U2U15 2003
782.42166'092'2--dc21

2003001816

Printed in the United States of America

First Edition

10 9 8 7 6 5 4 3 2 1

This Book is for Billy,
who was born the day after my first solo flight came out.

I also dedicate it to my ever-patient, ever-loving wife Caren,
my Ray of Hope, and my two older sons, Mike and Larry.

Contents

Acknowledgements

I must thank the following people, without whom this book would not have happened:

Jim Fitzgerald, my agent, who was responsible for so much great rock reading when he was an editor at St. Martins. He is one of the most musically inclined people in publishing, and I am truly blessed to have him in my corner.

Ben Schafer formerly of Hal Leonard, who bought an essay on Vince Guaraldi for a folio and then asked, "So what else have you got?"

John Cerullo at Hal Leonard, whom I've known and written for for twenty years, on and off.

The cast and crew at the Suffern Free Public Library, The Baruch College Library, The Hunter College Library and the Donnell, Lincoln Center, Main Research and Midtown branches of the New York Public Library, who were all extraordinarily helpful in researching this book.

All the publishers and writers of the source material for this book.

Rashas Weber of @U2, an excellent website that made some of this research easier and other bits possible.

Richard Carlin, my former editor at Schirmer, who actually instigated this project several years ago.

Mark Shulman, who got me critical information on venues.

Mike at Mr. Press for all the rush jobs.

Kerry Nolan and Jon Vena, my designated readers.

Thank you to the following authors and publishers for the materials in this book:

"Dublin Boys Top of Pops!" from the *Evening Press*. Reprinted by permission.

"Getting into U2" © Paulo Hewitt/Melody Maker/IPC Syndication

"U2" reprinted by permission of Tim Sommer.

"Operation Uplift" reprinted by permission of Scott Isler.

"U2 at War with Mediocrity" reprinted with the kind permission of Ethlie Ann Vare.

"Rocking with U2" from *Seventeen* magazine. Reprinted by permission.

"Once Upon a Time…" from *Star Hits* January 1, 1987.

"U2" from SCHOLASTIC UPDATE, December 4, 1987 issue. Copyright © 1987 by Scholastic Inc. Reprinted by permission of Scholastic Inc.

"America's Sexiest Men" from United Press International. Reprinted by permission.

"YMCA, U2?" reprinted from *The Advocate*, February 18, 1998. Copyright 1998 by Liberation Publications Inc. All rights reserved.

"U2: Keeping the Rock Faith with *Unforgettable Fire*" Wall Street Journal. Eastern Edition by Pam Lambert. Copyright 1985 by DOW JONES & CO INC. Reproduced with permission of DOW JONES & CO INC via Copyright Clearance Center.

"Band on the Run: U2 Soars with a Top Album, a Hot Tour and Songs of Spirit and Conscience" © 1987 TIME Inc. reprinted by permission.

"Luminous Times: U2 Wrestle with Their Moment of Glory" from *Musician*, October 1, 1987.

"Hating U2" from *Spin*, January 1, 1989.

"Me2" originally appeared in *The New Yorker.* Reprinted by permission of Elizabeth Wurtzel.

"Eno: The Story Behind *Original Soundtracks 1*" © Knight Ridder/Tribune Media Services. Reprinted with permission.

"The Future Sound of U2" originally appeared in the March 1997 issue of SPIN. Reprinted by permission of the author and SPIN.

"U2's Crash: Why *Pop* Flops" by Dave Marsh. Reprinted with permission from the August 25, 1997 issue of *The Nation*.

"Raw Power: Never Mind the Bollocks, Here's U2—and They Want Their Rock and Roll Crown Back" reprinted by permission of Anthony DeCurtis.

"Keeping the Peace" reprinted by permission of *ASCAP Playback.*

"Assessment: U2, Their Vague Majesties of Rock" © SLATE/Distributed by United Feature Syndicate, Inc.

"Bono's World: Part Rocker, Part Policy Wonk, U2's Singer Calls Himself 'The Thinking Man's Perry Como'" from *People* magazine. Reprinted by permission.

"Bono to the Rescue" appears courtesy of *The Onion.* All rights reserved.

"Washington Diarist: Actually" from *The New Republic*. Reprinted by permission.

"U2 Flips Zoo TV Channel to the Horrors of Bosnia" copyrighted VNU Business Media Inc. Used with permission from *Billboard* magazine.

"Trying to Do a Damned Thing," *Harvard Magazine*, July–August 2001, pp. 58–61.

"Bono" first appeared in Salon.com, at http://www.Salon.com. An online version remains in the Salon archives. Reprinted with permission.

"Bono Turns Up the Political Heat" from *George*. Reprinted by permission.

"Stop In The Name Of Love" from *Newsweek*, December 31, 1984 © 1984 Newsweek, Inc. All rights reserved. Reprinted by permission.

"In Sight" reprinted with permission of America Press, Inc. © 1987. All Rights Reserved. For subscription information, call 1-800-627-9533 or visit www.americamagazine.org.

"The Scripture According to Bono" © Scripps Howard News Service

"The Spiritual Journey of U2" copyright 2002 Religion News Service. Used by permission.

"U2's Hi-Tech Tent Revival" reprinted with permission of America Press, Inc. © 2002. All Rights Reserved. For subscription information, call 1-800-627-9533 or visit www.americamagazine.org.

"The New U2" from *On Being,* November 1, 1993.

"Honesty Goes out of Control" from *Sounds* magazine December 8, 1979.

"Irish U2, A Young Quartet, Plays at the Ritz" Copyright © 1981 by The New York Times Co. Reprinted with permission.

"U2: Peace with Honor" from *The Village Voice* May 24, 1983.

"U2 Starts National Tour on a Political Note" Copyright © 1987 by The New York Times Co. Reprinted with permission.

"*Achtung Baby*, It's U2 in Paris" from *Financial Times*, May 9, 1992, reprinted by permission.

"Reluctant Rock Star: How U2's Adam Clayton Learned to Play—and Conquer the World Onstage" from Bass Player magazine. Reprinted by permission.

"Perusing the U2 Catalog" by Jim DeRogatis from *Chicago Sun-Times*, May 6, 2001. Reprinted with special permission from the Chicago Sun-Times, Inc. © 2002.

"U2: Aiming for Number 1" © 1981, *The Washington Post*. Reprinted with permission.

"U2 Takes the Fifth" reprinted by permission of John Pareles.

"U2's Inspired War" from *Stereo Review* August 1983, reprinted by permission.

"*Under a Blood Red Sky*" reprinted by permission of Robert Christgau.

"*The Unforgettable Fire*" from *ROCK!* magazine, January 1, 1984.

"Love and Friendship, and You're All Invited" © 1987 VNU Business Media, Inc. Used with permission.

"Elvis is Alive?" copyright © 1988 Village Voice Media, Inc. Reprinted with the permission of *The Village Voice*.

"U2 Is Back out on Edge with Bracing Baby" from *The Hartford Courant*, November 19, 1991, reprinted by permission.

"U2 *Achtung Baby*" from *Stereo Review* February 1992. Reprinted by permission.

"*Zooropa*" from *Stereo Review* October 1993. Reprinted by permission.

"Millennial Dancing" reprinted by permission of Nicholas Jennings.

"*Pop*" first appeared in Salon.com, at http://www.Salon.com. An online version remains in the Salon archives. Reprinted with permission.

"U2: *The Best of 1980–1990*" copyright © 1998 by *Playboy*. Reprinted with permission. All rights reserved.

"U2 Comes Back from the Future" by J.D. Considine, *The Baltimore Sun*, reprinted by permission.

"Is This Desire?" originally appeared in the November 2000 issue of SPIN. Reprinted by permission of the author and SPIN.

"U2: Rattle and Ho-Hum" reprinted by permission of Armond White.

"U2 Hits the Road in *Rattle and Hum*" Copyright © 1988 by The New York Times Co. Reprinted with permission.

"U2' s U-Turn" copyright 1992 *Los Angeles Times*. Reprinted with permission.

"*Achtung Baby* Video Recording Reviews" reprinted by permission of Marianne Meyer.

"U2's Home Video *Stop Sellafield*: Good Music and a Message" Boston Globe by Steve Morse. Copyright 1993 by GLOBE NEWSPAPER CO (MA). Reproduced with permission of GLOBE NEWSPAPER CO (MA) via Copyright Clearance Center.

"U2 on the Tube—The Rock Superstars Conquer Prime Time" from TV Guide, April 26, 1997, reprinted with permission from TV Guide Magazine Group, Inc., © 1997 TV Guide Magazine Group, Inc. TV GUIDE is a registered trademark of TV Guide Magazine, Group, Inc.

"Do You Know This Man?" from *Select*, June 1, 1993.

"*The Joshua Tree*" originally appeared in *Playboy* magazine. Reprinted by permission of Bruce Hornsby.

"The Ground Beneath My Feet" © 2001 by Salman Rushdie, reprinted with permission of The Wylie Agency, Inc.

"U2 Q & A" from *LIVE!* magazine. Reprinted by permission.

"U2 at Madison Square Garden" from www.moby-online.com, reprinted by permission of MCT Management.

"McGuinness on the 'Principle' of U2 Management" copyrighted VNU Business Media Inc. Used with permission from *Billboard* magazine.

"Paul McGuinness: How the Fifth Man Turned Empire Builder" from *Music Business International*, October 1, 1997.

"Iovine Learns U2's All About El-E-Va-Tion to a New Demographic" reprinted with permission from the March 25, 2002 issue of *Advertising Age*. Copyright, Crain Communications Inc. 2002.

Preface

A few of us got together to watch the Super Bowl early in 2002. I was really looking forward to spending time with my friends, perhaps even seeing a good football game (although the Super Bowl is so often anti-climactic) and seeing U2 at halftime. The NFL had scored a coup in booking the band in the wake of their triumphant year and a half on the road supporting *All That You Can't Leave Behind*. They had reclaimed their place as one of the greatest rock bands ever after a decade that found them exploring, but alienating a lot of people with techno sounds and mirror-ball lemons.

Regardless, their recent tour had not been without its share of daring—yet tasteful—special effects. A friend who attended a show following the September 11 terrorists attacks reported that he was brought to tears when the names of people martyred in the attacks suddenly started scrolling behind drummer Larry Mullen, Jr. When the band broke into "Where the Streets Have No Name" during halftime and the names were again scrolled, I understood my friend's reaction. It was a gutsy statement for the band to make, but it was done so tastefully and sincerely that it was hard not to be moved.

Suddenly I felt that I'd been transported back in time twenty years to the end of U2's first American tour, which began in the Ritz in New York. That tour ended about three blocks away at the recently renamed Palladium (a couple of months before, when I had seen The Jam play there, it was called The Academy of Music). The Ritz was a club that held 1,500 people, max; but the Palladium was a sit-down theater with a capacity of about 3,500.

I had been hearing the U2 buzz for months, even before the Ritz show. It started when the British publication *NME*, which landed in U.S. newsstands just days after hitting London's, proclaimed U2's music to be "transcendentally eclectic, refreshingly realistic, naively passionate"; and that was just in one paragraph. While nonetheless compared to bands such as The Boomtown Rats and Virgin Prunes (more for geographical reasons than anything musical), the consensus on U2 was equivalent to Jon Landau's fifteen years before on Bruce Springsteen: "I have seen rock and roll future..."

Seeing U2 in concert at that early Palladium show, I felt what I imagine the people who first saw The Who at Hammersmith in 1966 or Springsteen at the Bottom Line in 1975 must have felt like. The show was epic, powerful, and exuberant. Bono prowled the stage like a frontman born; The Edge pumped even more energy out of his guitar, making better use of double-stops than anyone since Chuck Berry. The sound they made was mammoth, swathed in echo and energy. It sounded like nothing else before or since. When the show let out, over 3,000 people wandered up Fourteenth Street, drained, dazed, happy, and amazed.

Yet no one could have anticipated the extraordinary rise of U2—from a group originally lumped in with British neo-psychedelic revival bands like Echo and the Bunnymen to the greatest band in the world.

The articles in this book were put together so as to attempt to shine a light through many of the facets of U2, one or two facets at a time. Reflecting the periods in which they were written, the articles offer insight and context that few biographies could. Working like a paint-by-numbers cubist, I've tried to create a picture by balancing the parts. I hope I've succeeded.

Hank Bordowitz
Suffern, NY
Summer 2002

Foreword: The Last Great Rock Band

John Swenson

It's 2002 and we are in the post-rock era. There are no major rock groups left who haven't been around for a decade. Good second-tier bands, certainly, and a lot of minor-label bands. But the record industry is no longer built on rock, and unless we are DEVO, after all, it's not going to happen all over again.

U2 stands tall as the last of the great rock bands, informed by the spirit of the punk revolution of the mid 1970s, but inspired by the heroic gestures of the 1960s rockers who tried to make rock the medium for the self-realization and spiritual growth of a generation.

U2 was the most exciting rock band to emerge in the 1980s, an era when rock made its most damaging compromise with history by turning itself over to the visual-oriented needs of a "music" industry bent on becoming the New Hollywood via the promotional might of the fledgling MTV.

U2 picked up the banner dropped by rock's greatest live band, The Who, after the death of Keith Moon, a blow from which The Who never fully recovered. Like The Who, U2 matched a crushingly high-intensity, hard rock delivery with uncompromising ideals.

"Rock 'n' roll is full of lies," declared the young leader, Bono, who was unafraid to take on the past and eager to carve his own image onto the future.

The band's energy and control of live dynamics throughout its career have been formidable. As U2 became more and more popular, moving alongside The Rolling Stones in terms of stadium-level clout in the 1990s, the band rose to the occasion with the staggering Zoo TV tour, a multimedia extravaganza that set a new level for stadium-level productions. When that concept itself became a dead end, the band scaled back its dimensions—precisely on its most recent tour, and even then managed to pull off the most exciting rock performance ever staged during the Super Bowl halftime show. Bono's sense of knowing exactly what to bring to each dramatically different situation is a mark of true genius.

No punk group ever kicked harder than U2, but the band showed plenty of musical savvy as it played with virtuosity and arrangement intelligence. They knew rock had to be intense and visceral, but that didn't mean it had to be self-consciously stupid.

Nevertheless, punk taught the young band unforgettable lessons in the core value of rock energy.

"The ethic of '76," as Bono once called it, "which I really believed in, was the realism, the passion."

But U2 was going to be different.

"We weren't a punk band," Bono insisted. "We were loud and aggressive, so people said, 'Yeah, a punk band,' but we called ourselves U2 to take ourselves out of the usual category of the Sex Pistols, Clash, even Led Zeppelin—so that people would hear the name and say, 'What sort of band would that be, then?'"

Now the name is a household world, appropriated by countless Irish bars where the jukebox is stocked with CDs by the greatest of the Irish rock bands. Among other accomplishments, U2 turned the Irish popular music industry into one of the key elements of the economic revival nicknamed "The Celtic Tiger."

Bono hooked up with bassist Adam Clayton and guitarist The Edge by responding to a notice on the message board at Mount Temple School in Dublin placed by drummer Larry Mullen, who was looking to form a group. Only Mullen had been in a band, so the young rockers were free to develop a unique sound.

"We studied under a Renaissance music expert at school," Bono offered. "A lot of ideas must have come from that interest."

The band's first album, *Boy*, was quickly recognized as the most progressive rock of its time when it came out in late 1980. The record set the band apart from its punk contemporaries through the dense, nearly art-rock production style of Steve Lillywhite. Few groups have ever matched the sonic intensity of U2 with such mystical, space-rock arrangements.

U2 took London by storm. Bruce Springsteen hailed the group as one of his favorites and attended a London show.

By the time of the second album, *October*, the band showed such maturation that it was impossible to tell how far they might be able to progress. They were coining a new, dramatically personal rock style with mystical songs like "Gloria" and "Rejoice," and Bono's soaring tone shouting anthemic calls over the exciting rhythm leads fashioned by The Edge on guitar.

In 1982 U2 released *War*, an album that focused the band's concerns on Northern Ireland and the global tension that accompanied the Falklands/Malvinas war. Those general political ideas were balanced against Bono's own concerns about individual morality. "New Year's Day" and "Sunday Bloody Sunday" were a different kind of call to arms. The album was a commercial breakthrough, reaching Number One in England and going gold in America. During the U.S. tour that followed the release of *War*, U2 recorded a live concert at Denver's Red Rocks amphitheater. *Under a Blood Red Sky* captured the grandeur of U2's live sound and the amazing interaction with its audience.

U2 had left punk behind for good.

"I think punk rock may have left a bad taste in people's mouths," said Bono. "The fact that the Sex Pistols turned out to be an idea rather than a real band—and they were an idea, they were part of Malcolm McLaren and not that into what they were doing—combined with trendiness and faddism that is associated with modern music—I think it made a lot of people nervous."

Bono's lyrics personalized the politics, avoiding the take-it-or-leave-it demagoguery in favor of a plea for people to understand his feelings. He's a writer with a sense of purpose inspired by a humanist vision that makes his songs comment on each other until live concerts become a summation of the band's meaning; each album and tour updating the vision.

On *The Unforgettable Fire* the band set out to establish a new sound for itself. Producer Brian Eno was brought in to work with the band, shifting their focus just enough to allow musical risks and break new ground. "Pride (In the Name of Love)," Bono's tribute to a personal hero, Martin Luther King, is the perfect match of inspired lyric and heroic music: a truly shared vision from both Bono and The Edge. The emotional intensity contained in that song and played in various ways throughout …*Fire* charged the group's stage show with an even greater dynamic range than before. Brooding, atmospheric numbers like "MLK," "A Sort of Homecoming" and "4th of July" allowed the live performances to pit low, humming lullabies against high-flying rockers.

With *The Joshua Tree*, U2 pushed on to even greater heights. The album opened with three of the band's most emotionally powerful songs: "Where the Streets Have No Name," "I Still Haven't Found What I'm Looking For," and "With or Without You." You could write a classic opera around material this strong. "Where the Streets Have No Name" is the quintessential U2 song—a stirring mix of guitar flourishes, strong, romantic lyrics, and the Big Beat. "I Still Haven't Found What I'm Looking For" is one of the greatest pop songs of the twentieth century, expressing the spiritual and aesthetic quest that lies at the heart of what it means to be human, echoing the distant words of Homer, Goethe, Joyce, Shakespeare, and Yeats.

Superstardom is always followed by consolidation, which is where the live extravaganza of *Rattle and Hum* fits in, but the consolidation rarely leads to greater achievement. Not so with U2, as the band forged on courageously in the 1990s to mount the epochal "Zoo TV" tour in support of *Achtung Baby*, an album studded with such great compositions as "Even Better than the Real Thing" and "Mysterious Ways." The distorted crackle of The Edge's guitar on the opening track, "Zoo Station," and Bono's textured vocals, were a clear indication that the band was still in the process of evolving its sound.

Ever responsive to their fans, U2 attempted to respond to the widespread popularity of electronic dance music in the 1990s, but the sonic experiments of *Zooropa* and *Pop* inevitably left the band members wondering if they had gone off the rails. Bono mockingly acknowledged the kitsch elements the group was toying with by announcing the *Pop* tour dates at a press conference held in a K-Mart. In retrospect, it's amusing that the icon for the *Pop* tour was a giant lemon.

The members of U2 were capable of laughing at their own foibles, but they used going over the top with *Pop* as a cleansing experience and returned to doing what they did best: writing great songs and playing meaningful rock music without apologies. They are the only rock band from their generation to release an album after Y2K that can hold its own with their best work—the beautifully expansive *All That You Can't Leave Behind*, with its magnificent "Walk On," and the strangely prescient hymn to a city that was about to be dealt an unimaginable blow, "New York."

So here we are, back in the new millennium, contemplating the post-rock era. U2 still waves the banner, refusing to lip synch at the Super Bowl, demonstrating the awesome power that can still be summoned by this music in the proper hands. They are the last great rock band.

John Swenson

CHAPTER

1

AMONG PUNKS

They came together in the late '70s (you'll read the story of Larry Mullen's bulletin board message and the formation of U2 several times in this book) at the height of punk, inspired by the Clash and their do-it-yourself approach to music. Some of their earliest notices reveal that reviewers and critics didn't quite know what to make of these Irish boys who were set on nothing short of global domination from the git-go.

In retrospect, it's interesting to note U2's durability compared to the peers to whom they were frequently compared. The whole neo-psychedelic movement, with Echo and The Bunnymen leading the way, had faded from sight, leaving dozens of bands behind as the sort of musical residue that accumulates when musicians hitch their wagons to a movement. U2 was among the first genuine post-punk bands able to hang with the likes of the Skids and Stranglers. The English press recognized this early.

This seminal period resonates with those trying to make sense of the musical force that sprang seemingly out of nowhere to capture the imagination of rock fans of all stripes. That, in part, was the key: U2 resonated with followers of The Who as much as with people who liked the Clash, fit in as well on AOR stations as on college and the short-lived new-wave stations that sprang up during the early '80s.

All this led many to ask, "Just what are these very young guys playing? Where does it fit in the grand scheme of popular music?" Ironically, twenty years later, people still ask that question.

U2

Dublin Boys Top of Pops!

***The Evening Press,* March 20, 1978**

Four Dublin schoolboys carried off the top prize at the Limerick Civic Week Pop '78 Competition on Saturday night.

Sponsored by *The Evening Press* and Harp Lager Guinness, the competition was to find the most talented and entertaining pop group or showband.

The Dublin boys who attend Mount Temple Comprehensive, and are known as U2 (Malahide), headed 36 groups from all over the country and won for themselves £500, plus a trophy.

In second place was Rockster, also from Dublin, and the Limerick group Village was third. The only all-girl group in the contest, Harmony, from Tallaght, Co. Dublin, who got an enthusiastic reception, was unplaced.

The other finalists were East Coast Angels (Dublin), Graffiti (Clondalkin, Co. Dublin), Dragster (Charleville, Co. Cork) and Doves (Athenry, Co. Galway).

The adjudicators were Billy Wall, Head of Light Entertainment, RTE, Jackie Hayden, CBS Records, who will select one of the groups for a recording test, Paul O'Brien, President, Junior Chamber, Limerick and Disc Jockey Mike "Rave" McNamara.

The Mayor of Limerick, Cllr. Frank Prendergast, presented the trophy to the winners, and the cheque for £500 was presented by Mr. Colm Clarke, Limerick area representative for Guinness.

Mr. Harry Roycroft, also of Guinness, presented the trophy for the runners-up, and Mr. Alan Maxwell, Sales Promotion Executive in Irish Press Ltd., presented the trophy to the third placed group. Coordinator of the event was Mr. Eamon Walkin of Limerick Junior Chamber.

The Mayor, Cllr. Prendergast, said it was the ambition of the Civic Week Committee to cater for as many tastes as possible throughout the week in the city and all competitions were very successful.

He thanked *The Evening Press* and Guinness for their sponsorship and CBS Records who "definitely had some groups in mind for recording."

Mr. Colm Clarke of Guinness and Mr. Alan Maxwell for *The Evening Press* replied. Mr. Maxwell said Civic Week was a tremendous effort.

Mr. Jackie Hayden from CBS, a spokesman for the jury, said the standard was a credit to the musicianship.

U2, the winning group, was made up of 16-year-old Larry Mullen, of Rosemount Ave., Artane, an Intermediate Cert. Student at Mount Temple, Dave Evans (16), of St. Margaret's Park, Malahide, Adam Clayton (17), of Ard na Mara, Malahide, a Leaving Cert. student, and Paul Hewson (17), of Cedarwood Rd., Ballymun, who is also doing his Leaving Cert.

The group are just a year together and progressed from country music to "doing our own stuff." Paul Hewson said: "This means we can solve our money problems in a big way, particularly with regard to equipment. Now we hope to be able to buy a van."

The boys had to promote themselves. "No one in Dublin was interested in us and we came down here as a last resort," said Adam Clayton, group leader.

All the boys had praise for their school, which encouraged them, and gave them facilities to practice. In particular, they appreciated the help of Mr. Donald Moxham, History Teacher, and Mr. Albert Bradshaw, Music Teacher, at the school.

They appeared on RTE three weeks ago and they came to Limerick with the financial help of their parents—the trip cost them £60—and the support of their fans who traveled with the group to see them triumph.

U2

Getting into U2

Paulo Hewitt
***Melody Maker*, September 13, 1980**

"Four people, four individuals, four friends..." U2 are a band united by a determination to make music that moves people. Paulo Hewitt reports from Dublin where they're recording their debut album.

The Windmill studios are hidden away in a derelict part of Dublin town. The building is grey and the atmosphere a marked change from the carefree lightheadedness of Dublin's town centre.

A sense of cheerfulness remains, yet with an omnipresent hint of danger. As U2's Bono guides photographer Tom Sheehan and myself through some wayward back streets, a stone lands at our feet, bouncing off the brick wall beside us. Nothing dangerous, but our pace quickens.

U2 are at work on their debut album with the ubiquitous Steve Lillywhite at the controls, sympathetically directing the band. Today a song called "Another Time Another Place" is being laid down, and though it's not actually intended for the album, by the time Lillywhite and the band have gone through their paces, the finished item is just so good that it may very well end up on the record.

And even within the studio the air is one of excitement, nervous tension, and bubbling spirits. Bono, our courteous host, is the epitome of this.

His dress, his motions, his imaginative use of language, and almost fervent desire to be heard and understood...all this exudes an unmistakable quality of vitality and youthful enthusiasm still untainted by cynical world-weariness.

The rest of U2 are just as refreshing. Larry the drummer is straight, unblinkered, down-to-earth, smoothly dressed in Harrington and jeans.

Guitarist The Edge is quiet yet firm, offset by a sly sense of humor. Adam the bassist carries himself with an almost nonchalant air, totally at ease with his surroundings and the people around him.

"Four people, four individuals, four friends before they were in a band," says Bono.

"It is important. I was saying [of] session men: these people who can get into a band without any real creative expression. They just want to get in there, they want it for the next big thing, blah, blah, blah." The singer dismisses them with a sweep of his hand.

"The most powerful music is created naturally. Is not forced at all. It just comes out. In London, a band grows, comes out, has its bash, and if in a year nothing happens, they break up. If we were going to break up we'd have broken up by now. It makes a real bond of friendship."

And of understanding. A natural bond that plays such a large part in the band's unique music and stance.

It all began and grew in an experimental school, sparked off by a notice that Adam had placed asking for musicians.

Adam had arrived from public school and, in Bono's words, "stuck out like a sore thumb."

"He used to drink coffee in class and the teachers just got used to it. He got accused as being really quirky. He wore a kilt. He also took off his clothes at one rehearsal when he got very excited. The day they were having a meeting with the headmaster and his teacher was putting forward things like 'we need people like Adam in the school,' Adam was in the bush outside looking in. Of course he got caught."

"That's Adam," says The Edge. "He always gets caught."

Another example of Adam's quirkiness: as he plays bass he sniffs along. A problem at the moment. He's got a cold.

The band's school quickly became U2's focal point as they grabbed the facilities to practice and develop as a unit. Usually on a Saturday afternoon.

"The ideas came before the music," says the soft-spoken Edge. "We were together, so it just, sort of evolved into music. But at that stage it was just amusement, it wasn't anything particularly serious, though we all had deep interests."

On the musical level, it was Bono who finally discovered the band's true direction.

"Even from the beginning we wanted something like the power of The Who and something that was as sensitive as say, Neil Young; you know how on edge he can be, and we always wanted that," he explains.

"In the very start, even though we couldn't really get it together musically, there was something there and I call it the spark. I called it something you must have. We've built on a spark, we haven't tried to put a spark in the music.

"Like our main influences in this group are each other. They're not outside. They're very definitely each other."

U2 have progressed at a phenomenal rate for a band who are still so young. But what really impresses is the startling maturity that runs through their music, a maturity that has manifested itself in the group's ambitions and desires. Only when the time is right will they embark on certain ventures. For three years, for instance, they held out for a proper record deal even though the offers came flooding in. America is now beckoning, but only after due consideration will the band decide on the offer.

Their hometown of Dublin has played a large part in this ways of thinking.

"Coming in from Dublin into a London scene that everyone takes for granted, you really have an insight," says The Edge.

It's a very important part of the way we work, this insular type of development we've had where we haven't been exposed in the first nine months to a trendy, cliquey atmosphere that you have in London."

One thing he's certain about is that the music is designed to arouse his audience's emotions…though it's a wide-ranging panorama running the gamut of all emotions

Bono: "A range of different effects not just one — with emotion being the key word. Like aggressive live bands, I love that aggressive power, that type of push.

"At the same time, something like 'Shadows and Tall Trees' (a U2 song) is meandering, very sensitive, all those things, those words which you aren't supposed to say. But it's that kind of range and effect where people tune into the music and it takes them into various different places. It takes them to the top of the street, it takes them inside the house, into the bedroom, into the kitchen, out the backyard and across the street again. All over!"

The purpose of their music then is to take such qualities, normally unheard of or ignored, to the listener, to deliver it with a passion that will break down people's reserve and guarded cool. In much the same way their contemporaries, apart from the Joy Division/Magazine I/Talking Heads axis—are the Parkers, the Springsteens, and the Otis Reddings of this world. Tamla as well, I'd guess.

In the future, U2 will be releasing a debut that will be challenging and exciting. It's a characteristic of Dublin people. It's not just the hip London scene hiding under the camouflage of guarded reaction and manners. It's a whole country.

Which is why it's crucial that a band loaded with integrity and honest openness should succeed within the stultifying conservatism reflected in the national charts. As one who always believed that rock music was at least about some kind of challenge, some kind of intoxicating elixir concocted from such essential elements as adventure, pain, glory, excitement, and passion, plus a whole plethora of other ingredients, it remains to be seen whether Bono and his friends can pull it off.

Typically, Bono sees the problems ahead in his usual romanticized vision, another trait of his rich Irish heritage.

"I see it as a grid, and it's very easy to slip through that grid if you wear a suit and a tie or if you wear long hair and jeans and are that type of band. But bands who are individual can't slip through that easy.

"It is a problem on one hand because it does make it difficult to present the band to people who say, 'What type of band are they? Who do they sound like?' And of course we try not to sound like anything but ourselves.

"What I am saying is that it takes a while because bands like us do get through but they don't slip through the grid. They have to smash it."

If you have one ounce of spirit left in you, U2 can be a hammer.

Island Records Biography

December 1980

U2 always wanted to be hard to categorize. "The name U2 is ambiguous, it's in between...like the tightrope that we're all treading," says Bono, the band's vocalist.

The name could derive from the high-flying reconnaissance aircraft: U2's music certainly has stratospheric qualities. It could equally be a pun on the personal pronoun, an indication of the band's compulsive wish to communicate with their audience over and above conventional terms.

U2 are from Ireland although their music falls well outside that country's well-established showband tradition. But then U2 trade in surprise. The band's early reputation was built through just two singles—both released only in Eire—and a handful of London dates.

There's also one key fact about them that's much more unusual than many rock mythmakers pretend. U2 are a band formed naturally at school. U2 aren't seemingly rebellious older brothers with a murky history who have chopped a year or four from their ages for bios like this. Bono is 20 years old, guitarist The Edge is 19, bass player Adam Clayton is 20, and drummer Larry Mullen is 18. This doesn't make them any less than wise.

It was Mullen who, over three years ago, launched the band's first flight by pinning a message to the notice board at Dublin's Mount Temple School. He was looking for other musicians to form a band. Larry eventually teamed up with Adam Clayton—the only member of U2 with any previous experience in a rock band—Bono, and The Edge, who'd been given their names by a contingent of neighborhood friends.

U2 quickly developed a unique style, reworking and remodeling the classic four-man line-up whilst avoiding the clichés and excesses of both punk and heavy metal. The result was a soaring and emotional rock style that was powerful without being muscle-bound. U2 give you time to breathe.

U2, working away from the attentions of the London media and the record business, had time to develop without being rushed prematurely into the rock and roll circus. The band attracted their own audience in Eire. A three-track single, called *U23*, was released in late 1979 and went straight into the Irish charts. By the beginning of 1980 the band had won five categories in the Readers Poll of the Irish rock magazine *The Hot Press*. The last band to achieve that distinction was the Boomtown Rats.

Meanwhile, the band had tested the London air where they encountered the burgeoning factions of punks, skins, mods. Says Bono: "We looked down from the stage and saw all these strange little cliques...all these people in the so-called City of Freedom, y'know, the Permissive Society, trapped in little boxes.

"It was so sad. And we told them that. We said, 'we're from Dublin and we don't want to become part of your set of boxes, sorry and everything, but that's the way it is.'"

U2's first U.K. single for Island Records, "11 O'Clock Tick Tock," took such conformity as its theme, establishing U2 as one of the most exciting discoveries of the year.

It was followed by "A Day Without Me" and of course, U2's debut album, *Boy*.

U2 come from a country where the conditions for young rock bands have been inclement and discouraging. The band has changed the climate in Ireland; now they're set to do the same everywhere else.

U2

Tim Sommer
***Trouser Press*, July 1, 1981**

New music requires new classifications. Or is it no classification?

U2 is the sort of band that prompts the above riddle. The Irish group's sweeping and majestic music is "rock" in one sense, but simultaneously transcends all genres.

U2's uniqueness is probably due to the emotional depth-charges they detonate live and on record. Their debut album, *Boy*, is a glorious roar of hope, drenched in emotion. The band has a wonderful ability to find the musical correlatives to the ideas stirring in their young hearts and minds.

U2 singer and main songwriter Bono Vox, 20, projects warmth and openness from the moment you meet him; when introduced, he grasps your arm with both hands, making you feel immediately at ease. He's quick to pick up a comment that *Boy's* images and aural wash are startlingly vivid.

"What we were looking for in *Boy* was a sort of cinema sound, a Panavision—really textured and big, like a huge screen in a cinema. The lyrics are very picturesque; they don't tell a story as such, they're just various images in the album that link together to form one big picture. There are enough little groups around playing little sounds, very unimportant. We wanted a big sound. We're using a three-piece format—bass, guitar and drums—like the three primary colors. We're mixing them, trying to get the most out of them."

It works well. The Edge, U2's guitarist, lays down thick chords here, dreamy tonal support there, and even a straightforward solo now and again just to bring it all back home. Bono's expressive tenor is always in control; Adam Clayton's bass, with Larry Mullen's drums, make a solid foundation, no matter the dynamic shade. For all that, the music fits into a pop format, as full of hooks and memorable melodies as deeper moments that make you mull over—or just appreciate—what you're hearing.

U2 stands for hope—another singular trait. A lot of groups represent some form of nihilism, escapism, or despair; how many can honestly state the opposite case?

"It is a celebration," Bono says. "'Shadows and Tall Trees,' on the album, begins a pensive mood, as the character—who is me—looks around him. He sees this pattern developing, the repetition of everyday life. It really gets to him, really irritates him, as he realizes 'Mrs. Brown's washing is always the same.' I was listening to housewives talking; in Dublin there's this expression—'*I know, I know*,' they say to each other, 'I know'—but I realized that's very beautiful in many ways. It's often the everyday things that are beautiful.

"We chose the name U2 to be ambiguous, to stay away from categorization. People who work in print tend to tidy things up a bit—put a stack of bands in that way, a stack of bands in here. People don't fit into boxes. We all smell different, we all eat different, we all *are* different. There's a huge audience out there of individuals."

U2

Operation Uplift

Scott Isler
***Trouser Press*, July 1, 1983**

"Tell me, what do you like about U2?"

The question comes from Paul Hewson, better known as Bono, U2's singer. It's aimed at the *Trouser Press* writer. Who's interviewing whom here?

Hewson, 23, isn't being presumptuous, just disarming. It's the day before Ireland's U2 sets off on a two-month, 42-date tour of the U.S. that should certify the band's status as conquering heroes of 1983. *War*, U2's third album, has crashed into the upper reaches of American record charts. With FM radio plugging the "New Year's Day" single, very few people seem not to like U2.

Hewson doesn't want ego-stroking praise. He's genuinely curious about how his suddenly popular band is being perceived stateside. Why? Because U2 cares.

The Manhattan hotel room shared by Hewson and drummer Larry Mullen has a comfortably disordered appearance. A big acoustic guitar case (Mullen's; he's started writing songs) lies on the floor. The coffee table in front of the couch bears magazines, a basket of fruit, and an open box of chocolates with one piece in it. The band arrived in New York the previous day; before flying to North Carolina that evening, where the tour will begin, they want to see *Tootsie*. Hewson also wants to check out the city's hipper dance clubs—surprising, in light [of] U2's own rather "traditional" rock music.

"It's not how you play it, it's why you're playing it," the singer comments on the band's disregard of musical fashion. "Instruments are just bits of wood and metal nailed together, plastic skins stretched over boxes. It's what you do with them that's important."

U2 has taken its wood, metal, and plastic, and used the conventions of rock as a basis for evocative combinations of words and music. In June, Hewson will be declaiming his introspective (if exuberant) lyrics from the Los Angeles Sports Arena; the band is also considering playing New York's 20,000-seat Madison Square Garden. Not bad for a one-time punk outfit from Dublin. But what happened to the anti-big biz ethic that nourished U2 in the first place?

"If we stay in small clubs," Hewson counters, "we'll develop small minds, and then we'll start making small music.

U2 likes to think big.

Hewson is dressed all in black, but casual: black shoes, black pants, black peasant shirt. His spiky hair is long in the back; some dyed-blonde tufts in the front are the only touch of affectation in his appearance. Broad of face and stocky of build, he talks slowly and intently, hesitating between phrases. Overall he gives an impression of unforced sincerity.

U2's albums identify him only as Bono (pronounced "bonno"), a childhood nickname short for Bono Vox, shorter still for Bono Vox of O'Connell Street. His name, as well as guitarist The Edge's, is a legacy of growing up with friends who invented their own town, Lypton Village, and peopled it with arbitrarily renamed acquaintances.

"People think, 'They're into pseudonyms, they must be really pseudy-type people,'" Hewson says.

"'They want to hide their real names.' I can think of a lot better pseudonyms than Bono! Why couldn't I have thought of something like 'Sting'?"

(As a mini-revelation, *War* marks the first time Mullen's full name has seen print on a U2 album cover. "He's become a man," Hewson teases the youthful drummer; Mullen turned 21 early this year. "He now knows how to drink a pint of Guinness.")

Hewson didn't think of Bono; he was given it by an especially creative Lyptonian. As a "return serve," Hewson dubbed *him* Guggi, and that name stuck as well. Guggi now sings in another Dublin export, the Virgin Prunes.

More likely, U2's members abjured surnames out of folksiness. Nonetheless, Hewson is getting tired of misrepresentation. "Publications keep calling me Bono Vox," he sighs. "I'm not Mr. Vox."

U2's early history is intertwined with that of the Virgin Prunes. Before both groups stabilized, their personnels were interchangeable. The Prunes' Dik is older brother to U2's Edge—David Evans, to his parents.

The magnet for all these musicians—and would-be musicians—was a notice posted in school by Mullen, who was looking to start a band. ("If I see that in print again, I could do a nasty," Hewson warns.) It was 1976, and Mullen was 14. The drummer now resembles Billy Idol's kid brother in a blue denim vest over a T-shirt with rolled-up sleeves, blue jeans, and sneakers. His hair is '50s-rebel length and newly dyed blonde. He wears a solitary earring.

"I had two days of glory when I was tellin' people what to do," Mullen says. "Then Bono came in and that was the end. He took it from there."

It's not hard to imagine the outgoing Hewson taking charge. Back then, though, there wasn't much to take charge of, as no one was very proficient on their instrument. But the four—Hewson, Evans, Mullen, and bassist Adam Clayton—became friends, which seems as important to them as anything else.

They took the deliberately ambiguous name U2 to avoid categorization in those heady punk days. About a year after coagulating, in 1977, Clayton convinced manager Paul McGuinness to attend a gig.

"He came down to talk us out of it," Hewson remembers, "how we shouldn't do this, it's really a dead end." McGuinness came, saw and was conquered. The band re-christened him Magoo. "His first assignment was to get us served in the pub next door, 'cause we were too young," Hewson chuckles.

McGuinness formally took on U2 in 1978. The band was constantly improving and building a local following. After winning a lucrative talent contest, U2 was offered a record contract by the Irish arm of CBS. They issued a three-song single on that label, but refused to commit themselves.

In the spring of 1980, U2 signed to Island Records worldwide. "People there really believe in this group," Hewson says. "They never wanted us to be a pop group. We wanted '11 O'Clock Tick Tock' to be our first single. It was 4 1/2 minutes long, and was never going to get played on radio. They stood by us."

U2's first U.S. release was *Boy* in early 1981. The twin themes of adolescence and growth run through this debut LP, matched by swirling, misty music. Producer Steve Lillywhite's echoic approach gave U2 the phosphorescent quality of swampfire; Hewson's passionate stream-of-consciousness vocals combined with the basic guitar/bass/drums line-up to create an album that's both accessible and enthralling. For a new band receiving little airplay, U2 sold respectably well.

The group came over to tour, and fulfilled expectations with a dynamic stage show. Unfortunately, the climax of the trip occurred in Portland, Oregon, when two women walked into U2's dressing room and walked out with Hewson's briefcase, containing his notes for the following album.

"I'd like to meet them," he says wistfully of his robbers—"those big blue eyes." He pauses. "It's the $300 I want back! Keep the lyrics!"

Hewson may joke about it now, but at the time, the loss of his lyrics was no laughing matter. In between extensive tours of the U.S. and U.K.—U2 played over 200 shows in 1981—the band had booked studio time to record its second album. In the past, the group-credited compositions evolved out of sound check jams, with lyrics often improvised onstage. Now Hewson was forced to push his creativity to the limit.

That summer, with the backing tracks already laid down, the singer went into U2's recording haunt, Windmill Lane Studios in Dublin, and literally expelled lyrics through massive amounts of free association. Afterward, a harried Lillywhite helped piece together snippets of Hewson's extemporizing. The technique would have pleased James Joyce.

"It's best to do it under stress," Hewson avers with hindsight. "Maybe I have a few lines in my mind, or words or images. I play around with them, fill up a [vocal] track, move on, fill up another track. Then I go back with Lillywhite, and maybe Larry or Adam, and see a train of thought.

"I try to pull out of myself things I wouldn't be able to do with pen and paper. At the front of your brain is a lot of rubbish: You write about things you *think* you're concerned about, but that may not be what you're concerned about at all."

The album was entitled *October* for its month of release and the autumnal nature of its songs. To American ears it lacked the impact of *Boy* and didn't even dent the Top 100. But it entered the British charts at #11, serving notice that U2 was no one-shot wonder.

Hewson admits *October* "was quite an introspective record" and not "as immediate" as *Boy*. More importantly, its subject matter shoved U2 out of the Christian closet.

Hewson had started to talk about his deeply held but slightly unorthodox religious beliefs at interviews. While professing contempt for organized faith—understandably, having seen it divide his native land—he could take on an evangelical fervor.

"Christ is like a sword that divides the world," he told one reporter. "It's about time we get into line and let people know where we stand." It wasn't exactly sex and drugs and rock 'n' roll, but then U2 has never worried much about appearances.

To bolster *October* in the U.S., U2 toured here a second time. Swallowing its Irish pride, the group even accepted opening-act status for several shows with the J. Geils Band. Hewson, who says U2 doesn't "believe in playing a venue unless we sell it out," flatly denies the exposure helped U2's subsequent commercial breakthrough.

The band re-crossed the Atlantic and played some European dates. U2 finally retreated to Ireland by the end of the summer of 1982 to recuperate and plan a third album—the first they *could* plan since their debut.

As early as 1981 Hewson was hinting that Ireland's civil strife "was starting to affect me." Now he admits the concerns behind *War*, U2's current LP, were originally going to surface on *October*. His purloined lyrics were different from those on *War*, "but they had that same [feeling of] conflict."

War, released in early 1983, topped British record charts its first week out. Over here the record's gradual acceleration into the Top 10 has been less dramatic but more impressive, given chronic American indifference to new and/or imported popular music.

Lillywhite, who normally tries to vary his clientele, once again produced a U2 album. The band had been thinking of changing producers; having decided to strip down their sound on the new record, however, they realized Lillywhite was the most empathetic choice to carry out their intentions.

"I rang up Steve," Hewson says, "and in a flash he said, 'I'll be over.' He said we're his favorite group. It's a very close thing."

War opens with the claustrophobic attack of "Sunday Bloody Sunday," whose violent imagery tackles the Northern Ireland situation head on. But the mention of Jesus at the song's end implies it isn't just about politics.

"In the Republic of Ireland," Hewson says gravely, "if you make a statement against a man of violence you are in danger of coming into a certain amount of violence—a brick through a window. Some of the lines in that song were very strong in castigating the IRA. At the time I felt very angry. But that had to be tempered, 'cause I realized I was dealing with a blinkered situation, where people really believe in what they're doing; they're not just bad men. I'm prepared to say it's wrong, but I wanted to make it more than a song about the IRA. That's why I contrast it with Easter Sunday, the ultimate Bloody Sunday."

He acknowledges the lyrics were "tempered by other members of the band. They redeemed a very volatile situation." Still, "we have the right to speak out."

War speaks out on other topics as well: Poland ("New Year's Day"), atomic Armageddon ("Seconds"—"black humor on the bomb"), the senselessness of all armed combat ("The Refugee"). As on "Sunday Bloody Sunday," the specific is a jumping-off point for more generalized observations.

"I'm trying to get across the theme of surrender," Hewson says, "the white flag that applies to every area of your life—whether it's the factory, the campus or just being out on the street. I think the revolution begins at home, in the heart."

Whew. Does Hewson think everyone slapping down their money for *War* is getting the message?

"I'd like to say they are, but I couldn't. I'm sure there are many levels on which people come into our music. You may find 16-year-olds into the phenomenon of The Edge. I don't look down on that; I hope the music draws people in further."

On that point, the packaging sure is right. U2 has consistently shunned synthesizers and other trendy electronic hardware in favor of the good old power trio—the "primary colors" Hewson invariably mentions to the press. He has nothing against synth bands as such, but just likes some meat with his potatoes.

"It is a breakthrough hearing Human League on radio—they play synthesizers, they're non-musicians and they come from Sheffield—but the content of the songs is the same as Abba."

U2, on the other hand, is concentrating on message more than form?

"Well, 'message' always gives an image of a prophet [*pointing*]: 'This way!' It's not like that. We only use it in a very personal way."

The singer, who describes himself as an "aggressive pacifist," can be similarly convoluted explaining his music's conflicting components.

"There are few instruments that get across aggression as well as a distorted guitar; it's physically brutalizing. The power of a rock 'n' roll concert is that it stimulates you emotionally, as you follow the singer, and physically, as you dance and are hit by the music. It also has a cleansing effect; it's a great release.

"The brutalizing effect of the guitar has been used in a very negative direction at times. But our aggression is not, uh—masturbation. It's much warmer, much more communicative than that."

The master of U2's warmly brutalizing guitar, 21-year-old Edge Evans, is sharing a hotel room with bassist Clayton, 23. With his receding hairline and couple of days' stubble, and wearing blue jeans, black T-shirt, and checked wool jacket, the thin, soft-spoken Evans could pass for almost anything except a high-powered rock guitarist. A steely gaze and lupine face help explain his nickname.

Clayton, by contrast, sports a tie-dyed tank top, bracelets, a necklace, and studded belt through his black Levi's. His blond hair trimmed down from its former curly thatch, he looks like a serious hedonist.

According to Hewson, Clayton was bounced out of several schools before ending up at Mt. Temple Comprehensive with the other budding musicians: "People usually have no problems at our school, but he did! He was thrown out and became a full-time hustler for the group."

"I'd never been particularly interested in school," Clayton admits in cultured tones. "Then playing an instrument occurred to me."

Superficially, at least, Clayton is U2's odd man out. "Adam was more and more into the rock 'n' roll circus," Hewson says, while the rest of U2 was "getting more and more estranged from all that." Besides his distinctive (for U2) dressing up, he is the sole non-believer among his spiritually devout bandmates. Yet all concerned agree the group has no personality problems.

During the *War* sessions, Hewson says, Clayton "was becoming a caricature of himself, with a bottle of brandy. But there was never tension. There's always great love and respect for him, and vice versa."

"I don't think there are any particularly sensitive or vulnerable relationships within the band at all," Evans says. "We're pretty open; we're not afraid to talk to one another."

Something else all U2's members agree on is the band's continuing growth over the years. "We now know a lot more about what we do and how we do it," Clayton says. "In the past, we'd have a rough idea how a song was going to turn out, but we'd never really know how good it could be. Nowadays we're in control a lot more."

"I don't think U2 will ever get to the stage where there's a formula," Evans adds. "Our way of writing is always so much a part of experimenting, and a feeling at the time. It's not a conscious thing." Indeed, Hewson may change lyrics, or add them to a song (like "Twilight," on *Boy*) the band has been playing as an instrumental for a year or more.

"Essentially, there are no rules to what we do," the guitarist says. "That's what people can't understand."

Where do they go from here? The next U2 music will be a score for the Royal Dublin Ballet, to be presented this summer. That work may involve outside musicians on traditional instruments. Evans, who started out on acoustic guitar, hints at picking it up again. (He's also just recorded with Jah Wobble, Holger Czukay and Jaki Liebeziet.)

Hewson also implies U2's next album will mark a break with its past. "Everyone feels a weight off their shoulders," he says. "We feel like we're in a new group now. I can't sleep at night with thoughts about the next record."

What a come-on. How about some details? "We're not allowed to say," he laughs.

U2 admittedly hasn't revolutionized music through stylistic innovation. What they have done, though, is perhaps more daring: injected commitment into an escapist pop scene.

"We open ourselves up to people to such an extent it gets embarrassing," Evans says. "We sacrifice a certain amount of cool. There's so much theater involved in this business, and to a certain extent we've opted out of that. A performance must be larger than life, but to be worthwhile you must have an element of humanity. It has to be more than an intellectual pursuit."

Asked what effect he wants to have on audiences, Hewson replies, "Uplifting. That's the effect the music has on me. I hope that's the effect a U2 concert has: 'Let's all go get uplifted at a U2 show!'"

At least he's kept his sense of humor along with his ideals. At the same time, Hewson presents himself as a worldly character—a depiction that, to his credit, he doesn't bring off very well.

"Because we used a child's face on the cover and *Boy* was about innocence, people thought, oh, they must be four good Catholic boys from Ireland, wide-eyed to the world. I've probably been through more than a lot of people," he laughs.

"We were never innocent. We still have a lot to learn, and we've always felt if we didn't know something we should find somebody who did. But it would be complimenting us to portray us in that way. We're actually really nasty people." He laughs again.

Somehow that doesn't jibe with Hewson's belief in the power of music to change, just as he feels '60s music united a culture to stop the Vietnam War.

"It would be wrong for me to say, yes, we can change the world with a song. But every time I try writing, that's where I'm at!" Another self-deprecating laugh.

"I'm not stupid. I'm aware of the futility of rock 'n' roll music, but I'm also aware of its power. We're only coming to terms with our trade. We've yet to become craftsmen. Well, maybe we should never become craftsmen. It's great fun being in this band."

CHAPTER

2

ROCK HUNKS

Part of U2's durability undoubtedly comes from their stint as rock poster boys. Teen magazines loved them for their demographic appeal—just barely out of their teens themselves, U2 were close to the same age as the magazines' readers.

Not simply photogenic, the group also proved crucially videogenic at a time when MTV had more influence on teens and pop culture than radio and print combined. With the mid '80s marking the high point in the eminence of video as the barometer and harbinger of hit songs, the group's often innovative visual sense, along with their "presence" in the medium, ensured them high rotation throughout the MTV decade.

It was a big era for teen-oriented magazines and music. The newsstands were rife with titles like *Rock Scene, Rock Fever, Concert Shots* (all three of which I edited), *Star Hits, Teen*, and dozens of others with pull-out posters of the top pop and rock stars of the day. In 1984, U2 started appearing on the cover of many of these, and in articles that discussed their personal lives without revealing much.

The teen idol element certainly aided their rise from post-punks to pop hit-makers. Although "Pride (In the Name of Love)" was a Top 40 radio hit in 1984, its content was less superficial and more deeply passionate than the other pop hits of that year: Prince's "When Doves Cry," Van Halen's "Jump," and Madonna's "Like a Virgin."

Even during this high-exposure period, U2 managed to maintain a great deal of separation between their musical careers and personal lives. Residing out of the limelight in low-key Dublin helped, but their generally quiet way of life, on and off the road, was not the stuff of great gossipy copy. While grist for the teen mills, there was nothing much for Enquiring minds; U2's passion and integrity continued to rouse attention and interest in their musical contributions throughout this second phase of their careers.

Nor did this stop. Many of the qualities that made teen hearts throb—passion, black leather attire, youth, and political correctness—made U2 a fairly popular band in the gay community. Even twenty years on, the *Advocate* couldn't help noting the group's disco attire in the 1997 video for "Discotheque." As a female friend of mine, enamored with the band since the '80s, once remarked, "Sexy is as sexy does."

U2: At War with Mediocrity

Ethlie Ann Vare
***ROCK!* magazine September 1983**

It's a Saturday night at the terribly trendy Club Lingerie in Hollywood. People are wearing sunglasses in the dark. A new Welsh band, the Alarm, is playing, and some of their early supporters have come out to cheer them on. The doorman, more muscle than brains, is insisting on ID from a group of Alarm fans who have arrived. One of the newcomers turns on his heel in disgust and leaves.

"I'm Irish," grunts U2's The Edge. "I don't carry ID."

Welcome to America.

Late, inside, lead singer Bono Vox holds court. He has a beer bottle in each hand and more drinks being pressed on him by admirers. He puts an arm protectively around his wife Allie [*sic*], whose fresh-scrubbed looks make her as out of place as a dairymaid in a brothel. Drummer Larry Mullen tries to look inconspicuous, a shy boy uncomfortable with notoriety. Bassist Adam Clayton has already disappeared, a natural denizen of big-city nightlife.

A disparate group is U2, whose very contrasts propel the dense and urgent sound that has made *War* a worldwide hit. They met at school in Dublin and, as Bono puts it, "We built the group around the spark. The chemistry. We weren't great musicians; we were four people, none of us alike, but with great love for each other. The *group* was there, before anything."

Meet the group—a band which, with members 15 and 16 years old, had to play gigs in parking lots because their followers were too young to get into pubs. Today, the band sells out arenas and can awe the sensorially overloaded 150,000 at the US Festival. It's been a long journey in a short time.

"Edge is the 'head' of the group," says Bono (Bono's given name is Paul Hewson; Edge was born David Evans.) "Adam and Larry are the 'feet': the rhythm, the beat. Because I'm so emotional, people call me the 'heart.'"

Bono is physically smaller than you would imagine a man with such stage charisma and conversational presence. He is called the band philosopher, but insists, "I'm not all that good with my knife and fork." Still, he never simply talks. Bono Vox makes pronouncements.

"The Edge is a genius," he states. "An anti-guitar hero. He never practices, you know. Only takes his guitar out on 'formal occasions.' He rarely knows what time or day it is, and sometimes goes through a whole day and forgets to eat.

"Adam is more into the rock and roll circus. Adam is also a gentleman, in the literal sense of the word. He likes brandy and cigars.

"Adam and Larry are total opposites. Larry won't give interviews, except to the street press, fanzines. He wants to play music without all the trappings of being in a band."

And from this synergistic quartet came a musical force that grew like a groundswell. The first album, *Boy*, hinted at the fullness of sound and emotional impact they were capable of: "I Will Follow" was as hypnotic as a potion. Later came *October*, an LP that was jinxed from the start. Not only were the band's lyric sheets stolen from a dressing room by enterprising groupies just before the recording session, but the Island label had a falling-out with distributor Warner Brothers when the record was finally finished. Though songs like "Gloria" were admired, the album did not take off as well in the U.S. as it did in England.

But then *War* was declared: "New Year's Day," "Sunday Bloody Sunday," "Two Hearts Beat as One." These are not the only tunes lifted to new plateaus through Edge's tingling guitar work, they are also songs with emotional impact and—rare and unusual in today's radio—something to say about the state of the world as we know it.

"I think of *War* as our first record," says Bono. "*War* puts a torch to all this wallpaper music that's about right now. Everybody's writing about nothing. *War* is a slap in the face to a lot of these pop stars, a very aggressive record. I never intended to give people 'I Will Follow - Part Two.'"

Commitment to making a social statement is important to Bono. If the theme of *Boy* was growing up and the theme of *October* coping with manhood, then the theme of *War* might well be survival.

"People have to speak out," he says. "Things have to be done. We can't all lie down. But at the same time, I don't put on a '60s uniform."

"I don't see any real soul to music any more," sighs Bono with Irish-accented sibilance. Perhaps that's why he likes the Alarm, who, musically unalarming, at least are playing from their guts. "I came out of 1976, out of the naïve belief that we could destroy the star trip that was prevailing at the time. Now I realize that elitism and pose are worse now than they were in '76, and worse in the bands that came *out* of '76. More people are hiding behind their haircuts, behind a mask and an image.

"I no longer see any real commitment. I look for an X-factor in music, that feeling that the musician is giving of himself. I got that from John Lennon, from Bob Dylan. They didn't try to hide themselves. And I try to be honest with myself and about myself and my feelings. I give of myself totally."

Bono speaks of "breaking the barriers between myself and the audience," and one night at U2's live performance will see a lot of barriers shattered. In 1979 they played for an audience of nine at London's Anchor club, and they probably gave the same 120 percent there that they did at the US Fest. Bono leaps about the stage like a manic buccaneer, drawing sustenance from the approval of the crowd. He thrives on feedback. Backstage at the

US Fest, he was sweating, grinning, glowing after the set. "That was two year's wages," he panted. "And I'm not talking about money."

U2 has arrived. The band that since 1980 has been touted as "the future of rock and roll" is now the present of rock and roll. And if they seem at times pretentious, if they take themselves a tad too seriously, they do so on purpose. After all, it is that very seriousness that sets them apart from the glut of synth-pop costume bands on the market.

"We're not going through the motions—or the emotions—that may be in fashion," says Bono. "And we're not a synthesizer band. You tell people that. Tell them we're not a synthesizer band."

U2

Rocking with U2

Edwin Miller
***Seventeen*, August 1985**

U2's impassioned affirmation of life wraps listeners in a sweep of sound. Romantic images tug at the mind as this band of four strapping lads create ballads on smash albums such as *The Unforgettable Fire, War*, and *Under a Blood Red Sky* that speak to the people of today, even as they evoke a musical echo of old Ireland. Bass player Adam Clayton, whose light beard and glasses make him seem older than his twenty-five years, says, "I love the sound of the pipes and the violins. Although our music's not traditional, it has the flavor of the country." His partners, who are his age or younger, are vocalist Bono, guitarist The Edge, and drummer Larry Mullen. Oddly enough, when U2 got together some eight years ago in Dublin, they never thought of themselves as playing Irish rock: But when they toured America in 1980, the year they signed with Island Records, Clayton recalls, "People, would throw money onstage because we were thought to be a 'rebel' band." There were insistent questions about the North, referring to the bitter "clashes between Protestant and Catholic factions in Northern Ireland." Clayton and the band, however, live next door in the Republic of Ireland.

"People in the South think everybody's mad up there in the North," he says. Speaking of Ireland's political division in two earlier [wars] this century, he says, "The basic premise is that it should be reunited, but nobody has any idea how that's going to come about. When we realized we were Irish and didn't have any views on the subject—we started thinking. 'Sunday Bloody Sunday' came out of that," he adds, referring to one of their early hits. "But it's difficult to be objective about our work. People ask, 'Why did you write that song? What does it mean?' That's not something we can intellectualize. Bono," he points out, "writes ninety-seven percent of the lyrics, since he's got to sing them—but I never listen to them. We really don't think that much about what we're doing when we're writing; emotionally, we know if it feels right. All our decisions, artistic and political, are based on a kind of collective instinct." Speaking about his fellow band members, Clayton remarks, "Bono is pretty intense, very much an Irishman. He's loud and aggressive in what he's trying to do, and yet he has that lyrical side. For a long time, he couldn't decide which accent to sing in—he went from a cockney to an East Coast American accent. It took him a long time to establish his own singing voice, not authentic Irish but with an Irish flavor."

Of guitarist The Edge, Clayton says, "A Welshman born, he moved to Ireland when he was six months old. He's very neat and dapper, something of an eccentric and vague at the same time." Drummer Larry Mullen, he observes, "likes to get on with the job and doesn't intellectualize."

Clayton himself is English, a resident of Ireland since he was five, when his father, a pilot, went to work for Aer Lingus. He was educated in a private boarding school: "Until the very end," he says, "when I disgraced myself so badly with my lack of academic standards. My parents were fed up paying for my education and sent me to the local school. I didn't realize it then, but that was the best thing that ever happened to me—that's where I met the other guys, and we formed the band. I was about sixteen. I always hated school," he adds. "Nothing malicious. I just couldn't take studying seriously. I'd always be gossiping with someone, giggling, talking back to the teacher, getting the class on a different topic."

When Clayton was fifteen, he decided music was the one thing he was going to do. A good friend of his played acoustic guitar. "If you get hold of a bass," the friend said to Clayton, "we could form a little band." There was no other work Clayton fancied, so he cast his lot with rock and roll—not realizing what he'd taken on until much later.

Originally, the Dublin teenagers were stimulated by the punk rock scene. "Everyone knew punk was a rip-off, except people like us from the provinces," Clayton says now. "It was a London club movement, very tongue-in-cheek, but if you lived in Glasgow or Manchester and read the papers, you were so naive and wet behind the ears that you took it seriously. The idea was you didn't need to have rows of huge amplifiers to express yourself, you didn't have to be part of the Establishment, you just needed to stand on a chair with an acoustic guitar."

During the ensuing months, U2 members rehearsed when they could. Gradually, through fits and starts, they became increasingly dedicated to music. Tossed out of his second school, Clayton devoted himself to the band, but after two years, Clayton's dad told him that if he didn't get a job, he'd have to leave home—a prospect Clayton couldn't face, because, he says, "There was a telephone and food." He found a job driving a van, delivering china. Bono worked part-time in a gas station. The Edge was supposed to go to technical college but never did. Mullen was a clerk in a computer firm. "The most important thing to us was the alienation we felt," Clayton says, "the feeling that apart from music, we were a generation that didn't have much to look forward to." As the band developed, they first tried, unsuccessfully, to duplicate existing hits by such stars as David Bowie and the Rolling Stones. Then they wrote their own material, which was easier to cope with, but no one expressed interest in listening to it. They still couldn't decide where they fit into the musical scene, since they related to punk's energy but not its ideas. "We were confused by the sexual revolution," Clayton admits. "Promiscuity didn't appeal to us. And neither did the drug culture—longhaired people smoking pot and talking about the cosmos. We didn't have a social bracket to fit into, so we spent all our energy on the band."

Before the group finally clicked, U2 was turned down "by every recording company in England and the United States," Clayton recalls. "But we said defiantly, 'We're not going to lie down!' When we started touring, we realized there was a bigger world than Dublin. London was glamorous, the place to be. We did a couple of club dates there, but we couldn't relate to it and felt like fish out of water. The rest of England is more like Ireland in terms of the depression and fans' behavior, and we did much better.

"We're simple folk, basically," the bass player maintains. "People who enjoy U2 appreciate how awkward we feel at being 'rock stars,' because we're not—we don't dress up in satins and sequins, and it's the same with our audience. We reflect something audiences can feel comfortable with—U2 is a celebration of normality, with something deeper, about humanity. I don't like traditional religions because they really are political parties, but there is a spirituality in people that has to be acknowledged, call it what you will." As Adam Clayton sums up the essence of U2, he says simply, "Ear to heart."

Once Upon a Time...

Chris Heath
***Star Hits* magazine, January 1987**

U2 are successful the world over, have incredibly devoted fans and are deeply sincere about what they do. But what about their personal sides?

BONO

"I was one of those kids who was impossible to tie down from the very beginning," recalls Bono. "People used to—and family people still do—put up the cross (i.e., make a cross sign with their two index fingers) whenever I came in. They used to call me the Antichrist."

Paul Hewson was born on May 10, 1960, the second child of Bobby and Iris Hewson (their other son, Norman, was born seven years earlier). Paul can hardly have been a blessing—when he was born he cried incessantly, so much that when his father would come home from his job at the post office he'd prefer to stay in the car so that he could read the day's newspaper in relative peace and quiet.

The strangest thing about the family was that Iris and Bobby were different religions—she was Protestant, he was Catholic—still fairly rare and frequently frowned upon in Ireland.

"Their love was illicit at the time," Bono recently reminisced, "but it didn't mean anything to them. They just faced the flak and got married."

The way he tells it, Bono—or rather Paul Hewson as he was still then called—was slightly unusual from the beginning. His father remembers him once announcing that he'd "made friends" with a bee, while another time after a row he churlishly left a banana skin on the floor to send his dad a-tumbling.

Day in and day out he was apparently in a dreamworld of his own, preferring early on activities like painting to football, although he wasn't exactly, er, quiet. He cheerfully remembers his response when, on his first day of school, aged four, a bloke bit the ear of his friend James Mann. Bono simply "took that kid's head and banged it off the iron railing."

At St. Patrick's Secondary School, things finally came to a head. After growing less and less fond of his Spanish teacher he decided, rather unwisely, to take direct action—he simply lobbed a lump of dog poo over a hedge onto her. Shortly afterwards, you may be surprised to learn, he left.

After the Spanish teacher incident, young Bono was sent to a new school called Mount Temple—a modern experimental school where Catholics and Protestants mixed and where school uniforms and petty rules were seen as less important than the pupils' "personal development." There, things got much better.

Then, suddenly, his world was torn apart. In September 1974 his mother's father died—Bono's mother took it very badly and had a brain hemorrhage on the way back from the funeral. She died four days later. Legend has it that when Bono was told what had happened he went upstairs and strummed his guitar in misery. "That house was no longer a home," he says. "It was just a house."

In autumn 1976 things took a turn for the better. One of the other pupils at the school, Larry Mullen, put a notice up on the school board asking if anyone else wanted to form a band. Bono reckoned he was a pretty fine guitarist so he went along. After a while, despite the fact that he was pretty soon discovered as an abysmal guitarist and didn't have a brilliant voice, he became the singer. For one thing, he was overflowing with enthusiasm. For another he looked as if he was a pop type—he'd become the school's first punk with his spiky haircut, purple trousers, pointy boots, and chain from his nose to his ear.

Outside the band, though, his behavior got more and more bizarre. At home he fought with his dad, one time hurling a kitchen knife at Bobby Hewson's head, sticking into the kitchen door behind. He also formed a collection of friends who lived in a secret imaginary place called Lypton Village where they all had names like Dik, Strongman, Pod, Guggi and so on. (His own name Bono Vox came from a hearing aid shop called Bonovox.) One day he caused a public disturbance with them by deliberately dropping his trousers and bending over in the middle of the road.

At school there was the affair of the classroom fire and the stolen exploding rivets, and of the tantrums where he walked out overturning his desk. But there was also his serious membership of the Mount Temple Christian Union and a growing friendship with a girl called Alison Stewart. This bizarre combination was taking its toll—more and more he'd suffer from blackouts and nosebleeds.

Slowly, however, the band—at first called Feedback, then The Hype, then U2—became more and more successful. At first Bono tried a couple of jobs as well but they didn't quite work out. He took a post as a gas station attendant, the theory being that in the quiet hours he'd write songs. As luck would have it. it was then that the worldwide oil crisis erupted. "We had these lines for miles and the cars just kept coming, so I quit."

As U2's fame grew—first in Ireland for their *U23* EP, then all over the place for their *Boy* LP, Bono started to become more and more religious. Pod and Guggi from Lypton Village joined a group of Charismatic Christians called the Shalom, and soon Bono, Larry and The Edge were also attending twice-weekly meetings. Bono and The Edge even got baptized in the sea.

By the time of their second LP, *October*, pressure was being put on them to choose the church over music.

"We thought U2 might break up. I just lost interest," says Bono. "I thought rock 'n' roll was a bit of a waste of time."

Three of them even announced their decision to finish the band to their manager—he persuaded them to at least honor the tour they had booked already, and eventually they left the Shalom group. Bono is still very religious, though he prefers not to talk about it except in a song and person-to-person. "I am a Christian but I feel very removed from Christianity," he did say recently. "The Jesus Christ I believe in was the man who once turned over the tables in the temple and threw the moneychangers out...there is a radical side to Christianity I am attracted to. I think without a commitment to social justice it is empty."

Now married to his longtime girlfriend Alison and living in a converted tower near Dublin, Bono now spends his time just trying to work out how to cope with being a very famous pop star without turning into the "unimportant" famous pop stars U2 don't like.

For a few years, to fit in, he says he "drank too much and did far too many things out of this odd reverse guilt." Now, he says he's starting to feel the value of being irresponsible. "You read about the excesses of rock 'n' roll stars of the '70s—driving Rolls Royces into swimming pools. Well that's better than polishing them, which is the sort of yuppie pop star ethic we've got in the '80s."

Sometimes, though, it's not that much fun. "I've got people who want to kill me, people who want to make love to me so they can sell their stories to the newspapers, people who hate you or love you or take a bit of you. So you end up going back to your room and even if it's a suite in the finest hotel…it's almost like a prison cell. But, hey," he says, "if you can't stand the heat, get out of the kitchen."

THE EDGE

The Edge—his real name is Dave Evans—was born on August 8, 1961, not in Ireland but in East Barking, London. Soon after, the whole family—his Welsh parents Garvin and Gwenda with their eldest son Dick (a daughter Jill arrived later) moved to Ireland, and Garvin settled down as a contracting engineer, became an elder of the Presbyterian church, a keen golfer, and founded the Dublin Welsh Male Voice Choir (his mother also went to the Malahide musical society).

By all accounts, The Edge was very quiet as he grew up, wandering about on his own and learning a little piano ("I studied it for two years then packed it in at the ripe old age of 13") before discovering with gusto the joys of the battered old guitar his mother had shelled out $2 for.

Even after he joined the group at Mount Temple he still, for a long time, wasn't that matey with everyone—he was given a Lypton Village name,

Dave Edge [*sic*] (apparently because of the shape of his head and the fact that he was always hanging around the edges rather than being at the center of whatever was going on), but he wasn't invited to join in their activities. He did get up to the odd prank though with the group. When in June 1979 the band were playing a special "Christmas concert" he turned up at a local radio interview eating an ice cream and wearing a Santa Claus outfit.

Nevertheless, he's always been even more religious than Larry and Bono—he keenly joined in the Charismatic Christian group, encouraged the lifestyle where the three of them would rise at 5 a.m. to study the Bible, supported the idea that they should stop making pop music after *October*, and then announced his resignation once more in 1982.

At that time U2 used to get criticized a lot for their religion—Killing Joke calling them "vile Christian creatures" was only the tip of the iceberg. "People don't understand it," reflected The Edge, "so, they lash out. It doesn't bother me though—I'm past caring what people think about our belief."

He still feels, however, that it is his Christian belief which explains just how good U2 really are.

He also gets annoyed when people think U2 are a bit unadventurous because they're never caught doing the usual naughty rock 'n' roll stuff.

"I hate this idea of U2 as a nice, safe band. Maybe it's just because we don't play the rock 'n' roll game. We don't do drugs or get arrested or smash up hotels. All that is just conforming to rock tradition."

Eventually, The Edge was persuaded to stay on and is now recognized as one of the world's leading "axemen." He is married with two children, Holly and Pearse, and spends most of his time with them and his wife Aislinn, who he met at a Buzzcocks concert while he was still in school. She is, he says, the "stabilizing force" in his life.

"The great thing about her," reflects The Edge, "is she's not particularly impressed with rock 'n' roll."

ADAM

Adam Clayton has always been the odd one out in U2—he's the only one who's not deeply religious, he's the one who's most likely to be out partying, and he's the only one with a decidedly snooty English accent. He has the latter because he was born on March 13, 1960, not in Ireland, but in Oxfordshire, where his parents Brian (an Air Force pilot) and Jo lived at the time (he also has a sister named Sarah Jane and a brother named Sebastian).

The family moved into Malahide (just outside Dublin) when Adam was five—three years later he went away to boarding school where he went bird watching, learned some music and art and little else, although he was famous for his excessive politeness at all times. Before he left he told the headmaster "I am going to be a comedian, sir, when I grow up." At his next school, St. Columba's, he started playing bass, first on a cheap $20 guitar then on a $100 one his mum bought for him, but he fared little better. The last straw there was when he went on a smoking trip with two girls up a mountain.

"He stuck out like a sore thumb," remembers Bono. "He used to drink coffee in class and the teachers just got used to it. He got accepted as being really quirky. He wore a kilt."

Adam almost didn't get in the group at all, however, for when he saw Larry's note he ignored it, assuming it was part of some official school activity. However, he was then asked personally—he did, after all, have a smart bass guitar and had briefly been in a group called the Max Quad band at St. Columba's. At their first rehearsal, though, one problem with him was spotted. "People just kept coming up and saying 'there's something wrong' and we couldn't figure it out what it was," sniggers Bono, "until suddenly we thought—it's Adam. Adam can't play."

Fortunately, he soon learned. Over the next few years a new problem emerged, though—he was becoming more and more removed from the three Christian members. They'd sit together, discuss the Bible together and more or less ignore him: "I think it did send me a bit batty for probably a year or so," he now says.

Anyway, Adam was a bit more interested in the whole pop star lifestyle. "To be candid," he admitted later, "I would have liked to have been part of the fashion scene that was going on in London then (when New Romantics clubs were open). Being the weakest member of the band emotionally, I wanted to do that, but I couldn't."

Personally, he still may flip out every now and then (a few years ago he was banned from driving after being stopped by a policeman to whom he allegedly said "Stop messing around with a celebrity!").

"We're a bunch of noisy, rough Irishmen," he says, "who are arrogant enough to drag their tails all the way around the world and I think that's something to be proud of."

And he even has his own eccentric theory as to why U2 keeps getting more and more successful.

"Basically," he explains, "I think we're all nutters but somehow it works. It all comes out in the wash."

LARRY

Larry Mullen, Jr. very rarely gives interviews—he used to say he simply "doesn't enjoy them." He also explained that he will only sign autographs for people at certain times. On the personal side, he has spoken of how U2's travels in America have broadened his musical tastes.

"It was Larry's fault—he did start it," reckons Bono about U2, truthfully as it happens. Larry apparently put up a very embarrassed note saying he's stupidly wasted money on a drum kit and if anyone else had been crazy to have wasted some cash on an instrument they might as well console each other by playing together a little. "Yes," reflects Larry, "and I was in charge for about three days."

Larry was born on October 31, 1961—his father, Larry Senior, had trained for nine years to become a priest before opting out to become a civil servant at the Department of Health and Environment. His mother was called Maureen and he has an older sister Cecilia (another sister, Mary, was born in 1964 but died in 1970). Larry grew up 500 yards from the sea, smashed a plate-glass window with his head when he was four (he wasn't hurt), collected stamps and coins, and secretly listened to the radio.

At first he was encouraged by his parents to try the piano. "The teacher was a really nice lady," he recalls, "but one day she said, 'Larry, you're not going to make it.' She suggested I try something else."

Overjoyed, the nine-year-old Larry announced that'd he like to be a drummer. His mother got him a rubber pad to practice on but said he could only learn if he could raise the $18 for his first term's tuition—he did. He wasn't, however, mad about his teacher. "I carried on with this teacher for about two years," he says. "And I just got bored. This is terrible, but he passed away and...I mean, I was only a kid...and I said, 'Wow! Divine intervention! I don't have to do this anymore!' So I joined a military-style band."

He also joined the famous Artane Boys band. "They told me to get my hair cut," he laughs. "At the time, it was my pride and joy—you know, shoulder-length golden locks. So I got it cut a few inches and they told me to cut it some more. So I told them to stick it and I left." He had lasted just three days.

Larry finally got his own drum kit in 1973—a $32 one that his sister Cecilia had bought and set up in his room while he was out. By 1976 he was ready to form a group—hence his note. At the first rehearsal for the group that became U2—held in his parents' kitchen—a crowd of local folk gathered outside the window to see who was churning out these spectacularly awful versions of "Satisfaction" and "Brown Sugar" by the Rolling Stones: in the end Larry had to get rid of them by hosing them down with water.

These days Larry very, very rarely gives any interviews. In recent times the only statements of note he's made in public are his assertion in an American magazine that if U2 fans go looking for Joshua trees in the Joshua Tree National Park and take them home as souvenirs, "Joshua trees might be extinct by the time this album is over"; and his two statements at a recent New York press conference, firstly that "Abba, they were a big influence on my musical career" (sadly, a joke) and then a totally uncharacteristic outburst for several minutes when asked a question about their forthcoming Irish concert at the end of which the flabbergasted audience and the rest of the band gave him a round of applause as Larry smiled and said "fair play to me." Apart from that, he's man of mystery. "Lawrence," says The Edge, "can be so stubborn."

U2

U2

Deborah Sussman
***Scholastic Update*, December 4, 1987**

U2 is riding high. Their latest album, *The Joshua Tree*, jumped onto the U.S. charts at No. 7 and zoomed to No. 1. Their shows are always sold out. And they are generally considered the biggest rock group around—a band that makes music that fans can dance to and think about. So what does lead singer Bono have to say for himself?

"I'm very awkward. I'm not a very good pop star. "

Millions of fans disagree. But they also respond to Bono's honesty. Bassist Adam Clayton puts it this way: "I think (the fans) see four guys from Ireland who don't want to let go of their dreams."

The four guys from Ireland formed U2 in 1976, in Dublin. Drummer Larry Mullen, Jr., then 14 years old, posted a notice at his school asking if anyone was interested in starting a band. He wound up with Adam Clayton, guitarist Dave Evans, known as "The Edge, " and singer Bono Vox (who was born Paul Hewson).

From the beginning, U2 made music with a message. *War*, their first hit record in the U.S., contained the song "Sunday Bloody Sunday," about violence in Northern Ireland. "Pride (In the Name of Love)" is a tribute to Martin Luther King, Jr. On the new album, Bono sings a bleak, anti-heroin ballad called "Running to Stand Still."

Their commitment shows in their actions, too. They have played benefits for Live Aid, for the human-rights group Amnesty International, and for Ireland's unemployed.

U2 is a special mix of two things. First, U2 makes great music. Guitarist The Edge has called their sound "the tapestry effect." Adam and Larry provide the essential rhythm. Then Bono and The Edge add layers of chiming guitars and soaring vocals.

Second, the members of U2 put themselves into their music. As one fan explained, "I'm sick of everyday rock on the radio. U2 is more real. You can feel their fever." The passion in their lyrics comes from experience. Bono, for example, is the product of a mixed marriage—his mother was a Protestant, and his father was a Catholic.

What's next for U2? A film of *The Joshua Tree* tour is in the works. And Bono has been writing songs for a new album. He thinks that *The Joshua Tree* is the best record U2 has made so far. But he promises: "it will not be our best record by a long shot."

Whatever the members of U2 do next, you can be sure that they will continue to inspire as well as entertain their fans. "I think it's okay to be serious," Bono says, "as long as you're not boring."

U2

America's Sexiest Men

William C. Trott
United Press International, August 4, 1987

The 10 sexiest men in America include an Irish rock star, an Australian-born publisher and a computer-generated talking head. U2's Bono Vox ("beautiful to gaze upon"), publisher Rupert Murdoch ("swagger, daring ...a modern-day conqueror"), and Max Headroom ("the ultimate microchip off the old block") were among *Playgirl* magazine's 10 sexiest men in America for 1987. The annual list also included actor Tom Cruise ("pin-up beautiful"), Massachusetts Gov. Michael Dukakis ("brainy, seductive, scrupulous"), actor-director Dennis Hopper ("mesmeric eyes"), basketball's Michael Jordon, mystery writer Elmore Leonard, radio bad boy Howard Stern, and Dennis Farina of "Crime Story."

U2

YMCA, U2?

***The Advocate*, February 18, 1997**

No, you're not having a flashback, and that's not the Village People. It's Irish superstars U2, all dressed up for their new video, "Discotheque," now getting heavy airplay on MTV. On this first single from their upcoming album, *Pop*, the veteran rockers send up their own brand of soul-searching stardom and embrace the rebirth of music's gayest era: disco. But they've been way campier than this. The lads actually dressed as lassies for a version of their 1992 video "One," which was shelved at the time because it was judged to be too racy. Of course, nowadays that video is all over the tube. So what's next? Bono and friends in a remake of *Showgirls*?

U2

CHAPTER

3

STARS AND SUPERSTARS

In 1983 U2 hit the Top 40 for the first time with their paean to Martin Luther King, "Pride (In the Name of Love)," bestowing upon them mass acceptance and the pop stardom they had craved.

Their prominence grew steadily from the days when they played small clubs and halls to appearances on the auditorium circuit, in which they reached 3,000–5,000 fans a night at venues like Radio City Music Hall in New York. They became a staple on American rock radio with songs like "Gloria," "Sunday Bloody Sunday," and "New Year's Day." The *War* album instigated this rise, becoming the first U2 album to break into the Top 20 in the U.S. (they had conquered the U.K. charts almost the instant they appeared).

Clever marketing helped. The live, four-song EP (not a usual method of distribution in the U.S., but a stalwart in the U.K.) *Under a Blood Red Sky* also went on to sell well. While the band gained growing momentum with these records and the word of mouth about their incredible live shows, it was the release of *The Unforgettable Fire*, which featured U2's first hit single, that really began the groundswell. In the wake of this album, which sold a million copies within a year, the EP went platinum, as did *War*.

If *The Unforgettable Fire* set them on the road to hitsville, *The Joshua Tree* got them there in style. With two chart-topping singles, "I Still Haven't Found What I'm Looking For" and "With or Without You," U2 accomplished longstanding goals—including earning more money than they could ever know what to do with. "Bruce Springsteen," Bono recalled of an artist who had achieved this position several years earlier, "told us, 'Use what you need and let the rest take care of itself. Don't think about it too much or you'll go crazy.'" With that advice under their belts, U2 assumed their position as the band of the hour, the most popular group in the world. After ten years of climbing toward it, they'd reached the pinnacle at last.

U2

The Joshua Tree Bio

Island Records, March 1987

Summer 1978: U2 form in Dublin. U2 are: The Edge (guitars, piano, and vocals), Bono (vocals, guitar), Larry Mullen (drums), and Adam Clayton (bass).

December 1979: U2's first London concerts took place, and included club gigs like the Hope and Anchor (with an audience of nine people), and The Rock Garden. This period also saw the release of *U23*, a three-track EP which gave U2 their first chart success in Ireland. The record was released in Ireland only, and was unavailable elsewhere.

January 1980: U2 won five categories in *The Hot Press* (Ireland's leading rock magazine) Readers Poll.

April 1980: U2 were signed to Island Records.

May 1980: "11 O'Clock Tick Tock," U2's debut British single (produced by Martin Hannet) was released. The band spent most of the summer touring Britain.

August 1980: "A Day Without Me" was released. U2 returned to Dublin to begin work on their debut album.

October 1980: *Boy*, produced by Steve Lillywhite and recorded at Dublin's Windmill Lane Studios, was released. This record received unanimous critical and public acceptance. At this time, their third single, "I Will Follow," was also released. U2 embarked on a major British tour and played their first shows in Europe in Belgium and Holland.

November 1980: U2 returned from Europe and commenced their first American tour, performing at clubs on the East Coast.

January 1981: U2 collected nine #1s in *The Hot Press* Reader's Poll.

February 1981: U2 closed a major U.K. tour with a headlining show at London's Lyceum Ballroom. The demand is so great that over 700 people were turned away. They also made their first appearance on *The Old Grey Whistle Test*. The following day U2 flew to America to begin a three-month tour.

April/May 1981: The U.S. tour closed with concerts at New York's Palladium and the Santa Monica Civic Center. *Boy* charts America.

June 1981: U2 returned to Britain to play the Hammersmith Palais. The following month "Fire" was completed during a break in their U.S. tour at Compass Point Studios in Nassau. "Fire" gave U2 their first British chart single. The remainder of the summer was spent recording *October* in Dublin with Steve Lillywhite once again at the controls.

October 1981: The release of "Gloria" gave U2 their second U.K. chart single. *October*, the LP, charted at number 11 on its first week of release and within a month earned the band their first silver disc. Throughout that month U2 played an eighteen-date, sold-out tour of Britain.

November 1981: U2 returned to America for the first part of the *October* tour.

January 1982: U2 played their first Irish tour in over a year, finishing with a concert at the RDS in front of 5,000 people. Later the same month U2 returned to America to complete the *October* tour that included shows with the J. Geils Band.

March 1982: "A Celebration" was released and gave U2 their third U.K. hit single. During the summer the band headlined a number of European festivals and also played Gateshead, in northeast England with The Police. The autumn is spent writing the *War* LP.

December 1982: U2 played six sold-out U.K. shows, after which they traveled to Europe, and then Ireland, showcasing songs from *War* for the first time.

January 1983: The release of "New Year's Day" gives U2 their first Top Ten hit in Britain.

February 1983: U2 played 27 sold-out dates in Great Britain.

March 1983: *War*, produced by Steve Lillywhite, was released. It entered the U.K. LP chart at number one as the tour finishes. "Two Hearts Beat as One" was released and gave the band their fifth hit single.

April 1983: U2 began a three-month U.S. tour. Within a month *War* entered the U.S. Top Ten and the band received their first American gold record. The tour finished with U2 playing a series of stadium gigs to over 10,000 people a night.

August 1983: U2 headlined A Day at the Races in front of 25,000 people at Dublin's Phoenix Park.

November 1983: *Under a Blood Red Sky*, U2's first live disc, was released. It entered the U.K. charts at number two. At the end of the month the band traveled to Japan for their first concerts in the Far East.

January 1984: *Under a Blood Red Sky* was awarded platinum status. *War* notched up its twelfth consecutive month on the U.K. charts.

March 1984: In the 1983 *Rolling Stone* Critics Poll, U2 were voted Band of the Year.

August 1984: U2 played in New Zealand, their first shows in a world tour.

September 1984: "Pride (In the Name of Love)," the first fruit of the new U2/Eno/Lanois collaboration, is released, eventually reaching number three in the U.K., and earning the group their first ever silver disc for a single. U2 continued their world tour with shows in Sydney and played to over 30,000 fans Lu Melbourne. At the end of the month, U2 returned to Europe with four albums in the Australian charts and "Pride" at number four.

October 1984: *The Unforgettable Fire*, produced by Eno and Lanois, was released. The record charted at number one in the U.K. The tour continued with concerts in France, Belgium, and Holland.

November 1984: U2 played their first British concerts in over eighteen months, which included two shows at the Wembley Arena.

December 1984: U2 continued their tour with a series of concerts on the east coast of America, finishing with two concerts in Los Angeles and San Francisco.

January 1985: U2 toured in Europe.

February May 1985: The band headlined a massive U.S. tour that continued through May that included Madison Square Garden in New York City. *Rolling Stone* call U2 the "band of the eighties."

April 22, 1985: "The Unforgettable Fire" is released as a single in Britain. The following week it enters the U.K. charts at number 8.

June 22, 1985: U2 played The Longest Day Festival at the Milton Keynes Bowl. It is the band's only British date this year. The show was one of a series of European festival dates throughout the summer.

July 29, 1985: The band returned to Ireland to play at Dublin's Crole Park in front of 55,000 people.

July 13, 1985: U2 are one of the bands involved in Live Aid at Wembley Stadium.

February 1986: U2 won the Best Band and Best Live Aid performance categories in *Rolling Stone's* Readers Poll. The Critics Poll placed U2 in a tie for the number one slot with Bruce Springsteen and The E Street Band.

May 1986: U2 played Self Aid, an all-day concert in Dublin for the benefit of Ireland's unemployed.

June 1986: The band interrupted work on songwriting to play six American shows in aid of Amnesty International. The tour, A Conspiracy of Hope, also featured The Police, Peter Gabriel, Lou Reed, Bryan Adams, The Neville Brothers, Joan Baez, and Ruben Blades, among others.

U2 start work on a new album.

March 9, 1987: U2's new album, The Joshua Tree, *is released. The album, produced by Daniel Lanois and Brian Eno, was recorded In Dublin. The band prepare for a massive world tour, starting in America in April.*

U2: Keeping the Rock Faith with *Unforgettable Fire*

Pam Lambert
***The Wall Street Journal*, April 2, 1985**

Seen through the 16th-floor hotel window, the lowering sky is a study in grays. Not unlike his native Ireland, observes bass player Adam Clayton with a drag on the ever-present cigarette. His band mate Bono, known only to his father as Paul David Hewson, surveys the scene. In a voice muffled by singing three nights running to tens of thousands of screaming fans, yet still rich enough to pour over pancakes, he opines, "Every day is inspiring."

"Industrial cities interest me very much," Bono explains. "The spirit of the people seems stronger because the past few years have hit them so hard. Last night was a perfect example. Driving into the city, you see those dark satanic mills—that's a quote; Blake, I think. But when you play, the people just seem to explode. There's a lot in them and the music ignites it."

Residents of less gritty areas may dispute the young Irishman's observation, based though it is on seven visits to the U.S., including this sold-out tour spanning 30 cities that ends May 3. But no one present at that Detroit concert could challenge his assessment of the event. The meeting between 20,000 Midwestern teens and the quartet of Dubliners known as U2 resulted in spontaneous combustion.

When Bono, Clayton, drummer Larry Mullen, Jr., and guitarist and keyboard player Dave "The Edge" Evans took the stage, the vast maw of the Joe Louis Arena crackled with electricity. Fans rose to their feet with a roar and surged toward the small figures bathed in the spotlights. They held aloft matches, banners, the Irish colors, and white flags of peace. They stamped, they cheered, they danced. A few wept hysterically.

As palpable as the emotion in the hall was the band's atmospheric sound. Laying the foundation were Mullen's intricate, diversified drumming and the harmonic counterbalance of Clayton's bass. Above them soared the sonic tapestry spun by The Edge, from layers of guitar with echoey and chiming effects, keyboards, and electronic sequencers.

At times The Edge, whose nickname applies equally well to his angular physique and jagged style of playing, literally juggled his multiple roles, turning to play a few bars on the piano with a guitar still at the ready over his shoulder. Edge, whom Bono affectionately calls "the original poker face," carried it all off with characteristic unflappability. Sober and dignified in a dress shirt buttoned to the collar, he looked more like a church deacon than a "guitar hero."

Not so Bono. He whipped across the stage, tethered only by the slim cord of his microphone, exhorting the crowd to new heights of fervor with the keening voice that at times became a wordless sound color. By the third number he was already drenched with sweat. The concert built to the cathartic climax of "Pride (In the Name of Love)," the stirring paean to the spirit of Martin Luther King that has become U2's most popular single to date. Over Edge's ringing guitar, Bono tore into the song with the primal power of a Springsteen.

The 90-minute performance offered convincing proof that whatever else U2 may represent—and it's come to stand for a number of things—one of the primary reasons the group is the hottest in America is that it's a powerhouse live band. U2 sold out New York's Madison Square Garden for last night's concert in two hours. Fans in Providence, RI, slept outside the Civic Center box office in subfreezing weather to be among the first in line to purchase U2 tickets for tonight.

"To me, a rock 'n' roll concert is 3-D," says Bono. "It's a physical thing—it's rhythm for the body. It's a mental thing in that it should be intellectually challenging. But it's also a spiritual thing, because it's a community, it's people agreeing on something even if it's only for an hour and a half." Adds The Edge: "People tell us during our shows we sell very little in the way of hot dogs."

Early on, the four schoolmates who banded together in the late '70s began to write their own songs. They had quickly discovered they "weren't accomplished enough as musicians to cover other people's material," Edge recalls. It wasn't long, though, before The Edge began to develop the distinctive style that has led some critics to hail him as the most innovative guitarist of the decade.

Though far too modest to be comfortable with such praise ("our musicianship is competent but it's certainly not fantastic," he demurs), the

23-year-old does allow that in his use of echo effects, which others had previously employed in a far more limited way, he may be breaking new ground. "I'm not just playing the guitar, I'm playing a guitar and an echo unit," he explains. "I play to the effects all the time, I use them like an extra pair of hands. I use the repeats...almost like playing tennis against a wall."

Even before U2 signed with Island Records in 1980, the band began to build a fervent following through its live shows. But the group's commercial breakthrough came in 1983 with its third album, *War*. The record, which went platinum, packed a one-two punch; its songs were well-crafted and had something to say. There were the stirring pacifist anthems "Sunday Bloody Sunday" and "New Year's Day" (about the conflict in Northern Ireland and the Solidarity movement in Poland, respectively), as well as the curiously martial love song "Two Hearts Beat as One." (There were also other standouts that took a bit longer to come into their own, like "40," the band's final encore on its current tour. The song takes its name from Psalm 40, whose quietly inspirational words it quotes.)

At the same time, the electricity in the larger venues where U2 was starting to play spurred the emotional and highly theatrical Bono to new heights. Literally. At the mammoth US Festival the singer carried the band's symbol, the white flag he brandished during "Sunday Bloody Sunday," to the top of lighting tower six stories above the stage. His growing reputation for leaping into audiences and scurrying up scaffolding made good copy and electrified some spectators. It appalled others, who felt such antics detracted from the music. The verdict from the rest of U2: "You're either going to kill yourself, or someone else, or the band."

Bono now agrees. "If we continued in the way we were going, I think people might have come to see us wondering would I go into the audience and not come back...sort of like the thrill of racing cars: Will he crash at the next bend?"

With the *War* album and the highly successful live mini-LP *Under a Blood Red Sky* released late the same year, U2 acquired another image it hadn't particularly sought: that of Band-With-a-Message. Three of U2's members are professed Christians, and in the sex-and-drug saturated world of rock, the group came to be hailed—and decried—as something of a great right hope. The mantle of moral prophet fell most heavily on Bono, the band's lyricist and its charismatic voice. In frustration he told the *New York Times*, "How can you be the spokesman for a generation if you've got nothing to say other than 'Help!'?"

U2 may not exactly be a band of evangelicals, but the members do purposely strive for more substance in their songs than "pap music," as they put it, usually offers. Still, few of U2's songs are black-and-white manifestoes. The lyrics tend to be sufficiently ambiguous to permit several interpretations. For instance, the title track of the group's current platinum album, *The Unforgettable Fire*, takes its name from an exhibition of paintings the band saw by survivors of the Hiroshima and Nagasaki bombings. Yet the resulting composition is no anti-nuclear polemic but a hauntingly sad love song.

What counts is that U2 cares passionately about its music—both the songs it has written and those it will someday write. And that excitement appears to be keeping the musicians from just sitting back and savoring their success.

"If your ambition is for fame and fortune and you achieve that, then you are ambitionless and you've come to the end," Bono observes. "But that's not where we are.

"I think we're just being born as a group. Adam said it really well: We've spent the last five years learning to be U2 and we'll spend the next five finding out what U2 can do."

Band on the Run: U2 Soars with a Top Album, a Hot Tour, and Songs of Spirit and Conscience

Jay Cocks; reported by Elizabeth Bland
***Time* magazine, April 27, 1987**

He remembers it this way. Outside San Salvador, 30 or 40 miles up in the hills, mortars began to hit the village, and bombs cratered the hillside. Run.

That was his first thought. And this was the second: Where? It was open all around. The ground shook. The farmers looked at the traveler from Ireland and smiled and pointed. They tried to be reassuring. "That is over there," they said. "We are over here."

"I felt," says the traveler, thinking back in a safer place, "such a fool in the face of it. Those guys lived with it all their lives, and it meant nothing to them. But the fear I felt that day..." Just talking couldn't say it all. It would take a song.

When Bono tears loose on U2's "Bullet the Blue Sky," you can still hear the ache of fear in his voice, the closeness of the memory. The song is immediate and passionate, a cry of conscience on an album full of oblique social speculation and spiritual voyaging. *The Joshua Tree* is not, it would seem at first, a record for these times. Bono and the rest of the Irish band called U2 seem to be citizens of some alternative time frame spliced from the idealism of the '60s and the musical free-for-all of the late '70s. Their songs have the phantom soul of the Band, the Celtic wonderment of their compatriot Van Morrison, and some of the assertiveness of punk, refined into lyrical morality plays.

Their concerts are as revivifying as anything in rock, with a strong undertow of something not often found this side of Bruce Springsteen: moral passion. U2's songs speak equally to the Selma of two decades ago and the Nicaragua of tomorrow. They are about spiritual search, and conscience and commitment, and it follows that some of the band's most memorable performances—and, not incidentally, the ones that have helped U2 break through to an even wider audience—have been in the service of a good cause, at Live Aid or during last summer's tour for Amnesty International. This is not, then, just a band for partying down. "Partying is a disguise, isn't it?" Bono asks, and does not wait for an answer. This is a band that believes rock music has moral imperatives and social responsibilities. There is no one better than U2 at bringing "over there" back "over here," and setting it down right by the front door, where no one can miss it.

U2's sixth and best album, *The Joshua Tree*, in stores for little more than a month, hit No. 1 on Billboard's chart this week. The album's first single, "With or Without You," has made the band's heaviest mark on Top 40 radio and is already in the Top Ten. Other tunes on *The Joshua Tree* (the title was inspired by a California desert town where '70s rocker Gram Parsons died) are likely to keep it company. U2 launched a scheduled 18-month world tour in Arizona just three weeks ago, will play the U.S. through mid-May, perform in Europe most of the summer, then return to the States in September. "I guarantee you that when U2 comes back this record will be bigger than ever," says Andy Denemark, a director of programming at NBC Radio. "There's a lot of depth to this album."

He means depth of the commercial, not thematic variety, but he is right in either case. "People are always saying U2 is the largest underground act in the world," says their manager, Paul McGuinness. "I suppose that's true, but it is starting to change." And in a hurry, at that. Ask Thom House, who sold U2 concert tickets for local gigs via computer at his two video stores in New York and New Jersey. Crowds started lining up at his Manhattan store Thursday night, and at first, he says, "I had no idea why they were there. I chased them away, saying we were not selling tickets until Saturday. They kept coming back. We bought movie tickets and passed them out, so they could leave and come back. They stayed. It started raining. They stayed, hundreds of them. This group must rank close to the Beatles."

Just a second. The sound you hear is brakes being put on, and it is the band that has the heaviest foot on the pedal. "We don't think we're that good, really," says Bono, 26, who writes the lyrics and fronts the band both as lead singer and resident shaman. "We think we are overrated, and though we're concerned about living up to people's expectations, it scares us even to live up to our own expectations." "The band is at a frontier," says bass guitarist Adam Clayton, 27. "You don't get something for nothing. This tour is definitely frightening."

It is also taking on distinct phenomenological proportions. Even in Arizona, in the earliest stages, with Bono's voice raggedy from overrehearsing and with the band searching for a solid connection with both the audience and one another, there was a final fusion of performer and spectator that is one mark of great rock 'n' roll. Some of the songs, especially earlier efforts, can get tongue-tied by the unwieldy ambition of their lyrics and the discursiveness of the melody line. The audience shares a devotional intensity, however, that anchors the concert as a whole experience even when the tunes range free. Bono stalks a song as much as sings it, and the moment he takes the stage there is no doubt what his terms are: unconditional surrender. Clayton and drummer Larry Mullen, Jr., 25, have found some solid musical grounding, and the lead guitarist, The Edge, 25, can work a riff around to an epiphany.

(Of course you will want to know about those snappy nicknames before anything else. Bono, born Paul Hewson, got his off a sign advertising Bono Vox of O'Connell Street, a hearing aid store in Dublin. Not until later did he learn that the phrase meant "good voice" in cockeyed Latin, but he had long since dropped the Vox. Bono—say it Bon-no, to sound like the German city and not like the name of Cher's ex-husband—came up with the name for David Evans. "The edge is the border between something and nothing," he announced. "I am not a particularly edgy person," The Edge elaborates, "so it is funny." Now, then.)

It is on Bono, however, that all eyes stay fixed. U2 carries the day, but he carries the show. That has always been the way, ever since the band's first scuffling days in Dublin during the punk whirligig. "They were very bad," admits manager McGuinness. "But it wasn't the songs that were the attraction. It was the energy and commitment to performance that were fantastic even then. Bono would run around looking for people to meet his eyes."

Once met, those eyes are well remembered. They lock in for good as he travels the stage in a perpetual panther prowl. His presence is not specifically sexual, but it is intensely sensual and lends heft to his lyrical excursions. It also gives the spirituality and frequent Christian symbolism of the songs ("See the thorn twist in your side"; "I stand with the sons of Cain") a welcome grounding in earthly delights. "Their show is the best around," remarks an appreciative T-Bone Burnett, a guitar player and record producer (Elvis Costello, the BoDeans) of no mean skill. "U2 is what church should be." Lest such praise become a little burdensome, Larry Mullen keeps this reflection handy: "At the end of the day, it's just rock 'n' roll."

For audiences, though, that music can be a lifeline. A Springsteen song can tap right into your daily existence. A U2 tune like "Running to Stand Still," with a trancelike melody that slips over the transom of consciousness, insinuates itself into your dreams. Patty Klipper, from Parsippany, N.J., says, "First they opened my mind to their music. Then their music opened my mind to the world." The band's official fan magazine, called *Propaganda* and edited by their tour lighting director, is a neatly turned out publication that features the usual inside band stuff as well as some unexpected calls to political action. Fan publications usually urge readers to stay in touch with the musicians. *Propaganda* urges them to write letters on behalf of Amnesty International: "Please write to the federal authorities in Yugoslavia, asking for the immediate and unconditional release of Dr. Nikola Novakovic and all other Prisoners of Conscience. Write to: President of the Presidency of Bosnia-Herzegovina...Begin your letter 'Your Excellency...'"

His Excellency is not likely to invite the band to fall by for plum brandy and cabbage rolls, and U2 is probably not at the top of the White House invitation list, either. They are dead serious about their liberal activist politics although careful not to be sanctimonious. Clayton talks worriedly about some fans turning to the band "needing to be healed," and Bono says, "I would hate to think everybody was into U2 for 'deep' and 'meaningful' reasons. We're a noisy rock 'n' roll band. If we all got onstage, and instead of going 'Yeow!' the audience all went 'Ummmm' or started saying the rosary, it would be awful." The band shares a kind of ecumenical, nonspecific spirituality. Bono, The Edge, and Mullen are Christians, although of a particularly loose-limbed variety.

The Edge: "I suppose I am a Christian, but I am not a religious person." Bono: "I feel unworthy of the name. It is a pretty high compliment. But I feel at home in the back of a Catholic cathedral, in a revival hall or walking down a mountainside." Mullen: "I am a Christian and not ashamed of that. But trying to explain my beliefs, our beliefs, takes away from it. I have more in common with somebody who doesn't believe at all than I do with most Christians. I don't mind saying that."

Clayton, who alone has not announced formally for Christianity, says simply that for journalists "religion was an easy angle, a hook to hang a story on. We all believe in much the same things but don't express ourselves in the same way." This, along with Clayton's inborn rebellious instincts and up-tempo temperament, caused some intramural tension that has only lately been resolved. "I was in the wilderness for a few years, so there was a natural antagonism within the band that people picked up on. Now the spirituality contained within the band is equal to all the members." Clayton, tan and muscular, with an army recruit's haircut and a pair of steel-rimmed spectacles that makes him look like an insurrectionist with a bass instead of a bomb, remains U2's most sulfurous presence, lending a slight but leveling tension to the stage show. Still, the band's fervor comes from deep springs, not simply from sheer showmanship. "Great songs and all that great heart," says Lou Reed, a formidable musician whose influence can be heard on "Running to Stand Still." "U2's not a pop group. They are in this for real."

For high stakes too. The band's commitment, to its audience and its music, sanctions and encourages the kind of social concern that in the Reagan '80s became unfashionable, even antique. The album that *The Joshua Tree* displaced from the top of the chart is a revisionist rap record by the Beastie Boys, three well-born white teens copping street attitude but assuming social postures that teeter between preening smugness and snide irresponsibility. After arriving in Arizona, U2 discovered that Governor Evan Mecham had canceled the state's observance of Martin Luther King, Jr.'s birthday. U2 considered canceling the concerts but did something better: made a contribution to the Mecham Watchdog Committee and played "Pride (In the Name of Love)"—a tribute to King—with a joyful vengeance. But it is not just that U2 is on the side of the angels. It has given a new charter and a fresh voice to conscience. "A sense of humor is something I value," Bono says, "but we don't play rock 'n' roll with a wink." Without sermonizing, they have become a rallying point for a new and youthful idealism. After Live Aid and Farm Aid and after the Amnesty tour, after heated and heartfelt music from Jackson Browne and Little Steven, it is no longer corny or uncool to be concerned, to get involved. And especially after the breakaway success of U2, it seems that audiences are ready to take heart and to reach out. There are, as Bono sings in the opening of "In God's Country," "new dreams tonight." "Nobody knows how it works," Adam Clayton says. "You turn the music up as loud as you can and hope people like it." Mullen admits, "I do believe our music is special. But you have to separate the music from the people. The music is special, but I don't think we are. We are ordinary people." They are earnestly going about trying to "demythologize" themselves, as T-Bone Burnett puts it, cutting themselves down to manageable size, the better to handle their superstar stature. It is a posture that is both defensive and pragmatic, disarming and perhaps just a shade desperate. "People respond to our naïveté," Clayton insists. "I think they see four guys from Ireland who don't want to let go of their dreams."

It was Larry Mullen who set the dream in motion. He posted a note on the bulletin board of Mount Temple, a public high school in Dublin, asking if there was anyone interested in forming a rock band. That was in 1976, and he was 14. "Stories simplify how big a step that was at the time," says Clayton. "That one action of Larry's has affected the rest of his life and, indeed, everyone's." David Evans (yet to be called The Edge) was a top student in his Mount Temple class, but he had been spending spare time "strumming away" on acoustic and electric guitar. When he saw that notice, he felt a decidedly nonacademic stirring in his soul. "Ah," he thought, "this could be it." Mullen had been playing drums since the age of nine, charging money for household chores ("I should have done them anyway, I know") in hopes of getting his own kit. His parents finally gave him part of a set—made by a toy manufacturer and retailing for $15—at which young Larry happily flailed away until his father, an environmental-health inspector and part-time optician, suggested he try to get a group together. "You are not going to get anywhere," the senior Mullen pointed out, "if you continue playing on your own."

The Saturday after the school notice went up, six or seven Mount Temple students appeared in the Mullen kitchen and started playing Rolling Stones tunes. "During the course of the afternoon," Mullen remembers, "I saw that some people could play. The Edge could play. Adam just looked great. Big, bushy hair, long caftan coat, bass guitar and amp. He talked like he could play, used all the right words, like gig. I thought, this guy must know how to play. Then Bono arrived, and he meant to play the guitar, but he couldn't play very well, so he started to sing. He couldn't do that either. But he was such a charismatic character that he was in the band anyway, as soon as he arrived. I was in charge for the first five minutes, but as soon as Bono got there, I was out of a job."

The boys who became U2—the name, suggested by a local musician pal, refers ironically to the high-altitude spy plane—all knew of one another, vaguely, from school. The Clayton and Evans families were friendly. The Edge, whose family is Welsh, and Bono (still generally called Paul Hewson back then) had briefly gone to the same guitar teacher. For his part, Bono had a distant but still vivid impression of Clayton, who was raised outside London and in Kenya, and had moved to Dublin with his mother and airline-pilot father at the age of eight. He had come to Mount Temple from boarding school "pretty freaked, terrified I was going to get beat up. I thought the quieter you kept, the more wary people would be. Intimidate them and not give anything away." It worked. "Clayton was an incredible rebel, in the true sense of the word," Bono recalls fondly. "He would come into class with a flask of coffee and put it up on his desk and start to drink. The people would blow their heads."

Clayton's other prop was his bass, a gift from his parents ("I'll play till I'm bigger than the Beatles!" he promised them), which he handled with similar élan. It became clear after a little time, however, that there were certain limitations to style. The Claytons were dubious when the band started to talk about turning pro. "Quite sensibly," The Edge remembers, "they realized this business is very hard and that Adam is not the world's most gifted musician and what possible chance has he got of making it. My folks probably made the same calculation." "Adam's amazing," says Bono flatly. "He just pretended he could play the bass, when in fact he couldn't. And at the age of 16, he pretended he knew the music business inside and out." He, of all the four, saw the band as his future.

He had to. Bono was dubious at first about joining up ("I thought rock was ugly"), and The Edge at these early stages "didn't ever consider the band as anything other than a worthwhile thing to do on Wednesday afternoons." Mullen, the youngest of the group, could only dream of a career, while Bono and The Edge were getting on with their education and taking their final exams. Clayton, however, had been booted out of Mount Temple, and worried about "commitment" from the others. He hustled hard, trying to force their hand, and made contact with McGuinness.

The band, which had gone through a variety of names, including the Hype, was better with chutzpah than with chords. "You see," says Mullen, "we couldn't play. We were very, very, very bad." In the first hot flush of punk, this did not greatly matter, and after seeing them in 1978, McGuinness, who had done mostly film production work up until that moment, agreed to become their manager. "It looked to me like they would be a great rock band," he says now, adding, "I've only had to be right once."

McGuinness farmed himself out for the occasional production job and began to "live off my wife." The boys, still living at home, would occasionally be driven to dates by a stray mom or dad. This sort of early scuffling can break a band or bond it, and with U2 it seems to have brought the group closer. After a bit. "The first couple of years," says Clayton, "we kind of hated each other. It was very competitive, and everyone was trying to come out on top." As the band gigged around, scrambling to get heard by record companies and earn a little living money, there were third-party suggestions that one member or another be dropped in the interest of strengthening the band's musicianship. All such notions were rejected out of hand. "We never, ever felt that being a great musician was a necessary qualification for being in U2," says McGuinness. "The individuals were much more important than whether you could play."

There were other ties, ones that stayed strong beneath the surface tension. Grief could be shared, understood. When he was 15, Bono's mother died from the effects of a stroke she suffered at his grandfather's funeral. Mullen lost his mother in a traffic accident in 1978. "The thing that has kept us going," he says now, "is the fact that we are friends. This whole band is based on our friendship. If it had originally been based on our music, we would have failed."

After some patchy times and a couple near misses with record companies, McGuinness struck a deal with Island in 1980 that allowed an unusual amount of creative independence ("They had to accept the record without any question"), and the band released its first album, *Boy*. That same year, it paid its first visit to America, opening in Boston for a band of what Bono calls "some local renown. We started to play, and all the people started standing up, turning over the tables. The place was packed. Steam was dripping off the ceilings, and they wouldn't let us leave the stage. We had one, two, three encores. I just looked at Edge and said, 'Hey, wow, if this is America, I want some more! This is it!'" When the star attractions finally made it to the stage, the club was empty.

It would take U2 a couple more years and two more albums before it could compound that Boston frenzy worldwide and come up with the first song that could stand as its anthem. That was "Sunday Bloody Sunday" from 1983's *War*, a tune about the divisive heat and blind violence of modern Ireland that curried no favor on either side. *War* was U2's best work until *The Joshua Tree*; the year after its release, Island, detecting seismic vibrations, renegotiated the band's contract with McGuinness. "Now U2's in an absolutely unique position," he reports. "They own outright every song they ever wrote, and they always will."

The contract also made them flush, and that of course has further quickened the collective conscience. Bono has been flabbergasted to read that he and his wife Alison, another Mount Temple grad, live in a seaside castle near Dublin. "It's a little round tower," he laughs. "Three levels, three rooms." Domesticity presents its own problems. Although he, like the rest of the band, cherishes a bit of personal distance and privacy, Bono acknowledges, "My life is just a mess. When I am away, I'm not at home. When I'm home, I'm not at home. I come in when she is going out." Ali, who is studying politics at Dublin's University College, "is the dark eye," in the words of her admiring husband. "She will not be worn like a brooch. We have a stormy relationship because she is her own woman." While in Arizona, worried that she sounded a little depressed on the transatlantic phone, Bono asked his in-laws to "keep an eye on her. They must have rung her right away, because I got this phone call saying, 'I don't need a baby-sitter!' and she slammed down the phone." Ali made an unscheduled appearance in Arizona 48 hours later and stayed five days.

Mullen, who added Junior to his surname after his father began to receive large tax bills meant for his prosperous son, lives on a beach near Dublin. His girlfriend does office-temp work, so she is free to join the tour at frequent intervals. "I live in a nice house and don't feel bad about it," he says. "But I don't drive a flashy car, first of all because I don't want to, and second of all because I think that would be rude in a country like Ireland, where there is high unemployment." Clayton lives in Dublin ("an incestuous place"), though his dreams of taking off for "another climate, a beach somewhere" are tempered by the sure knowledge that "I'd always return." With his wife Aislinn, who works for a boutique, and their daughters, The Edge also lives in Dublin, although he frets, "My life revolves around the music, the keyboard. My family should make a difference, but I am not able to spend enough time with them."

Politics and the past make perpetual demands, of course. The band underwrites Mother Records, an outfit that gives young bands their first shot. "We're trying to provide an opportunity for Irish groups," McGuinness says. "You don't have to be Irish, but it helps. We do have one Scottish group." Besides the trip to El Salvador last year, Bono and Ali found time for seven weeks of relief work in Ethiopia, and Mullen tries to stay tapped in to the roots: "All the neighbors knew my mother, and I try to drop in on them occasionally, just to keep my foot in." Celebrity, however, does have its inconveniences. "When you go into a shop, and you're in the only successful band to have come out of Ireland since whenever, every father and uncle and grandmother knows who you are. It is embarrassing when you want to go buy some socks."

There are further signs of changes and counterbalances as well. Although Bono has received lyric credit on the last two albums, the songwriting has traditionally involved the whole band, "chipping away," as Mullen puts it, "chipping away and doing it until it feels right. It takes an awful long time and is incredibly frustrating." Sometimes the system works well—"Pride (In the Name of Love)" was written at a sound check in a total of seven minutes—but The Edge is mulling over further streamlining. "I think in the future Bono and I will work together more closely," he says. "It seems to be a quicker way. When you've got everybody there, it can be very fun, but slow." However this may affect the rest of the band, they are all agreed on one point. "*The Joshua Tree* is the best record we've made to date," Bono declares, "but it will not be our best record by a long shot."

Bono has been reading Walker Percy, Flannery O'Connor, and Raymond Carver and has promised to write new songs during this tour. He has already begun one, based on a recent video shoot at a grungy Los Angeles location and a chance encounter with a gay Vietnam vet. "I spotted empty bottles all over the roof with the label Wild Irish Rose wine," he says. "So I started this song. It is about suicide. The opening line is 'This city of angels has brought a devil out in me.'" (Well, the band has been listening to a good deal of country music.) He yearns to write a song that, as manager McGuinness puts it, "could go into the language."

It may have already been done. "I Still Haven't Found What I'm Looking For," the second cut on *The Joshua Tree*, has one of those seemingly casual melodies that, a little like a high-flying version of the Police's "Every Breath You Take," is heard once and slips directly into the collective memory. It manages to work much of what the band believes in, yearns for, and has gone through, in the past and in prospect, into a single simple, elegant reflection:

I believe in the Kingdom Come
Then all the colors will bleed into one
But yes I'm still running
You broke the bonds
You loosed the chains
You carried the cross
And my shame...You know I believe it
But I still haven't found
What I'm looking for...

Let them run on, then. They are not likely to get caught. And they already know the way home.

U2

Luminous Times: U2 Wrestle with Their Moment of Glory

John Hutchinson
***Musician*, October 1, 1987**

A lot can happen in half a year. In the last six months, U2 have gone from being a beloved middle-level rock group to The Biggest Band in the World. Almost alone among their generation of groups they have upheld rock's best values while also winning a stadium-size audience. Which is not the motivation for creating music, but which is surely a heck of a trick. This year almost every popular musician ends up talking about U2. Sting, finishing up his new album in New York, recalls the farewell appearance of the Police on the final night of the 1986 Amnesty International tour: "The last song we played, we handed our instruments over to U2. Every band has its day. In '84 we were the biggest band in the world, and I figured it was U2's turn next. And I was right. They are the biggest band in the world. A year from now it'll be their turn to hand over their instruments to someone else."

We've got to be careful here not to measure success just by seats sold or dollars generated. The Bee Gees were once the Biggest Band in the World. So were Fleetwood Mac and the Monkees. If you just count cash receipts, the B.B.I.T.W. right now is probably Bon Jovi. And in 1965, Herman's Hermits outsold the Beatles. No, if we're going to bestow such grand and stupid mantles, we must be clear: U2 are—right now—the band that best combines great talent with mass appeal, who capture and set to music this moment better than anyone else with a prayer of reaching so wide an audience.

In the six months since the release of *The Joshua Tree*, the entire climate around U2 has changed. This Irish quartet, who had never had a record in the Top Ten scored two Number One singles and a Number One LP right out of the box. Their spring tour of the U.S. was a triumph, and their autumn return promises to bring down the stadiums. Perhaps more important, they have continued to quietly release new songs—by now almost another album's worth. The flip sides of U2's singles "With or Without You" and "I Still Haven't Found What I'm Looking For" gave buyers four new songs—"Luminous Times," "Walk to the Water," "Spanish Eyes," and "Deep in the Heart." In August they upped the ante by packaging "Where the Streets Have No Name" with *three* new tracks: "Race Against Time," "Silver and Gold" and "Sweetest Thing." Add in their two new collaborations with Robbie Robertson ("Testimony," "Sweet Fire of Love") and Bono's contribution to the new T-Bone Burnett album ("Purple Heart") and you have an idea of U2's creative energy in 1987.

Sitting in their manager's Dublin office above Windmill Lane, the studio where their albums are recorded, Adam Clayton and Bono listen to acetates of the three newest songs. "Race Against Time" opens with a low drone, moves into a heavy bass riff—played by Edge, and sounding as though it has been inspired by a rhythm on the Irish hand-drum, the *bodhran*—and then is augmented by "treated" guitar. Bono, dressed in black, his hair swept back into a ponytail, taps his feet, swaying slightly from side to side; Adam smiles and beats time with his hand. Then a distant voice rises: Bono sings in an Ethiopian language, and follows it up with the phrase, "race against time." It is an infectious groove ("Larry did this in one take," says Adam with a grin) and has an African flavor. It is vaguely reminiscent of Peter Gabriel. Bono tells me that the song was inspired by his visit to Ethiopia, and refers to the famine there. "It reminds me of the desert," he says. "The desert is so empty, but it aches with a strange kind of fullness."

Next up is "Silver and Gold," a version of the song Bono wrote at the Sun City sessions. It's tough and raw, with Bono in husky and confident voice, underpinned by a sinuous bass line, and with Edge demonstrating his newfound prowess in blues-based guitar. "Sweetest Thing" opens with a piano, picks up tempo and moves along with tight, fast-moving percussion and fluid bass. Bono dips in and out of a falsetto, singing, "I'm losing you" in a way that recalls John Lennon.

Three new tracks, all of them memorable, and they're hidden away on the back of the third single off *Joshua Tree*. Just what are these guys doing? Riding the crest of a wave, U2 are brimful of confidence and have a rock-steady belief in the power of their music. They're willing—indeed, determined—to stretch their talents to the limit. Bono says, before the interview begins, "We're nowhere near our peak yet. We're only just beginning to tap a completely new set of ideas."

It is the day after U2's gig in the vast NEC arena in Birmingham, England, which, with the exception of an outdoor concert in Cork on the following Saturday, brings the first leg of their world tour to a close. The Dublin evening papers announce that Bono has been listed in the top ten of "The World's Sexiest Men." At this moment, though, Bono doesn't look too sexy. He's tired, unshaven, and his voice is a mite hoarse. On the way into Windmill Lane, where the outside walls are covered with U2 graffiti, he was encircled by a small crowd of fans, mainly female, who asked for autographs, shook his hand, and shrieked with excitement. He said a few words and was escorted, almost at a run, to the doors of the studio. While he waits for the other members of the band, Bono chats quietly. "It's strange coming home like this," he murmurs. "You come back to Dublin, to your family and all the familiar places, and it seems like another world."

If Dublin looks a little different to Bono, U2 looks different to Dublin. Earlier in the summer, when the band played two nights at the Gaelic soccer stadium Croke Park, the newspapers were filled with stories about the local boys making good in the U.S.A. The predictable backlash quickly came from Irish journalists who questioned the efficacy, if not the good intentions, of U2's concern for the world's underprivileged. Those shots have rankled the band, but not as much as the fact that critics have spent more time analyzing the U2 phenomenon than U2's music. Being without honor in your home is a traditional burden of being The Biggest.

Edge arrives at the office looking like a hippie. He is still the diplomat who smoothes over rough patches. Larry Mullen, newly vocal after years of refusing interviews, is the most down-to-earth in his comments, which are generally wry and good-humored. Because Larry kept his silence for so long—and maybe also because he looks like James Dean—he got an image as reserved and serious. So journalists have recently been delighted to find out what a funny guy the drummer is. At a New York press conference last spring a reporter asked the band if Larry's status as a sex symbol in Japan had spread elsewhere, Mullen, who had not spoken a word the whole time, raised his head, leaned forward and said, "Not yet, but we're hopeful."

As our conversation begins, Adam considers his replies carefully and at times gets a little acerbic. Bono, as ever, is the most vociferous. He restrains himself at first, but gradually becomes more involved, at times becoming quite agitated. Some of his pronouncements, read in print, may seem overly earnest and perhaps a bit pompous, but in person his fiery character is charming. If he sometimes talks faster than he thinks, you nonetheless feel that his sincerity is genuine and that his comments are always heartfelt; his integrity burns right through any skepticism.

In a few years somebody else will be the Biggest Band in the World. But Bono, Adam, Larry, and Edge will still be making music from their hearts, and lots of us will still be listening. In fact, when all this current hubbub dies down, the music will probably be easier to hear. Then we can forget about charts and political litmus tests and get back to the real soul of U2. "Isn't it incredible," Larry Mullen smiles, "that when you reach a certain stage everything suddenly becomes *important*. Everyone has been talking about the U2 phenomenon and not so much about the music. That's the bottom line, after all."

Musician: Let's get this out of the way first: How seriously do you take the Irish criticism that you're only playing liberal songs for white middle-class audiences in America, and that U2 is ineffectual as a force for change?

Bono: That assessment is wrong; it's actually inaccurate.

Edge: Our perspective is Irish. Sure, that isn't as relevant to a black kid in New York as to someone in Dublin, but there's a spirit in what we do that I believe can transcend cultural barriers. The success of U2 is based on the fact that it does that. We find in our European shows that we have a language barrier, yet some of the audience members seem to understand what we're getting at better than our English or Irish audiences.

Bono: It's fair to say that we don't have a big black audience in the United States, and we really regret this, but it has nothing to do with the color of their skin. It's cultural. Black music has a different sensibility in American urban areas; at least it's different from an Irish urban situation. We have a large Latin audience in the Southwest and in Florida, and to say that it's primarily middle-class means nothing. Working class in America is middle-class by Irish standards. I think that that critic's description of the audience at the Amnesty International concert at the Giants Stadium as "mainly white, middle-class and content as a field of flowers" is misleading. I've never met a man whose contentment is derived from his class—never! Why should a person who is middle-class be necessarily more content than a working-class person? This is a completely empty-headed argument intellectually, and that critic ought to have been more rigorous.

Adam: It's irrelevant. Why is he trying to impose class structures on music? Is Frank Sinatra any less of an artist because you have to pay a small fortune to see his concerts?

Musician: But do your socially conscious songs actually achieve anything in terms of change, or are they simply a handy release valve for the consciences of thousands of young people?

Bono: I don't think that it's an artist's duty to provide answers, and the idea that a rock 'n' roll band is going to change the political infrastructure of a country is, I think, just naïve. We, as a group, don't have to justify any reaction to our music. Literally, if people went home and battered their wives after a U2 concert, or stuck syringes into their arms, or even committed mass suicide [laughs]—we can't be responsible for the exact response to our music. But, as it happens, the "Conspiracy of Hope" tour doubled Amnesty International's membership in the United States. Significant?

Musician: Yet it was reported that Amnesty International said that the number of young new members was more of a burden than anything else.

Edge: Not true. That was a spokesman who didn't know what he was talking about. We contacted Amnesty International when we heard about that, and they said that, on the contrary, the young people who joined Amnesty International because of U2's interest and the "Conspiracy of Hope" tour are greatly valued and are highly effective.

Bono: There are people who have been working for twenty years for that to happen! I read the article where that point was made, and not only was it bogus, but it was dangerous. It actually *encouraged* apathy, and that, I'm afraid, is the great middle-class disease. And I'll bet you one thing—that the guy who wrote that article isn't from Cedarwood Road [one of the less privileged areas of Dublin]. In my experience, the only people who talk about class structures are middle-class. As it happens, I *really* respect the U2 audience. I think they're extraordinary and, indeed, a kind of phenomenon in their own right. They come from different backgrounds, and it seems that, more than any other audience in rock 'n' roll, they have found a way of channeling their energy into hope.

Musician: At your homecoming concert at Croke Park there seemed to be an incredible feeling of solidarity between the band and the audience that I've never seen at an outdoor gig of that size. But Bob Geldof, in the British TV documentary on the show, said that the audience's newfound optimism would probably only last as long as the bus ride home. There were a large number of drunk, semi-hysterical kids in the crowd.

Bono: [*angrily*] How many? All of them?

Musician: No, but a significant proportion, I'd say.

Bono: A small minority of a rock 'n' roll audience of 50,000 is a lot of people. If even ten percent of them are assholes, it's a crowd, a frightening mob. But have you ever tuned into the police radio at midnight on Christmas Eve? It's unbelievable—you'll hear things like

"They have a priest up against the wall." There are more people hurt at Midnight Mass on Christmas Eve in Dublin than at a U2 concert! Some people obviously drink too much. I've drunk too much; I've fallen over; I've called the fellow in front of me names and then put up my fists when he turned round. But a lot of the U2 audience are working men with wives and kids—a guy might work overtime so he can get to the concert. And why should we put the responsibility on him to sign up with Amnesty—the guy probably hasn't got the time to have his kid baptized by the local priest! You can't make these grand assessments of the whole audience. Go home with them; get on the bus with them! When was the last time Bob Geldof got on the bus to go home to Finglas? And who knows—maybe next time the kid will think twice about who he votes for, instead of only once.

Adam: I just don't think it's true that people forget everything on the bus home—not at all.

Bono: Even if it is true, it doesn't detract from what U2 does.

Larry: U2's music has many different elements. If someone comes along to a concert and is inspired to join Amnesty that's one part of it, but someone else may feel emotionally overwhelmed by the music, and someone else again may just come along to jump up and down and bop. They're all relevant; they're all important. They're intertwined, and to put emphasis on one element is wrong.

Bono: And that's the story of U2's relationship with the press. They put emphasis on one thing or another, instead of taking the situation as a whole. The press like grand statements, but not necessarily statements about truth. That's where we sometimes differ.

Edge: They can simplify the message to a point where what's really being said by the band is no longer evident. What we're about is possibly too complicated to be explained in a few lines in a review, and even to attempt to explain it like that is wrong. I think a review can give an impression, but it can't sum up U2 in total, or give all the story.

Musician: Where are journalists getting it wrong?

Adam: We can't tell you, man. Just listen to the records!

Bono: The most serious misconception is in oversimplification. It's easy to mock us because we have belief in, and respect for, our audience—in a way that is unusual for a rock 'n' roll band. It's easy to paint it as a populist ploy, or as stupidity and naïveté. But we came out of that audience, and we're now onstage, playing to it. Whether the U2 audience will be any more significant than the audiences of the '60s or '70s remains to be seen.

Edge: We're just trying to figure out how to live in this world. That's what it's all about.

Bono: I'm sorry. I apologize if I got carried away with myself. This is an issue that riles me a little bit. I probably haven't expressed myself that well, because I'm still thinking the matter out—I haven't really thought it through enough to give an accurate response. But it worries me that people judge us by their own assumptions regarding what the band is about. When *The Unforgettable Fire* came out there was a negative reaction to it in the United States—it wasn't a straight rock 'n' roll album, but we started to experiment, and experimentation is almost not allowed, because pop is the dominant force in music in the '80s. People are impressed by record sales. Why? I also think that a great deal of rock criticism is at an all-time low at the moment. It's got to the stage in Ireland where journalists have decided to criticize U2 just for the hell of it! That's not a good enough reason. What rock 'n' roll criticism has to do is own up to its own limitations and uncertainties. And then there is the problem of being an Irish band in Ireland, where a whole generation is on the slippery slope, and they're holding on to us, trying to turn us into some kind of icon.

Musician: How do you rid yourselves of that burden? And how can you keep in touch with that generation?

Bono: I don't know. I don't know how we're going to do it. I'd say the odds are against us doing it. All this responsibility has been thrown upon us, just because we're a rock 'n' roll band.

Musician: But you've taken a lot of it upon yourselves—it's a brave thing to have done.

Bono: I suppose we do make music that we want to hear. That's all. But I'll tell you what I think. I see something changing—I think people are looking for art that doesn't just reflect the chaos, but *challenges* it. And that's why I believe there will be a re-examination of soul music, country music, gospel, and folk—music made by *people*. As one French writer said about us, what's so extraordinary about being *human*? To a lot of the intelligentsia, the most offensive aspect of U2 is our lack of self-consciousness. But rock 'n' roll is not an intellectual art form; it's much more to do with instinct. With U2 I'd like to achieve a balance between the head and the heart, and I'm not sure that we've got it yet. But at least that's what we're aiming for. I'd like to make a rock 'n' roll album now that has at its core a sense of abandonment—there are so few artists owning up to what it's like to have both fears *and* faith.

Adam: Our music is about *humanity*; it doesn't create fantasies.

Bono: A filmmaker like Francis Ford Coppola doesn't have to justify *Apocalypse Now* in the way that we have had to justify songs like "Sunday Bloody Sunday" or "Bullet the Blue Sky." He sees things in a particular way, and expresses them in a movie. We accept it, look at it, and examine the film. With U2 that doesn't seem to be the case. This word "responsibility" crops up all the time in assessments of U2, but do critics judge Coppola by the reaction of cinema-goers to *Apocalypse Now?* Shouldn't we ask that question about rock criticism? People said, "How can you write a song like 'Sunday Bloody Sunday' when you don't live in Derry?" But they didn't ask Coppola if he was on the river being smuggled into Cambodia. Of course he wasn't—he's *a writer*! I think that rock 'n' roll criticism itself has to be reappraised—it has to be more intellectually rigorous. It's turning in on itself, and the same standards should apply to rock as apply to other art forms.

Musician: Tell me about the three songs on the B-side of your new single, "Where the Streets Have No Name."

Edge: They're different. They're three extremes of what U2 can do. The first one is a version of "Silver and Gold," where you'll find some of the rawest rock 'n' roll that you can hear. We've got a beautiful song called "Sweetest Thing," which is pop as it should be—not produced out of existence, but pop produced with a real intimacy and purity. It's very new for us.

The last one is called "Race Against Time," which is a study in rhythm. It's like taking some of the rhythms of traditional Irish music, where there is no emphasis on the two or the four—a strange, twisting, rhythmic experiment. I actually played bass on the track, but it was inspired by Adam. He has the knack of playing parts that no one else would ever think of. My bass playing is very predictable, but this is one of my more unusual parts.

Bono: On the "With or Without You" EP there are three songs that all deal with obsession, with that kind of sexuality. I'd like to have done a whole side, a whole record, blue. That EP is something close.

Musician: "Luminous Times" is very somber—it's almost like a track from Low or Heroes.

Edge: It's a great track. Some of those songs would definitely have been contenders for the album, but what happened was—and it is a classically "U2" thing to do—we had quite a lot of time to work on the record, but right in the middle, the Amnesty tour came up. That took us out of circulation for about two months, because of the dates, recovering, getting the gear back, and getting back into the studio. We ran out of time. There would have been two records, depending on which songs we decided to finish. There was this one album, the "blues" album that Bono was talking about, and another, much more "European," which is kind of the way I was led. "Luminous Times" would have been on it, as would "Walk to the Water." In a funny way you aim somewhere, but the album itself makes up its own mind. We hustled to try to finish it, and to get our own views across, but it is a democratic band, and neither my nor Bono's feelings came through completely. What we ended up with was *The Joshua Tree*.

Musician: Why didn't "Spanish Eyes" make it onto the album?

Edge: It wasn't ready. That's the only reason. I discovered this cassette of something that Adam, Larry, and I were playing around with, and it evolved in the course of an afternoon's recording in Adam's house. It was forgotten, and months later I dug it up and played it to the group. We then realized it was great, but it had got lost in the confusion.

Bono: Marc Coleman, our assistant, has been through my cassette collection, and he found about a hundred songs that I've collected over the last five years. There are acoustic bits and pieces, bits of the band at sound checks—and he reckons that at least half of them are goers.

Musician: The song that Marc engineered—"Deep in the Heart"—is very free form. It's unusual for U2.

Edge: That's exactly what it is. It's a bit like the "4th of July" of this record. With "4th of July," Adam and I were in this room playing and we didn't even know we were being recorded. It was the same with "Deep in the Heart."

Adam: It was actually recorded on a 4-track cassette machine. It was the only recorder set up.

Bono: "Deep in the Heart" was a simple, three-chord song idea that I'd written on the piano, about the last day I spent in Cedarwood Road, in my family house. After I left and went out on my own, my father was living there by himself, and there were a lot of break-ins. Heroin addiction in the area was up and kids needed the money. Anyway, my father decided to sell the little house, and before he moved out I went back there and thought about the place, which I'd known since I was small. I remembered a sexual encounter I'd had there—"Thirteen years old, sweet as a rose, every petal of her paper-thin...Love will make you blind, creeping from behind, gets you jumping out of your skin. Deep in the heart of this place..." The simple piano piece that I had was *nothing* like what these guys turned it into to, which is an almost jazz-like improvisation on three chords. The rhythm section turned it into a very special piece of music.

Larry: Yeah, like Edge says, these moments just come along when you're not expecting them. The great thing about U2, and probably about Adam and myself more than anyone else, is that we *struggle* with our musicianship all the time. We don't know what to do. We don't know what the format is, we don't know what a great rhythm section is supposed to do; we're still discovering. Even now—and I hope that this is something that doesn't disappear—it's the struggle, the fight to get it right, that makes U2 what it is. The day that U2 stops fighting is the day that U2 will not be the band that it is now.

Musician: Do you listen to other drummers, Larry?

Larry: I'm very rarely inspired by them. I get more inspiration listening to Christy Moore playing the bodhran than listening to Steve Gadd. But I look at drummers. When we did the Amnesty tour, I asked Manu Katche if I could sit down behind him and watch. He was freaked and didn't know what I was doing, but I just wanted to see what real drummers get up to! I like to watch, as opposed to listening. It's just jealously, I suppose, based on the realization that a good drummer can do things that I can't. There are two angles to drumming, which you can see by comparing Manu Katche with, say, Omar Hakim, who's an incredible technician. They both sit at the kit in the same way; they both have similar attitudes and the same flair, but Manu has a feel that I really admire. On the Peter Gabriel tour he was offered work on four albums, I think, and I got anxious for him, because I saw the risk of him becoming a session-head. Another drummer I really like is Andy Newmark, for his precision. He never put in any frills. I remember meeting him in a hotel a long time ago, and I said, "Look, I'm having a problem with tempo, and I'm a bit embarrassed about using a click." He said, "I use a click all the time in the studio." He talked to me for maybe an hour, and he explained to me how to work with a click, how to rehearse—all those sorts of things.

Musician: You have control of your studio drum sound?

Larry: Yes, complete. But Edge or Bono might suggest something—we work together on it. Nothing that I do is really my own; everything is influenced by the others.

Musician: Do you and Adam work together in the early stages of laying down the backing tracks?

Larry: We've found it very difficult working together, because neither one of us knew how to play in a band. I'd say, "What are we meant to do here? The bass line goes like that, and I want to play it *this* way!" An awful lot is battling through it. It was only on *The Joshua Tree*, and now live, that Adam and I are complementing each other. We've never done that before. It's not through our own fault—we never learned how to do it.

Adam: I take my cue from Larry's drumming, to be honest. Once Larry has decided on a beat for a song, I try to emphasize it with the bass. We'll rehearse the bass and drums sometimes if we're having a problem with a song.

Larry: But that's only a new development. At the beginning it was much more difficult, because Adam wasn't playing what a normal bass player would, and I wasn't always doing what a normal drummer would do. So there was conflict, not in terms of personality, but as far as the playing was concerned. Things weren't sounding right, and so we worked really hard, listening to dance music, trying to find out how a dance record is made.

Adam: On the recording of the first three albums we didn't do the backing tracks as a band. The backing tracks were usually guitar and drums, and I'd put down the bass later. I had the luxury, once the song was there, of being able to figure out a bass part. I hated using cans in the studio, because you can't hear anything, so I would do the bass part in the control room, where I could hear the bass and drums. Now we don't bother with cans at all; we use stage monitors.

Musician: You worked on two songs on Robbie Robertson's new album. I can see some similarities between you and the early Band—a kind of pioneering spirit and a visionary quality. And like the Band, you've looked closely at America from an outsider's perspective.

Edge: We spring from the same source, perhaps. That comparison is an interesting one, because, as Robbie said—what was his turn of phrase?

Bono: "I was fifteen and I guess I had the *fever*!" Robbie puts on sunglasses before he plays up the neck of the guitar. There was messing about and there was playing for real. When he played for real he looked the part—he was incredible to watch. He had the Hawaiian shirt on, and the shades, and he was belting it out. As a singer he's totally underestimated, and, indeed, he underestimates himself. He has an extraordinary voice.

Edge: What we're doing now, and what we were interested in doing then, was finding out about the original blues music—not the rehashed white blues, which was so awful—which has the spirit of what we've been trying to express since the beginning: the feeling of alienation and loss, the feeling of not being at one with your circumstances. Their music has pain in it, depth and a sense of personal commitment.

Musician: You don't think that white guys can sing the blues? When I bought the John Mayall and Eric Clapton Bluesbreakers album in 1966 it sounded pretty authentic to me, as I imagine your music sounds emotionally authentic to your fans.

Edge: By the time we had arrived that whole scene had gone.

Bono: Clapton is a true bluesman, there's no question about that. The blues doesn't belong to any color.

Edge: Yeah, it's all about feeling. I'm sure that Eric Clapton is more of a bluesman than, say, Robert Cray—but I'm judging purely on instinct. There must have been blacks who felt the blues more than whites, but at the same time I think it's possible for white guys to feel the same emotions—like Keith Richards or Eric Clapton. Those feelings make the blues.

Bono: I think it is inverted racism to believe that the color of your skin prevents you from being a soul singer or blues player.

Adam: What we're discovering now is that pop music, or commercial music that you hear on the radio, is just not for us. It doesn't fit in with what we're trying to do. We understood Irish traditional music first, realized that it had a long history, and with that kind of understanding we were able to go through to country music and appreciate its depths, and eventually end up somewhere in the Delta. That's what we're focusing our attention on right now, rather than on studio technique.

Larry: But it would be wrong to suppose that when one of us gets into the blues, suddenly everyone says, "Wow! Let's go for it!" We all have different tastes. My interest in blues music is from Bono's perspective, which is that of soul singers. That's what attracts me, as opposed to the actual history of the blues, of which my knowledge is obviously very limited, because I grew up in the '70s.

Musician: I hear you want to record a country album, Larry.

Larry: I've had it planned for a long time, but I still haven't got around to doing anything about it. When this tour's finished, I'll get down to it seriously.

Musician: I'm told you have a great voice—that's what Maria McKee says, anyway!

Larry: Well, this is true. [*Guffaws from the band*] You think Robbie Robertson is underestimated!

Bono: Go on, give us an aul' song!

Larry: I did say to Maria that if I did get this country record together, I'd like her to come and help me sing, and maybe write a few songs. Unfortunately, I can't play guitar, and when I did start to learn, I did something to my hand and I couldn't get it round the neck. These guys think that I didn't bother to try [*laughter*], but it's completely untrue, and I *will* learn how to play. My initial interest started when I got into Johnny Cash through Bono here—he was always talking about the *At Folsom Prison* album—and then I became friendly with a guy who loaned me all his country records. I've always known Patsy Cline songs, although I never really understood them, but now I listen to Johnny Cash, to younger people like Steve Earle and Dwight Yoakam, and the Judds, especially.

Bono: Larry gets love letters from the Judds!

Musician: You've been writing country and blues songs, Bono?

Bono: I wrote one for Roy Orbison called "She's a Mystery to Me." "When Love Comes to Town" is the one I wrote for B.B. King. I haven't sent them out yet—I write them, then I lose them. Anyway, they're not fully demoed yet...

Edge: The best story is about the time that Bono, T-Bone Burnett, Bob Dylan, and I were up one night writing a song, and Bono lost the lyrics! So I hope Bob has them…

Bono: There's another song I wrote about B.B. King's guitar, called "Lucille," but that's a country song. "When Love Comes to Town" goes like this: [*sings softly*] "I was a sailor lost at sea; I was under the waves before love rescued me; I was a fighter, I could turn on a thread, but I stand accused of the things that I've said—when love comes to town I'm gonna catch that plane. Baby, I was wrong to ever let you down, but I did what I did before love came to town!" The last verse is a gospel verse: [*changing tempo*] "I was there when they crucified the Lord; I held the scabbard when the soldiers drew the sword. I threw the dice when they pierced his side, but I've seen love conquer the great divide!"

Musician: Robertson said that when you're writing lyrics for a band you've got to write on the group's behalf, not just for yourself. Would you agree?

Bono: No.

Edge: Not actually true, but accidentally true. There's such a strength of commitment within the group that ninety-eight percent of Bono's lyrics could have been written as if they were for the band.

Bono: But a writer has to be selfish.

Edge: It's not that Bono would ever be precious about his lyrics—he always comes to us and discusses them. We may only be his first critics, but in that sense there is an input, and occasionally someone from the band will contribute.

Bono: Edge will sometimes walk up to me and say something like, "I still haven't found what I'm looking for," and I'll turn it into a song. The original statement came from Edge, and it occasionally happens that a song will work out that way. But I think that the group would support me if I went out on a limb, even if it's something they don't fully believe in.

Musician: T-Bone Burnett said that Bono is an inheritor of John Lennon's gift for making grand statements, and that U2, with its capacity for musical expansiveness, is one of the few bands able to "fill" a stadium.

Bono: Well, John Lennon was an artist of *performance*, in a way, and U2, onstage, is the same—there is a *performance* of music that has previously been made. We work with what we have before us. If it's a small club, like in the early days, I might get off the stage. We once played to seventeen people in Birmingham and I would sit down with them in the middle songs. I'd drink from their glasses, and pour the rest over their heads. If we're playing in arenas, we'll adapt accordingly. U2 music tends to float a bit, and it suits us not being hemmed in by a small room. When we're recording we use the studio as an instrument, and we work with the stage as an artist might work with a canvas. We make big music that isn't easily contained.

Adam: You see our love of music is not just for the sound, but for the fact that you can communicate with people through it. That's what I believe U2 is all about. It's an ability to reach people, to touch them, to have a relationship with someone through your music. There are no physical limitations to that. You try to provide the biggest platform on which you can get through to people—and for them to get through to you. It's a two-way process.

Edge: But we never sit down to write a "big" song or a "big" lyric. We write songs because we want to express something.

Bono: I find that people make assumptions about U2 based on the singles, or on the *Under a Blood Red Sky* film. They accept the rhetoric that *War* is a very brash record, but on that LP is a song called "Drowning Man," which is the most intimate musical piece. *The Unforgettable Fire* is a very intimate album, and a very personal one. "Pride" was the odd song out, and if someone judges the album by that one single, then he's missing out. I take it as a compliment if someone says that we're making grand statements, but I'm just not interested in that. As a writer I'm now more concerned with complexities and gray areas than I ever was. We made black and white statements in a particular period in the group's history, when we kind of went through the John Lennon Handbook; Lennon wrote a song called "Sunday Bloody Sunday."

Musician: There are plenty of comparisons between the Beatles and U2 these days.

Edge: I don't know if there really are any significant comparisons to be made, beyond the fact that, like the Beatles, U2 is a band. Otherwise, I don't know...There's a guy who argues that there is a twenty-year cycle to everything, and that *The Joshua Tree* and *Sgt. Pepper* are exactly twenty years apart! [laughs]

Bono: When we were kids, everyone wanted to be in the Beatles. Now we are! [*laughs*] I'm only kidding! THAT'S A JOKE! In the '80s, which is a barren era, we look back at the '60s as a great reservoir of talent, of high ideals, and of the will and desire to change things. We're turning the '60s into the twentieth-century Renaissance, and trying to relive the period. Therefore people want to turn U2 into the Beatles.

Larry: The only good thing about the references, for me, is that the Beatles, like us, didn't take themselves too seriously. They had a laugh, made music seriously, and that was it. We're not spokesmen for a generation.

Musician: So let's talk about the music. "Where the Streets Have No Name" is a classic introductory album track. It really sets the pace and the context for the rest of the album.

Bono: I thought that the intro sounded like an orchestra tuning up. It was a treatment of an Edge keyboard line.

Edge: Yeah, Brian [Eno] did one of his Russian things on it. It was a natural choice for the beginning of an album, and we actually tailored the intro for that position. Had we put it elsewhere on the record we would probably have shortened it, because a lot of U2 songs start out longer than they finally end up. But we loved it the way it evolved, so we left it as it was. To be honest, though, when you're making a record the running order just develops, as the songs tend to give us clues when we're working on them.

Musician: But there does seem to be some kind of a structure to **The Joshua Tree,** ***although perhaps it's a rationalization after the fact. The first two songs are "transcendent" songs, and they're followed by love songs and more socially oriented material.***

Bono: There is a beginning, middle, and end to the LP. I actually object to the fact that we had to put it on two sides—I'd have liked it all on one side, and nothing on side two.

Edge: This side one/two business isn't something we subscribe to, although we used to take advice like "Stick anything that's going to keep radio happy on side one, and put all the experimental, interesting stuff on side two."

Bono: "Running to Stand Still" was always meant to be followed by "Red Hill Mining Town" and that's one reason for having the CD—although I'm not a big CD person myself. I like the crackles.

Musician: What do you consider the highlights of* The Joshua Tree, *with the benefit of hindsight?

Larry: The inner sleeve, basically!

Adam: I think the power of "Bullet the Blue Sky" is something we never conjured up before. That's what I like.

Edge: But whenever I hear that track I think about how far it *could* have gone. As a guitar player I'm only barely getting into that style. The guitar playing is much better live than on record, where I was only exploring possibilities.

Musician: Was the guitar multi-tracked?

Edge: It was a live take. The guitar break towards the end has an overdub on it, but the basic track is live. We should get into this now, because it's a classic example of this kind of recording. When we were planning this record, one thing we wanted to do was to take up where we left off with *The Unforgettable Fire* in terms of recording techniques—getting the sound of a live performance. There is no way that recording each instrument in a separate acoustic environment, and trying to blend them back together again, from tape, is going to get the same result as musicians playing together. You don't get the sound of the room, you don't get the chemistry. So we did *The Joshua Tree* in Adam's house, in my house, and also in the "live" room here in Windmill Lane. Everybody was in the same space, playing with eye contact and a great deal of feeling. The sound of "Bullet" is the sound of U2 playing in a room. It is essential for that song that we have that feeling. It's the same for a lot of the other tracks too, like "Running to Stand Still."

Bono: I tend, as a word writer, to think in terms of a running order. It would be on my mind a lot. The whole process of U2 involves four people, and we all have different opinions. Side two would have been different if I'd had my way. I wanted it to go further into the swamp. There was a very different piece before "Exit," and a gospel song to go before that. I had this idea that we should start with U2—with "Where the Streets Have No Name"—and then dismantle U2 during the record, and be left with nothing recognizable as us. This didn't completely come to be, because in the end we took decisions on the strength of the songs. I would battle more for the big idea, for the structure of the whole record, but in the end what we went for—dare I say it—was the Beatles' idea that each song has its own identity.

Edge: The music is so different from anything we did before, in terms of where the music springs from. If we'd taken the notion to its extreme people wouldn't have known what was going on. It would have been quite good to see people totally floored by it, but we also wanted to present what we felt was the strongest material.

Musician: Do you consider your music primarily as art, entertainment, or a vehicle for meaningful messages—be they social or spiritual?

Edge: I don't think we ever consider anything other than "This is a song we want to write." No one ever says, "This is great entertainment!"

Adam: You're talking about all the things that make up a song—you can't separate them.

Bono: The people who try to do that are those who are on the outside looking in. We're on the inside, and we can't see in front of our noses. To try to turn us into prophets—or for that matter wanting to put us on in Las Vegas—is missing the point.

CHAPTER

4

EXPERIMENTS AND BACKLASH

U2, the band of the '80s, now faced a new decade. They had achieved great success. The big question was, "What next?" Their first answer was two-fold. They would explore their roots. American rock musicians knew their roots—blues rockers started playing because they loved Muddy Waters and Albert King; others were drawn to Motown. Over time, these origins were obscured by infiltrating influences and almost altogether erased by punk. Now U2 wanted to find out where their influences came from, and much of the answer was in America.

On tour in the States they explored such root elements as the blues with B. B. King, gospel in Harlem, and the Sun sound at the Memphis studio that bears that name. With director Phil Joanou U2 documented the tour on film, and as the fan furor over *The Joshua Tree* grew, so did the dimensions and distribution of the film.

Ironically, U2 discovered amid the *Rattle and Hum* experience that, while it's good to know your roots, digging for them is a lot like living in the past. This did not appeal to the band that tried to think five minutes into the future at all times. So, at the end of the tour, at the end of the line, at the end of the '80s, U2 came very close to breaking up.

But they didn't. Instead, they reinvented themselves, energizing their music with the coarser sounds of the contemporary punk scene—industrial music. They sequestered themselves in Berlin, one of the most happening places on the planet at the time—the Berlin Wall came down while they were recording. From inside the tumult of a reunifying Germany, the boundaries between the industrial West and the Communist East disappearing around them, U2 created an entirely new sound and captured it on *Achtung Baby*.

Taking the music on tour, they decided that their earnestness alone was no longer enough to sustain and entertain a stadium of concertgoers. So, taking a page from both David Bowie and Madonna, they created Zoo TV. Zoo TV turned the tour into a spectacle, with huge video screens and sensory stimuli extending way beyond the simplicity of four guys performing on a stage.

Finding this experience liberating they were compelled to write about it. Once off the road, their enthusiasm and excitement still high, they went into the recording studio and recorded what amounted to a companion piece to *Achtung Baby* called *Zooropa*.

From *The Unforgettable Fire* on, U2 had successfully joined creative forces with producers Brian Eno, who had helped craft some of David Bowie's most challenging works, and Daniel Lanois. After coming off the road from *Zooropa*, the band decided once again to team with Eno; not as band and producer, but as true collaborators. The *Passengers* project, while a noble effort to create soundtracks for essentially hypothetical films, proved a bit too oblique for many of U2's fans.

Consequently, when U2 went back into the studio, it was time for them to again change gears. With mixmaster Howie B. on board for the recording sessions, rumors spread like kudzu that they were making a dance record; and the new album's first single, "Discotheque," seemed to bear that out. *Pop*, instead, took all of U2's themes to the extremes. Musically, it drew heavily on the sounds that informed *Achtung Baby* and *Zooropa*. Lyrically, it may be their most spiritual album; it certainly is one of their darkest. As many fans found it off-putting as found it exhilarating.

If the album was confusing, the PopMart tour was downright perplexing. Featuring a golden arch of speakers, a custom-made video screen touted as the "world's largest," a 100-foot-tall swizzle stick complete with a 10-foot-tall olive, and a 35-foot-tall lemon / mirror ball that dropped the band onto the stage for their encore, it appeared that U2 had taken the excesses of Zoo TV to its limits.

As for countless others, for U2 the '90s were a decade of decadence. While to some it was all about self-indulgence and commercialism, for U2, it was all about art.

U2

Hating U2

Ted Mico
***Spin* magazine, January 1, 1989**

U2 set out to become the biggest band in the world. Now they're fighting to avoid being crushed by their own myth.

It's midnight, Sunday night in Dublin, and the crowds around most record stores are lining up around the block. A tramp wandering by joins the crowd, hoping to see a miracle, preferably someone who can turn water into elderberry wine.

"Are you also waiting to get a copy of the new U2 album?" one of the congregation asks.

"Agh. *Them*. Christ no," he grumbles, and scuttles over to the nearest alehouse.

Ah. Them. Suddenly nothing is that surprising anymore. For U2, anything is possible. The band's new album, *Rattle and Hum*, went double platinum in Britain on advance sales alone. Dublin record stores were forced to open at midnight on the day of its debut to avoid riots. It is now the fastest-selling album in British record history.

U2 are without a doubt the biggest band in the world. Their last album, *The Joshua Tree*, has now sold in excess of 14 million copies, and the group's global tour last year put them in front of over three million people, grossing over 40 million dollars. In the face of such titanic adoration, U2 *should* feel on top of the world. Instead, the day after, Bono looks like he's stranded on the wrong end of a bottomless pit.

"I'm going to destroy the whole fuckin' U2 myth, the U2 godhead," he says, looking half-cooked and slightly bemused. He won't do a proper interview this time around because he thinks he has nothing to say, and wants to leave the explaining to guitarist The Edge and bassist Adam Clayton. The irony is that at the moment he has lots to say, but little or no voice to say it with. Today he's in a bad way. The following day he's king of the castle again. It is typical for him to oscillate between extremes, tipping into bouts of melancholy. Being Bono for just one day would scramble most rational minds. So what's it like to be Bono all the time?

"It's very…difficult at the moment. I don't know. If I talk too long now I'll say something I'll regret." He shakes his head and adjusts his hat. "It's important that I keep things together, but it's not easy sometimes. Everything I say becomes some sort of statement, something of vast importance. I could go on stage, unzip my pants, and hang my dick out and people would think it was some statement about something."

U2 are still learning to live with the conflicts they've inherited with their acclaim. Many believe Bono the awe-inspiring star can't cope with Bono the ordinary human being, which is usually a recipe for mental meltdown. In a nearby pub, The Edge and Adam sit opposite one another and muse over the singer's predicament.

> *Edge:* "He has his moments. As a character he's a little strange. We hold together because we look after one another. If Bono gets too freaked out there's always someone there to tell him to get it together."

> *Adam:* "Bono can go pretty far out there. It's not as simple as sex, drugs, and rock 'n' roll. You can lose your mind very easily under the pressures he's under sometimes."

For over three months last year, as the band invited a 40-member film crew along the second leg of *The Joshua Tree* tour through the States, U2's every waking move was captured on celluloid. Bono couldn't even relieve himself without some voice in the next cubicle shouting, "Turn over." It must have been the nearest a rock star has ever come to being a U.S. presidential candidate.

> *Adam:* "Oh no, no. Being a presidential candidate is the closest thing to being a rock star!"

> *Edge*: "We were stupid enough to agree to do the film in the first place. We only had ourselves to blame."

In fact the blame rests on manager Paul McGuinness, who understood that U2 would have had to stay on tour for almost three years to satisfy all their fans. Instead, the film *Rattle and Hum* offers all U2 fans the chance to sit in the back seat of a movie house and still be in the front row of the U2 stadium event, a silver screen kiss embracing the intimate and intimidating.

How did the project get started?

> *Edge*: "For two years we had a lot of approaches from various directors with scripts, saying, 'We could set it in Dublin and you could play a band involved in the troubles in Northern Ireland and suddenly break out...' It was absolute shit. Then it occurred to us, or rather Paul McGuinness, that maybe there was something to the idea of a film, trying to capture what the band was going through at the moment on film. Then we started to spend money—a load of money, and we thought, 'What are we going to do now?'"

The film eventually cost around $5 million of the band's own money, a lot for an absent-minded excursion. The band wanted *Rattle and Hum* to rival their three favorite rock films: *Gimme Shelter*, Martin Scorsese's *The Last Waltz*, and Jonathon Demme's *Stop Making Sense*. Inevitably, there's also an unintentional sprinkling of their other fave chestnut, *This is Spinal Tap*.

> *Edge*: "*Gimme Shelter* has got real drama because of the shooting and the Hell's Angels. That's why it's so stupid for a rock 'n' roll band to make a film. There's no drama in being on the road. The only dramatic thing was Bono breaking his shoulder. And where does that lead you? To the hospital and back again. So the fuck what?
>
> "At this point I'd like to say that we have *no* interest in acting whatsoever. In fact, we've no interest in the film business whatsoever. At least if you're a musician you can write a song, record it with someone else, and it can be on a piece of plastic a week later. Making films is virtually impossible without an army of technicians and a huge budget."

Director Phil Joanou filmed over a quarter of a million feet of concert film, which meant that to watch the uncut film would have taken over one week and nine hours—a little arduous for even the most ardent U2 fan. Although

Joanou himself filtered off most of the dud footage, the band was still heavily involved, sifting through every frame with a final veto over the film's content. The movie shows U2 rehearsing "When Love Comes to Town" with B.B. King, watching street players in New York, working with gospel choirs in Harlem, searching through Elvis's sock drawers at Graceland, and dusting off microphones in Sun Studios. But *Rattle and Hum* is *not* a rockumentary. It doesn't tell you anything about U2 you don't already know.

> *Edge*: "The only criteria for the film was, 'Do we find this interesting?' The holiday film aspect of things like the ambulance taking Bono to hospital after he fell off the stage was funny for a week, but it wears thin after a while. The things that sustained our interest were the musical bits. Musically it's pretty much all over the place, but it's real, it's there."

Somebody once said watching yourself on film is like watching pornography.

> *Bono:* "*I* said that. It *is* like pornography."

> *Edge*: "The idea for the film was that Phil would make us all look like movie stars. The deal was that we'd all look like Montgomery Clift."

So what happened?

> *Edge*: "He double-crossed us, the bastard."

> *Bono:* "They tried to film me standing still, but I kept moving about. It was ridiculous. In the end they had to keep chasing me down the street."

On camera, Bono's so fidgety and hyper he can't even act fidgety and hyper. He only appears in the film when on stage.

> *Adam:* "There's really little point in trying to look that good anyway. This is the year of John Cleese as sex symbol. We've no chance. We won't even get a look in."

Except for drummer Larry Mullen, who steals the show.

> *Edge:* "That's true. He is the star of the film. Larry always had the pose. The bastard. Larry is really the Pete Best of U2. We should have thrown him out the first month. He was much too good-looking then and still is. We never found our Ringo!"

How important is this film to U2?

> *Edge*: "The only important thing about this film is that we've survived it. Of course, whether we survive the bullshit hype with our marbles intact remains to be seen. Having avoided a lot of the bullshit for so long, this film will mean us walking straight into a mountain of it."

Appropriately, the band have spent most of this year in Los Angeles, recording tracks for the album and weeding through the film. The last time they played in L.A. was at the Olympic stadium, where the Olympic flame was lit for only the fourth time: twice for the actual event, once for the Pope, and once for the band.

> *Bono:* "L.A. is a strange place. As long as you think it's strange, then you're all right. *I* think it's strange, and *I'm* pretty damn strange too."

> *Edge*: "We don't belong anywhere, but we don't belong any less in L.A. than we do in Galway. I was living in Beverly Hills, a millionaire's suburbia, a total mindfuck, but if you go ten miles down the road you're in the middle of Watts, and you see economic apartheid in operation. If you're a black guy walking down a street in Beverly Hills, you'll get picked up in two minutes flat. There's something honest about living there. At least you're facing it."

> "To write a song you have to know about people. Some of the most interesting people I met in L.A. were doormen or street bums. That's one of the great things about Bono. He really understands and is interested. No matter how big or successful he gets he'll always be fascinated...especially by women, but we won't get into that."

> *Bono:* "I remember what you said last time: 'Bono will remain a star as long as he doesn't become a celebrity.' It's so true. Even Charlie Sheen had an imaginary conversation with me. He went on this TV show telling everyone he'd met me. He said, 'I was wasted on booze and I asked Bono, 'How do you do it? How?' And Bono turned to me and pointed to the bottle and said, 'You won't find it in there.' Can you believe it? It was the last date of the tour and I'd already drunk a whole bottle. I couldn't even speak, let alone preach. It's incredible. Everything gets twisted."

Since 1980, U2 have sold well over 30 million albums and have been No. 1 in almost every chart in the world. *Rattle and Hum* seems like a deliberate attempt to sabotage their position, to undermine the U2 myth. If *The Joshua Tree* was, to use Bono's phrase, "the big picture," then *Rattle and Hum* is a piece of spontaneous doodle, reducing their scale to more human proportions. They seem determined to exhibit their frailty, their vulnerability.

> *Edge*: "It wasn't really a deliberate attempt to do anything other than record the songs as straightforwardly and with as much feeling as possible. People can put a whole heap of significance on something that's incredibly straightforward and unpretentious. These are the songs we wrote and this is that album we wrote."

Five of the songs were recorded in one day at Sun Studios, and the film even shows the band screwing one of them up. Occasionally U2 can tilt the world off its axis. In this episode they couldn't even tilt a pinball machine.

> *Adam:* "That's what rock 'n' roll is. It's about playing the songs and not being too precious about them."

> *Bono:* "What other band in our position would learn the chords of 'All Along the Watchtower' five minutes before they went on stage and would record it? No one."

> *Edge:* "You see us trying to work out what the fuck we're going to do with the songs. There's a lot of doubt around. From the beginning, most U2 songs are riddled with doubt. That's the thing about faith. Faith is meaningless without the doubt. Without doubt there is no faith."

> *Adam:* "You always have to ask questions. Part of the problem with music today is that people are too afraid to ask questions. Rock 'n' roll is a term that's been heavily abused. It's not something you can buy in a record shop. It's an attitude."

Do you ever feel guilty about the lofty position you've attained?

> *Edge:* "No. I just take each day as it comes. This band is full of contradictions. The song 'God Part II' is really Bono trying to express his own internal feelings of conflict. I have doubts, but I don't feel guilty."

> *Adam:* "We'd feel guilty if we abused our position more, but you soon learn it's not worth it."

In "God Part II," Bono sings lines like, "I don't believe rock 'n' roll can really change the world," yet he is one of the only people who really *does* believe in the recuperative powers of music. He believes he can affect some small changes. Last year he told me it was this conviction that kept U2 going.

> *Bono:* "People think, 'Oh yeah, there they are, U2 marching off to war. There goes Bono running all over the stage. And unlike Mick Jagger, Bono doesn't do it with a wink. *That's* the problem. Bono actually believes in the people that come to the concerts and *believes* in what he's doing. Oh how embarrassing. Oh dear, oh dear.'
>
> "I'll tell you though, Jerry Lee Lewis and Elvis Presley believed in what they were doing too. The problem in the '80s is that people stopped believing in rock 'n' roll—to believe in it has become something to scoff at."

Although Bono's always been quick to deny any association with agitprop orators ("We don't really want to get involved—especially not in America's political playground!"), his outspoken statements and immense popularity have given him the political muscle to wrestle with issues under the arc light of public attention. Last year the band was courted by both the Kennedys and Jesse Jackson. But the star system that allows him the platform to lambaste TV evangelists in "Bullet the Blue Sky," the South African regime in "Silver and Gold," and terrorism in the film's half-acoustic version of their anthem "Sunday Bloody Sunday" (recorded a day after the tragic Enniskillen bombing in Ulster) is the very same stardom that reinforces the injustices he abhors. Idols are living proof that the system works, the dream can be attained.

No other band benefited so much from the exposure provided by Live Aid, yet U2 themselves were so unhappy with their performance, or the reasons behind it, that they almost split up. Adam pulled the band back together by demanding they record *The Joshua Tree* first and disintegrate later.

Are things still volatile?

> The Edge laughs off the suggestion. "We split up last week, but we're back together again. I must admit that we've been getting on much better this last while. There used to be rows about everything. I think it's much easier being a big group because it allows you more freedom. It was much harder making our first few albums."

> *Adam:* "It *is* always hard, but you tend to mellow a bit as personalities. All that celebrity bullshit that you get when all you want to is play fucking music. How do you deal with that?"

How do you deal with that?

> *Adam:* "We drink a lot." He fingers the pint before continuing. "The only thing that gets me through the day is music. Because I know what's the truth. It doesn't matter if I'm walking down the street or riding in limos."

U2's musical isolation has been cited as the main reason they've now adopted roots in Sun Studios, Memphis.

Why do four Irishmen now want to be Tennessee children?

> *Adam:* "I think the journey starts here in Dublin, with what we have in our traditional music. We hear immigration songs and songs of exploitation within Irish culture and then it went to America, going via the plantation supervisors who were Irish and then it mixed with the black blues and gospel music. That's where the journey starts. It's not adopting. It is a part of us.
>
> "Rock 'n' roll *is* an American thing. It's where it all started. When you start scratching the surface of it, you go back to the lifestyles of people. When we went to Graceland to see Elvis's home it was obvious he was a simple country boy and you saw it in his house. That's really what this album is about. A return to simplicity."

Why not move forward?

> *Adam:* "Because who wants to play stadiums for the rest of their life? We really want to play a gig at the Marquee. That's really what it all comes down to, just enjoying playing in the band and seeing things happen when we come together. That's what's important. Not stadiums and lighting rigs zooming around the country."

The only differences between big dreams and wet dreams is the laundry bill, and from the moment Bono, Edge, and Adam answered Larry Mullen's "Musicians Wanted" ad on the school notice board, U2's sole goal was to become the biggest band in the world. The rest, as they say, is hysteria. Now the biggest band in the world wants to be a garage band again.

Edge: "That's the irony of life. There's no way around it really. It's been said that rock 'n' roll died in 1959, and there's something to that. I think that the music we tend to go back to all the time is something very fragile and hard to pin down. It's in the early Elvis records, it's in some country records, in the Band. You find it in obscure bars in New Orleans and places like that. You'll never hear it on the radio. I couldn't begin to explain what exactly it is, but I know that people like T-Bone Burnett and even Dylan spent their life finding this music. We're just getting a feel for it now."

Adam: "It's freedom. That's what it is."

Edge: "Is it?"

Adam: "Absolutely. When we were 16, we plugged in a guitar we couldn't play but it made a sound and we thought, 'We can go anywhere with this.' You have to hold on to your freedom. We're a big band now, but we could lose our freedom."

Like Prince, Marvin Gaye, and Al Green, U2 have found a skein that binds sex and spirituality. Bono even describes U2's music as "soul music."

But haven't you substituted sex for celebration, seduction for elation? "Where the Streets Have No Name" can transport an audience, make them go places, but can't make them come.

Adam: "I think you misunderstand how much sex there is on the record. There's a lot there and sex is a very difficult thing to keep together."

Edge: "I think there's a very honest sexuality about the record which I find more interesting than a blatant *Spinal Tap* type thing. The subtle spirituality of gospel music is what attracts me. It's strange and twisted, because that's far more what it's all about."

Adam: "Spirituality and sex are so close. If you try and have sex without spirituality it's not sex. You have to be able to do both or else it's not a good fuck. That's what we saw in that roots music. The prim and proper people call it gospel, but the people who know what it's about call it sex music, because that's what it is."

I'm still uncertain exactly where to pinpoint* Rattle and Hum *in the great U2 scheme of things.

Adam: "What we could have done is not put out this record and waited another year and a half and that would have been the end of what we are now. We wanted something more immediate."

And because it's a soundtrack, no one can make direct comparisons to* The Joshua Tree *and you don't have to compete with past triumphs.

Edge: "It's true. We never really thought about it like that, but you're right. As a big group we feel it's our responsibility to fuck up the charts as much as possible. This album, to be honest, is just treading water. I mean, I like the songs, but this is only a fraction of what we can do. It's like a little Polaroid of U2."

Have you written the great song yet, the tune to take to the grave?

Edge: "Not yet. 'Still Haven't Found' came close. There's better to come."

Adam: "I'm proud of what we've done. I listen to the records and I know they're weak sometimes, but I believe in them. I realize that I haven't wasted my life."

Edge: "Adam will listen to our old records and for all their flaws will find something. I can't listen to any of them. The only record I can sometimes listen to is part of *The Joshua Tree* because it reminds me of my favorite Velvet Underground records. I don't know why."

So what of the future?

Bono: "We're going to keep releasing record after record until everyone'll be sick of us."

U2

Me2

Elizabeth Wurtzel
The New Yorker, **February 17, 1992**

In recent years, some of the most exciting and vital—as well as contradictory and irritating—popular music has come from Ireland: spirited doses of drunken jigs and Hibernian rhythm and blues combined with a glum, deadly serious outlook conditioned by potato famines, civil war, the I.R.A., hunger strikes, Bobby Sands, Bloody Sunday. It's no wonder that the Irish James Brown wannabes in the film "The Commitments" claim to be "the blacks of Europe," living as they do in a country so weighed down by poverty and despair. Some twenty-five years ago, Van Morrison brought his Belfast rock and roll across the Atlantic, and introduced Americans to his version of soul music and soul-searching—a hybrid of Irish folk traditions and contemporary rock. Morrison was the Irish Invasion's maiden voyager, but neither his sound nor his pudgy, untelegenic presence bears much resemblance to the biggest Irish phenomenon of the last decade: U2. In fact, the only thing these artists have in common is a deeply Irish outlook—a striking mixture of bleakness and joy, which can sometimes seem maudlin but never fails to fascinate and confound an American sensibility accustomed to rock stars who prefer to keep an ironic distance from the fray. As Brian Eno wrote recently in *Rolling Stone*, "Cool, the definitive eighties compliment, sums up just about everything that U2 isn't. The band is positive where cool is cynical, involved where it is detached, open where it is evasive. When you think about it, in fact, cool isn't a notion that you'd often want to apply to the Irish."

The first that most Americans heard of U2 was in 1982, when the clangy, adolescent angst single "I Will Follow" landed on the soundtrack of the teen exploitation flick *The Last American Virgin*. That song helped introduce U2's debut album, *Boy*, to a collegiate audience that, after the fast burn of the angry young men of British punk, was mired in the intellectual pretensions of new wavers like Talking Heads or in the attitude dancing of haircut-synthesizer bands like ABC and A Flock of Seagulls. The shock of U2 in Reagan's America was that we suddenly had among us a new band that mattered, at a time when nothing much seemed to matter—certainly not in pop music.

Lately, the focus has tended to be on U2's lyrics and on the messianic posing of its lead singer, Bono (who is classic black Irish—tall, with long dark hair, a sharp nose, and a stately, religious bearing), but in the beginning the band's most noticeable feature was its sound. U2 was a noise band—a beautiful noise band. Its most distinctive trait was the innovative use of string harmonics by the band's guitarist, who is aptly called The Edge; he could create a ringing sound that was like steely bells and chimes and then soberly retreat into what sounded like a rake scratching across the strings. The use of harmonics wasn't new in rock music—the classic example is the guitar introduction to the Yes song "Roundabout"—but The Edge pushed it the farthest, splitting octaves, plucking out chords, and repeatedly banging on single notes at machine-gun speed. The best U2 songs unfold with a signature rhythm that is sensual and sexual: a strong, steady buildup followed by a powerful, jolting release.

Urgency and yearning were apparent in everything U2 did, but they were expressed more in The Edge's metallic guitar, in Larry Mullen's battle-cry drums, in Adam Clayton's portentous bass, and in Bono's unadorned wail than in anything particular the band was saying. The musical assault was so total that you could hardly decipher, much less analyze, the lyrics. What Bono and the boys were all hot and bothered about may have had something to do with Ireland, or with sex and love, but mostly it seemed to be a venting of free-flowing anger which any alienated, rebellious youth could relate to. The FM radio hit "Gloria" (possibly an homage to Van Morrison), from *October*, U2's second album, seemed to be about a girl, but it also seemed to be about every frustration you could think of. U2 was a political band in that no love song it played wasn't also about how hard it is to love in a loveless society.

That a band as apparently uncompromising as U2 achieved such popularity proves that from time to time critics and consumers come out on the same side. U2 repeatedly topped the *Rolling Stone* polls, was named Band of the Eighties by that magazine as early as 1985, and by 1987, made it to the cover of *Time* as "Rock's Hottest Ticket." Its work was so huge commercially that industry people were only half joking when they said that U2 bankrolled Island Records. Given all this adulation, a backlash may have been inevitable, but somewhere along the way — perhaps after the breakthrough success of the third album, *War*, with its sloganeering antiwar messages "Sunday Bloody Sunday" and "New Year's Day"—U2's public persona became as annoying as its music was riveting. Suddenly, U2 was not just a band, not even just an Irish band; but *the* Irish band, the emissary to the world of a broken nation. The band in general, and Bono in particular, began to take on an air of martyrdom, which usually came across as pompous. And pomposity is a cardinal—though perhaps unavoidable—sin of rock and roll; while almost all rock stars seem to suffer from it at one time or another (it's hard not to be pompous with millions of people adoring you and hanging on your every word and thought), its universality does not make it any less tedious. U2's tendency in interviews to make self-important pronouncements about missions and quests was bound to alienate those in the audience who thought rock and roll should above all be fun, even when it was delivering a message.

U2's image, more than that of any other band I can think of, always seems at odds with its work. For instance, *The Unforgettable Fire*, the band's fourth studio album, scored a hit with a tribute to Martin Luther King, Jr., called "Pride (In the Name of Love)," which achieved a rock and roll ideal in that it was not only lyrically stirring and provocative but also ridiculously catchy. If a song can inspire you to think and make you want to dance (or jump or shout or tear down the walls), then the artist must be doing something right. The trouble was that the sense of emergency never seemed to let up. In concert, night after night, Bono would get onstage, sing as if the fate of the planet depended on it, and fill the space between tunes with speeches about Amnesty International, revolution in Ireland, apartheid in South Africa, politics in America. His expertise and his passion seemed to know no bounds. Even the band's champions admit that Bono tended to undermine the self-contained brilliance of the music with his inarticulate spiels about, say, the Irish Republican movement, which he would deliver to arena audiences and to reporters backstage. Eamon Dunphy in his generally fawning U2 biography, *The Unforgettable Fire*, says of one of Bono's discursive discourses on "Sunday Bloody Sunday," "In all of this, the real richness and diversity of a marvelous song is lost in the proselytizing which is little more than well-meaning rhetoric, devoid of intellectual rigor."

This is not to say that audiences don't expect or don't approve of social protest in rock stars and the music they make; at this point, it's practically de rigueur. But U2's rage has a relentless, monolithic quality that can become frightening in its lack of humor. What finally redeems most "serious" artists of popular music—people like Bob Dylan, Joni Mitchell, Bruce Springsteen, and the Beatles—is that their bodies of work also contain plenty of songs that are funny and lighthearted, that kick back and relax. Even the angriest British punks, like the Clash and the Sex Pistols, had a sense of humor; in "Anarchy in the U.K.," Johnny Rotten can be heard laughing in a sinister, devilish cackle that's scary but also indicates that there is humor to match the hatred. Humor, after all, is not just about finding a situation funny—it's also about admitting doubts, showing confusion or embarrassment, offsetting sanctimony with human fallibility, and having perspective. In fact, part of rock music's ethos is that at times it's better to laugh at a hopeless situation than to cry about it. Laughter is a universal language not because we all laugh at the same things but because we all laugh, period. But not U2.

The band hit its nadir in terms of public reception with the release of *Rattle and Hum*, a black-and-white documentary film in which U2 promised to teach us Americans a thing or two about our musical history. The presumptuousness of this effort—who do these guys think they are, telling us about Elvis Presley? —may have helped to make the movie the band's first encounter with flat-out rejection from its audience. Just as Sting was able to recruit an all-star lineup of black jazz musicians to back him up for his film *Bring on the Night*, U2 used its money and fame to add B.B. King and Bob Dylan to its bill and to do some recording at the legendary Sun Studios, in Memphis. The result felt like purchased credibility and overstrained integrity. U2 sang about Billie Holiday in "Angel of Harlem," did a gospel choir reworking of "I Still Haven't Found What I'm Looking For," and flaunted this newfound connection with black music like a pair of torn-up, stone-washed jeans that a teen-ager buys in a shopping mall hoping to achieve ready-made, a look of wear and tear.

And yet, despite my qualms about that project, I found myself listening to the soundtrack album over and over again, and in particular to "Desire," "Hawkmoon 269," and "All I Want Is You," three love songs of such bewildering intensity that they seem proof, at last, of the feminist adage that the personal is political. On "Hawkmoon 269" (a song not included in the film itself), Bob Dylan plays a Hammond organ while Bono can be heard bellowing, "Like thunder needs rain/Like the preacher needs pain/Like tongues of flame/Like a blind man's cane/Like a needle needs a vein/Like someone to blame/Like a thought unchained/Like a runaway train/I need your love." On paper, this may seem overwrought, but U2 and all its hyperbole make perfect sense when The Edge Orchestra begins to play and Bono spills out his guts—and the result is gorgeous music. Given the quality of U2's talent, I always thought that if the band ever got away from topics like God and war and bloodshed and got in touch with the everydayness of everyday life it would make a great album, one that successfully combined the effervescent and effortless with the sententious and sedulous — good vibes with a heavy heart.

The musical and lyrical principles behind the most winning songs on *Rattle and Hum* were applied to all the material on *Achtung Baby*, U2's latest album, which is not only the best work they have ever done but quite possibly the best album of 1991. Partially recorded in Berlin— the most hyperactive of European cities at the moment — the album is elegant and guttural, a far cry from the band's last studio effort, *The Joshua Tree*, which won a Grammy for Album of the Year but took the band about as far away as it could possibly get from the Anglo-Irish punk roots that invigorated its early work. Many of *Joshua's* problems (and triumphs) could be attributed to the involvement of Brian Eno, the former keyboardist of Roxy Music, who is an extremely atmospheric producer; he is often credited as the inventor of new wave "ambient" music, which merges the peaceful easy feeling of the Windham Hill sound with a more compelling artistic vision. Until *The Unforgettable Fire*, U2's studio albums had been produced by Steve Lillywhite, who helped the band develop a rollicking, thunderclap effect that was haunting without losing its hardness. From *Fire* on, the primary producers have been Eno and Daniel Lanois, a French-Canadian musician who has worked magic for the Neville Brothers, Bob Dylan, Robbie Robertson, and others in his New Orleans studio. Lanois is also an atmospheric producer, but the full force of this pair's influence was not felt until *The Joshua Tree,* on which every song seems bathed in a moody mist, with a keyboard haze in the distance, while the once pronounced drum sound has been thoroughly suppressed. Because of scheduling conflicts, Eno's role on *Achtung Baby* was more peripheral; left alone in the studio with Lanois and an engineer called Flood, the boys in the band were able to unleash their less polished instincts once again.

And not a moment too soon. Last year, when the Pet Shop Boys recorded a campy medley that mixed the fluffy "Can't Take My Eyes Off You" with U2's high-minded "Where the Streets Have No Name," it was clear that U2 needed a new direction. And since 1987, when *The Joshua Tree* was released, musical sensibilities have gone through some changes. With the popularity of rap, hip-hop, and other dance music at one end of the mainstream spectrum, and heavy metal and hard rock at the other, the new emphasis in today's pop is on grooves, grunge, noise, and nastiness. While U2 always manages to sound as if it means it, many of the bands that have risen to the top recently, from PM Dawn to Nirvana, sound as if they *dig* it. U2 had to get the riff and the rip back into its sound. So on *Achtung Baby* there are no more high horses—just wild horses; no more running for your life— just running to you.

This is an album unashamedly about relationships, but it's not merely a relationships record — it is, above all, an album of rock and roll. Its opening track, "Zoo Station," begins with discordant guitars, muffled vocals, and industrial wah-wah drones, and sets the tone for the rest of the album, balancing between funk and heavy metal, garage feedback and glam-rock. This is the first U2 album that appears to have taken inspiration from current chart trends—the blaring noise-making of My Bloody Valentine, the druggy euphoria of Happy Mondays, the alternative-dance sounds of the KLF, and even, occasionally, the guitar assault of Sonic Youth. Just as love songs in the hands of their usual practitioners can be tedious and trite, heavy-metal effects—screechy guitars and a speedy, jarring backbeat—are pretty boring when performed by heavy-metal bands. But when U2 applies the principles of dissonance to its usually seductive studio sound, the band regains its early rawness and adds some novelty to tired licks. Brian Eno wrote in *Rolling Stone*, "Buzzwords on this record were *trashy, throwaway, dark, sexy* and *industrial* (all good) and *earnest, polite, righteous, rockist* and *linear* (all bad). It was good if a song took you on a journey or made you think your hi-fi was broken, bad if it reminded you of recording studios or U2."

U2 is not the only band to consciously put hard and heavy sounds into its normally gentler music. This was a year that gave heavy metal a new cachet in the music scene. The Pixies, a Boston-based band that has been enjoying plenty of alternative radio airplay, recently released the best album of their career (and another of the best albums of 1991) with *Trompe le Monde*, an amalgam of their cute, eccentric melodies and the Metallica-like speed metal that the band members had come to like so much. The result is as raucous as anything you might hear on an Anthrax album, but it retains a quirky coolness, an intellectual edge that signals from the start that this isn't the usual arena rock that most people can write off as big, loud, and dumb. And now Neil Young, whose *Rust Never Sleeps* has been acknowledged as a seminal metal masterpiece, has come up with Arc, a thirty-five minute sonic manifesto that he calls "New Age metal."

Considering *Achtung Baby's* periodic harshness, it might seem odd that this is U2's "love" album, but it is precisely the harsh sound that keeps the romantic urges expressed here from degenerating into sappiness. And the love that is sung about on *Achtung Baby* is tough, coarse, and complex. On "Who's Gonna Ride Your Wild Horses," a dazed and confused song of heartbreak recalled somberly against an icy guitar line, Bono offers a litany of abuses that his lover has subjected him to— "You're an accident/Waiting to happen/You're a piece of glass/Left there on the beach"—but then, despite all this misery, shyly begs, "Baby... can we still be friends?" And "So Cruel," with its lovely string arrangements, winding keyboards, and frothy, hypnotic melodies, is reminiscent of Tommy James's "Crimson and Clover," except that every lovingly sweet line is contrasted with a bitterly ironic counter line: "I disappeared in you/You disappeared from me/I gave you everything you ever wanted/It wasn't what you wanted." And so it goes, not all of it quite so sad and sorry, but all of it complicated and musically varied, from the psychedelic warble of the hit single "Mysterious Ways" to the more typically U2-ish aggression of "Until the End of the World." Even the foreboding thud of "Acrobat," which sounds as though it might be political, with martyr-complex lines like" Don't let the bastards grind you down," unfurls as a song about love facing the long run. It comes as a relief to discover, after all this time, that the guys in U2 are as hormonally charged and concerned with love as the rest of us.

After *Born in the U.S.A.* rolled its anthemic, larger-than-life juggernaut across the country and sent Bruce Springsteen up the caste system from mere rock star to multi-platinum supernova, he decided to make a record that was smaller in scale and softer in subject matter. For the first time in a career that had relied heavily on the capacity to tell sagas of working-class heroes and of the lives of ordinary people, Springsteen delivered a body of material that studied the vicissitudes of love, commitment, and marriage. The result, the brilliant *Tunnel of Love*, appeared in late 1987, and proved that not all love songs had to be silly. With the popularity of this album, Springsteen made it possible for other serious artists to express their maturity of thought not just through political awareness and astute social commentary but also through writing about love and relationships with an emotional depth that requires some semblance of adulthood. While it was once left to girl-with-guitar types like Joni Mitchell and Carly Simon to ponder romance endlessly in song (Mitchell's *Court and Spark* actually turned love into a concept album), Bruce Springsteen now made it perfectly proper for *men—real* men, and not just California crooners like Jackson Browne—to do the same thing.

Similarly, *Achtung Baby* is U2's effort to bring its unwieldy public image down to size, to make the political more personal. While *Joshua* is large enough to cast light and shadows over miles and continents, *Achtung Baby* is small and private, a homey antidote to political activism and burnout. It's as if the band had finally learned, as Bono sings on "Mysterious Ways," that "If you want to kiss the sky/Better learn how to kneel (on your knees, boy!)." Bono seems to be saying that it's not just the big issues that matter—that the life you live in the hours when you're not trying to save the world is important, too. In her new book, *Revolution from Within*, Gloria Steinem attempts to give feminism a more personal, internalized interpretation, transcending party politics; it seems appropriate that on the new U2 album one of the sweeter ballads, "Tryin' to Throw Your Arms Around the World," recycles an old catchphrase of Steinem's to illustrate the dangers of becoming a loner with a cause: "A woman needs a man/Like a fish needs a bicycle/When you're tryin' to throw your arms around the world." Ultimately, the public embrace is retracted and turned homeward, as Bone promises in the chorus: "I'm gonna run to you... run to you...woman be still/I'm gonna run to you...run to you...woman I will."

On the whole, this was a year marked by an increasingly intelligent approach to love songs from several surprising sources: Chris Stamey, formerly of the dBs, sang of breaking up and falling in love again on *Fireworks*; Matthew Sweet contemplated his divorce on *Girlfriend*; and R.E.M., that staple of college radio and musical polemicism, turned their attention to politics of the human variety on *Out of Time*, an album that was recently nominated for seven Grammy awards. What it means, that both U2 and R.E.M., the two most popular bands to come out of the alternative-music scene of the early eighties, chose to make a similar departure in the same year is hard to say. Most bands start out singing about girls (or boys) and mature into serious social commentary, but these two groups have followed the program in reverse order. Not that *Achtung Baby* and *Out of Time* sound at all alike; the comparison holds up only if you consider them both thematically—*Out of Time's* antecedents are strictly of the folky, funky American variety. But both albums mark an emotional breakthrough in which arrogance gives way to doubt and confusion—both bear witness as mountains of rock-solid superego dissolve into buckets of messy id. Perhaps this means that the nineties have truly arrived, perhaps it means, that the men's movement is actually having an effect in unexpected places—among rock stars, who suddenly need to express their most intimate feelings with more ardor than ever. Or perhaps all it proves is that the generation *after* the baby boom is also getting old. Whatever is going on, though, I only hope that it doesn't become a trend. After all, a mind is a terrible thing in the hands of the wrong person, and while the talents of U2 and REM—not to mention their experience—enable them to handle this type of interpersonal, mixed-genre ambitiousness with the requisite grace and ease, I'd rather see new bands on the rise try to compete with the garage-rock ethic of sudden stars like Nirvana than end up with weepy, sloppy, second- and third-rate versions of either of these masterworks.

U2

Eno: The Story Behind *Original Soundtracks 1*

Tom Moon
Knight-Ridder News Service, November 5, 1995

It started with a producer's simple "Why don't we try..."

The members of U2 and their producer, Brian Eno, were finishing up 1993's *Zooropa* album. The work had progressed more quickly than most U2 projects, but near the end, Eno says, the band hit "a stone wall."

"In the studio, it's easy to get to the screwdriver level, where you're debating about the slightest things and getting obsessive," Eno said last week from his New York hotel, recalling the genesis of *Original Soundtracks 1*, on which he and U2 perform as the collective Passengers. *Soundtracks* arrives in stores Tuesday.

"I suggested we do some improvising sessions, just turn the tape on and play, so we were working with a broad brush rather than the one-hair brushes we'd been using. It was designed to open us up a little, and it proved to be a good way of originating music."

The recordings were so fruitful that Eno proposed more. After the Zoo TV tour, the band returned to the studio—without an agenda, he said, or a specific project in mind. From the sessions' 25 hours of taped experimentation came *Soundtracks*, which reflects both the band's pop instincts and Eno's predilection for ethereal, "ambient" music that moves slowly and doesn't demand conscious attention.

As always, Eno's touch is evident throughout. The 47-year-old pop visionary, who has midwifed important works by David Bowie, Talking Heads and others, is a master of moods. Where other producers work to capture unusual instrumentation, Eno develops textures, a nearly tangible sonic world that suggests whole ways of being. He electrifies otherwise mundane material by limiting the range of sounds. His austere productions create heart-pounding drama from the wispiest sources. "I completely admire economy," explains Eno, in what could be his mantra.

In order to guide U2 toward a more exploratory way of making music, Eno devoted considerable time to preproduction. He generated a number of sequences and rhythm patterns, which were ready to use at a moment's notice. He decorated the walls with rare cloths from Africa, India, and the Arab world. He installed a huge monitor and stockpiled a wide range of videos. "When things started getting dull, you'd just pop in a different tape," he said.

One cut on the 14-song *Soundtracks*—"Miss Sarajevo," a song that features Bono and Luciano Pavarotti—was inspired by a TV documentary of the same name. Other pieces on the album, which was finished in less than two months, were commissioned for films or suggested by existing films.

"News footage from 1953. Animations from students at the Royal College of Art. Films from the Orient. Everything. The idea was to have enough different types of things to suit whatever musical situation."

"More and more of my energy goes into preparation, because then the act of actually making the music is relatively fast," Eno said. "This is in opposition to the way most people generally work—they're inside the music all the time. What I tried to do was think about what eventualities to expect. I needed to have things in reserve."

Eno, who has produced U2 landmarks including *The Joshua Tree*, says that vocalist Bono, guitarist The Edge, bassist Adam Clayton, and drummer Larry Mullen, Jr. have always taken an improvisatory approach to songwriting.

"A lot of their material would come from them standing around playing. What they would do then is say, 'OK, let's get (the fragments) properly structured.'...They were generating the seeds that became songs.

"I love that sense of discovery. So I told them on this project, we'd just work with whatever we got. What we'd generate was not a map of the material, but the material itself."

Eno—who said he wouldn't be surprised if other passages from these sessions turn up on the "rock and roll" record U2 plans to release next summer—played synthesizer and acted as the archivist, notating particularly inspired moments in a log. He devised various "games" to keep the musicians on their toes, such as requiring everyone to switch instruments for a segment.

Though it sounds like the inclusion of Pavarotti was another game, Eno says the legendary tenor suggested the duet.

"He was really easy to work with—he (recorded) the high notes first. People always assume that classical music is earnestly correct in the way it works, but those guys really know how to cheat. We've got nothing on them."

When the nightly sessions ended, Eno would retrieve the important moments, then mix them. His mission was to capture the development of certain episodes or ideas, but to keep things at a manageable length.

"Listening to the original improvisations as they came off the floor, you feel the excitement of the process. The dynamic between things falling apart slightly and coming back together again is an important aspect of improvisation. You have to be careful not to disturb the organic flow of the thing."

As Eno talks about the editing process, it's clear that he's not satisfied with all the cuts. Like many multimedia and electronic music artists in the years before the computer boom, Eno feels limited by the current technology. His goal is to offer listeners more options, different ways of experiencing the same music.

"Like 'Always Forever Now,'" he said, citing another *Soundtracks* cut. "The full-length (version) of that is really fabulous. What you would really like to be able to do is have records or movies or whatever where you could offer choices. The listener could get radio length, a slightly more expanded 'standard' length, and a 'train-spotter' length for people who want all the gory details and the whole sweep of the thing."

The Future Sound of U2

Ann Powers
***Spin* magazine, March 1997**

"Come on, Adam, row!" Bono shouts, mastering his sea legs and giving a hearty shove to his oar. Adam Clayton shakes his silvery, close-shaven head and smirks. Truth is, Clayton's the one moving our yellow dinghy across Dublin's Grand Canal in the murk of this summer midnight. We're crossing a waterway in the Quays, the labyrinth of locks where the River Liffey meets the Canal and the River Dodder to form a basin that feeds the city's industrial mills. Ireland's famous green finds no foothold here; this is a place not of poets but of forgotten laborers. Few new buildings warm the landscape. Our passage lies between the two of them: Hanover Studios, which looks like a displaced beach house with its whitewashed wood and big windows, and the cheerily imposing condominium that houses Windmill Lane.

The members of U2 trek from studio to studio several times a day, working on their new album, *Pop*. Before The Edge's 35th birthday a few days ago, they traveled these 25 yards by car or foot across a nearby bridge—not much of a trip, until you factor in the inevitable pack of tourists waiting outside for snapshots. This raft, a gift to U2's guitarist from the recording crew, allows for discreet escapes. It also offers Bono, whose scruffy reddish hair and stocky workingman's body make him look like the type of Irishman who could have made a life hauling cod off boats, a chance to play the salt.

Trying on personae is one of Bono's favorite activities, and our brief encounter with the waves allows him to run through a few. As Clayton navigates, Bono sings. He bellows, really—improvised arias, "Michael Row the Boat Ashore," whatever seems to suit our watery environs. "Ahoy!" he shouts toward the lit apartments of the condominium, nearly tipping us into the dank water. "Maybe we should use the motor," Clayton suggests. "Ah, we're almost there," Bono replies. A handful of stars glow in the indigo sky. "I love the sea life!" he declares, and for a moment it seems like he might take hold and steer the raft downriver, following the Liffey toward the soft mouth of the Irish Sea.

As much as he might like to let the current pull him toward some new adventure, Bono stays on course. This moonlit interlude can be no more than that. He and Clayton are in the middle of a recording session, and DJ Howie B., renowned captain of the U.K.'s rapid-growth ambient-electronic music scene, awaits them in one of the Windmill Lane studios. We secure the dinghy to the cement bank and climb up into a parking lot. Jumping the security gate, we ascend three flights of stairs and enter the messy den where Howie stages his unending psychedelic show. "Hanover is the daytime," Bono whispers to me, "but Windmill Lane is the night." Four or five overlapping light projections fill the walls, geometric shapes in Day-Glo green and orange and pink. Howie, a dark Scottish imp in a striped soccer jersey, stands at the gigantic console, fiddling with his latest version of U2's soon-to-be-released single, "Discotheque." The sweet smell of hashish tickles our nostrils. Clayton plops down on the couch and rolls his own herbally enhanced cigarette. Bono asks the second engineer for a glass of red wine.

"It's magic," says Howie of the sound flowing out of the room's speakers. Howie thinks a lot of things are magic, including his current role as what drummer Larry Mullen, Jr., calls U2's "disco guru." A manically prolific ambient music constructionist who's made albums under his own name and as Spacelab, as well as remixed cuts by such genre-busters as Everything But the Girl and Bjork, Howie's been ensconced in Windmill Lane since early on in the recording process, serving as a trusted gauge of what's wicked and what's washed up as U2 forge their allegiance with this still-forming sonic universe.

Right now, as Howie hears it, nothing's more magical than Clayton's bass line, which anchors the direction of the "Discotheque" remix (producers David Morales, Steve Osborne, and David Holmes have also crafted mixes of "Discotheque"). Clayton takes in the praise from a dim corner of the couch, his sleepy smile taking on a bit of a glow. "Discotheque" 's pulse bubbles up and fills the room; Edge's wah-wah guitar does the bump with Clayton's popcorn bass line and spars with Mullen's manic disco drumbeat. The double-tracked vocal captures a sleazy blend of seduction and disgust. Bono, drawn in, wants more. "Let me redo the middle part," he says, cajoling. Howie doesn't need much persuasion. He cues up the tape. "Ready to go," he announces.

"When we do it live, I want to put 'Love to Love You Baby' in here," Bono says slyly as he begins. "Discotheque" 's throb builds. Invoking Donna Summer sets Bono off, and as he riffs on the phrase "You've got heaven in your heart" his moans grow sultry, woozy. He ends the repetition with a twisted, choked falsetto note, then plunges into a growling rap about all the forces that can enslave a man. Meanwhile, Howie's shifting the levels, matching Clayton's bass to the tenor of Bono's words. Finally, the music sweeps over Bono's vocal, and the track ends. Bono falls back into the couch. "Magic," Howie proclaims.

When Clayton and Bono row me across the river, it is August. *Pop* should be finished any day now. Yet the band, Howie, and producer Flood remain submerged in 12-hour recording sessions that have so far produced fewer than five complete songs. Island, U2's label, is discreetly champing at the bit; the veteran crew at Principle Management simply shrugs its collective shoulders every morning. "Nearly all the records have been finished in a spirit of crisis," explains Paul McGuinness, U2's manager for nearly 20 years and the group's unofficial fifth member. "Maybe that's good. Maybe it's necessary. You can see how hard they're fighting for this record."

While Bono and Clayton submit to disco delirium across the river, the goings-on at Hanover prove the aptness of McGuinness's words. As Mullen watches Winston Churchill on TV, Edge and Flood try again and again to capture the ideal guitar part for a track called "Gone." "I've just got to come up with a mix that's emotional and heartfelt, economical and clear," mutters Flood, longtime U2 engineer-turned-head honcho, his ever-radiant smile hardly hiding his frustration. In bomber jacket and wire rims, the renowned producer of PJ Harvey and Nick Cave looks like a computer nerd trying to hack the perfect code. Edge, patient as a farmer, sits in a straight-backed chair; he's always willing to try again. At any rate, neither man will settle. They'll be here another two hours; several weeks later, they'll trash the track entirely and rebuild it from its core.

Though a summer-camp playfulness pervades U2's work environments, with their many comfortable lounging areas, kitchens well-stocked with cookies, caffeine, and alcohol, and a catering staff providing nightly three-entrée meals, the mood within the studios themselves can often grow as stern as an SAT testing room. U2 do not permit supermodels to drape themselves attractively over the engineering boards; they do not take long lunches with visiting Hollywood stars. Sometimes on Thursdays—Pie Day, because the caterers offer crusty shepherd's tarts that night—they'll drop by the Kitchen, the bar in the basement of the Clarence Hotel, for a 2 a.m. beer. Other than that, what they do is work.

"There's none of the naughty-boy syndrome, where musicians just skip out for the day," reports Flood.

"No, there's no skipping," Howie concurs. "Edge does go to his cooking classes, though. Every Monday afternoon at 4-o'clock."

Edge's interest in soufflés aside, the *Pop* sessions show U2 making music with even more intensity than usual. The extra pressure comes from the band's determination to break once and for all from the style that made them famous. In the 1980s U2 invented the modern-rock sound that many Alternative Nation bands, from Live to Stabbing Westward, still steal from—big guitars, earnest vocals, wide open spaces in every song. But since 1990, the band of the '80s has been tunneling away from that sound. The retreat was inspired, partly, by what rock became after it went "alternative." Bono hates that category, and has scornful words for the artists who fall under its mantle. He decries their glamorization of heroin ("talk about pseudoreligious") and their smug antifashion attitude. Most of all, he condemns the notion of a certain brand of raw rock as the music's only authentic form. He considers this "particularly male, white, Anglo-Saxon aspect" to be an insult to anyone who understands the value of a good hip shake. "Is something authentic because it's in runners and a plaid shirt?" he fumes. "Is it authentic because it has no ambition? If that's the case, give me some fucking plastic pants, and quickly."

That's easy for Bono to say now, after spending the '90s wearing nearly nothing but vinyl. But at the end of the '80s, U2 was the very band he's just derided. The gigantic sound and transcendent imagery that made them post-punk's ultimate rock heroes collapsed with the commercial and artistic failure of 1988's documentary film and double-album soundtrack, *Rattle and Hum,* which made them look like minstrels and fools.

The new U2 began with *Achtung Baby*. Recording that album, in Berlin with Eno at the helm and Flood manning the engineer's board, transformed U2; they went on to mount one of the most ambitious tours in rock history: the Brechtian media frenzy Zoo TV. Then they made *Zooropa*, an album sexed up with an electronic shimmer and rife with images of a future lived through holographic billboards and crashed cars. *Zooropa* took U2 as far from the monastic mysticism of *The Joshua Tree* as they could go. It freed U2 from itself.

The next step was for its individual members to free themselves from U2 for a while. They took a year off after completing the *Zooropa* tour in 1993. "It was the first long break U2 ever had," says Clayton. "We'd worked for 14 years straight." He spent most of the next 12 months in New York City, studying music and getting his head together after the tour's excesses. (These days, Clayton orders Club Orange sodas in bars and, besides a little smoke now and then, is substance-free.) Mullen, too, recharged his batteries in New York, then returned home to Dublin to prepare for fatherhood; his longtime companion, Ann Aecheson, gave birth to a baby boy in May 1996. Edge nurtured a new relationship with Morleigh Steinberg, the Los Angeles-based choreographer who was the "Mysterious Ways" belly dancer on the outdoor leg of the Zoo TV tour. Bono spent time with his wife, Ali, and their two daughters, but also hopped around the globe, collaborating with fellow one-name wonders like Sinatra and Pavarotti.

Finally, bit by bit, U2's foursome started to want to be a band again. "Without really discussing it much," says Clayton, "we realized we were all listening to the same music." The druggy, atmospheric soul trances of Portishead, Tricky, and Massive Attack, then sweeping Europe and seeping into the corners of America, had captivated all four players. Reunited in

London in the fall of 1994 and calling themselves the Passengers, U2 and producer Brian Eno explored these new avenues. Ambient in the good and bad senses—sometimes haunting, often barely there—the Passengers album, *Original Soundtracks 1,* let the band get loose in a way they'd never allowed themselves before. But it definitely didn't cut it as the newest U2 breakthrough. "I don't like that record," says the famously frank Mullen.

To carry the band to another level, *Pop* would have to offer more than just mood. For Edge, this meant establishing a new relationship with the guitar, taking into account the mind-altering noises being made by bands who'd rejected the instrument. "The sounds that a guitar is capable of creating are at this point cliché," he insists. "The challenge is to find things you can do with the instrument that are not already used up." Clayton and Mullen, who'd taken on the synth-rock challenge with their 1996 update of the *Mission: Impossible* theme, would have to figure out how to translate the lessons they'd learned from those cold machines into the warm language of U2's rock 'n' roll. To aid them in fusing rock's aggressiveness with dance music's wide musical and emotional range, U2 gathered a top-notch group of musical talents: Howie B., Soul II Soul grandmaster Nellee Hooper, and Steve Osborne of the British electronic duo Perfecto, offered a virtual living encyclopedia of current studio trends.

All of which might have simply served the dilettantish whims of a veteran rock band trying to stay fresh if U2 were not pursuing a more profound goal with *Pop*. Having refreshed their rock sound with dance elements and synthesized flourishes, the band now wants to enact a true fusion of the two often-warring genres. "We're trying to find the access points connecting lots of different music," says Clayton. "We're actually trying to make a kind of music that doesn't exist yet," adds Bono. "That is a terrifying place to be."

The '90s house-techno-ambient evolution proved to be an ideal conduit for U2's new ambition. Steeped in the black music history they'd already been exploring on *Rattle and Hum*, the new dance music was spiritual and iconoclastic, aggressive and sexy. The contradictions that classic rock had imposed between mind and body, black and white, tradition and invention—contradictions that had ultimately entrapped U2—fell apart in the wash of sample-happy syncretism. With *Pop*, U2 hoped to match that music's ferment of dizziness, humor, love, corruption, sex, surrender, pain.

"We wanted to make a record," Bono concludes, "that would actually feel like your life."

As they sprawl around Hanover's extra-long, pine dinner table at the beginning of another arduous night, the only hint of U2's self-conception as a team fighting a mighty battle is the uniformity of their haircuts. Three of the four (the classically cut Mullen is the exception) wear the barely-there *Trainspotting* do currently fashionable among British clubgoers. The effect differs on each one: Bono seems more rugged, older; Clayton, brashly chic due to his Warholian tint; Edge, surprisingly hatless, looks like a rock 'n' roll Captain Picard. It's weird that these men, known for refusing trends, would all give in to such an obvious one. But in the context of the recording sessions, the common style reads like a shared commitment to change.

"They're egoless," says Flood. "You don't find many bands where that's true for all the members. They're trying to achieve something that sounds like them, but in a whole new way. And as Bono puts it, good is not good enough. They're only after greatness."

Most rock stars indulge in ways that have to do with their lower impulses, grabbing as much sex or money or sycophancy as they can get. U2 indulges in another way—by feeding their hunger as artists. "People find it hard to accept artists working above their station," says Edge. "But the most interesting stuff comes from people doing things they shouldn't really be doing, acting outside of the boundaries of convention. I'm not in the least bit apologetic if people think we're pretentious."

U2 have always acted more like artists than rockers, even down to the famous pals they've made in recent years. Novelist Salman Rushdie is a well-known U2 fan and friend. Luciano Pavarotti invited the group to his annual charity concert in Modena, Italy, and subsequently appeared on the Passenger's semi-hit, "Miss Sarajevo," adding an aria that lifted the song to another level of grace. And filmmaker Wim Wenders, a longtime *companero* of Bono's, is currently working on a production deal for a science-fiction film, *The Billion Dollar Hotel*, based on a Bono concept about a group of outcasts who populate a futuristic Los Angeles flophouse.

U2's members see their associations with such notables as an antidote to the soul-draining boredom of the average rock scene. "Personally speaking, I don't really like hanging out with musicians," Clayton admits.

"It's just...it's hard to really talk about anything. Sitting and talking about Peavey amps is not my thing." But artists are not the only answer to this ennui. Perhaps Clayton, who spent several months of 1994 engaged to supermodel Naomi Campbell and remains the only romantically unattached member of the band, prefers that old-fashioned gentleman's pursuit—the company of beautiful women? He smiles. "That's always fun. If you can't find intellectual conversation, that will do."

Clayton's dalliance with Campbell seriously increased U2's fabulousity quotient, as the English fashion princess began carting her friends (notably Christy Turlington and Helena Christensen) around the globe to catch Zoo TV concerts. It's pretty standard rock star behavior, hanging out with models, but U2 very publicly approached it as high camp, as if they were doing it for intellectual, not libidinal, reasons. It was all part of the band's switch from over-the-top sincerity to ultravivid irony.

"I used to find it uncomfortable to be around a lot of things," says Bono. "Then I found these goggles. I put them on and I found that I could go anywhere." The goggles were part of his getup as The Fly, one of his Zoo TV costumes; they were also imaginary shields that kept him from seeing the jet-set scene U2 entered into as anything but a giant game. Edge, also, tried to avoid too much entanglement. "It was really fun and good," he says. "But I also was aware that something that started off as being very ironic had the possibility of turning around and biting us if we weren't careful."

More than his bandmates, Bono's taken that risk by playing ambassador to the stars, showing up at Cannes or behind the bar at the hottest new Soho nightspot. But he claims he'd never want to get stuck in the in crowd. "I hang out with every set," he says. "Anyone will tell you that. From the penthouse to the pavement but under the pavement. I'll go anywhere there's an idea hatching or a great party being thrown."

"Bono has an acute sense of how trends are evolving," says Wenders, "of what people need, and what people feel."

There's a line in the *Pop* song "Miami" that captures Bono's longing for both excitement and protection: "We could make something beautiful," he sings, "something that wouldn't be a problem." In *The Joshua Tree* days and before, any encounters with what a Christian would call temptation posed a problem, not only for U2's souls but for their image. Partaking of the usual perks of the rock superstardom would make the band seem hypocritical. "We always had girls sleeping in our rooms, but we never considered them groupies," says Bono. "Our female fans would show up with *Siddhartha* under their arms, and they'd want to talk."

Such oddly chaste behavior stemmed, in large part, from U2's reputation as spiritual seekers. Edge, Mullen, and Bono once belonged to a fundamentalist Christian commune (Clayton, forever secular, sidestepped that phase), and every album has contained its smattering, small or large, of Jesus imagery. The chime of Edge's guitar, coupled with Bono's striving wails, formed a sound that aimed heavenward: all head and heart, no hips. It's no coincidence that the band's fascination with '70s soul and '90s dance music coincided with a dive into life's carnal joys and perils. "The challenge for us is to factor our spirituality into the mix along with our sexuality," says Edge.

On *Pop*, Bono's lyrics still address spiritual matters, but instead of the heartfelt yet sometimes ponderous pronouncements of albums past, his phrases can now elude linear comprehension. They're like little shards of theology thrown out above the din. In "Wake Up Dead Man," Bono calls for Jesus' return, sounding like a drunk calling for another whiskey, and trying to remember how he got to this terrible place: "If there's an order/In all of this disorder/Is it like a tape recorded/Can we rewind it just once more?" He answers himself in "If God Will Send His Angels," a bitter refrain that seems to sink into disbelief—"Nobody else here, baby/No one else here to blame"—to make the point that only human actions can solve earthly problems, divine presence or none. Even on a song as seemingly hedonistic as "Playboy Mansion," Bono returns to matters of the soul's survival in this secular world. "Then will there be no time of sorrow/Then will there be no time for shame," he sings, a psalmist dreaming of rapture in a consumer's paradise.

"I enjoy the test of trying to keep hold of what's sacred, and still being awake," says Bono. "It's one thing being in that holy huddle; it's another thing taking yourself out there into the world."

The Clarence Hotel was built in 1852 at 6-8 Wellington Quay, in the heart of the neighborhood known as Temple Bar. For years it served as a humble stopping point for rural folk and visitors from the rougher north side of the Liffey. As kids, Bono and Edge (then Paul Hewson and Dave Evans, respectively) frequented the hotel's bar, where they could nab an illicit pint of Guinness. They were students together at Mount Temple, a progressive high school on the outskirts of town, just starting to fool around with the idea of a band. "For us the Clarence was like a secret place," Edge recalls. "The people who used to go there were priests and judges from across the road."

It's not likely that you'll see many men of the cloth wandering the Clarence's pristine, airy halls these days. Bono, Edge, and prominent Dublin entrepreneur Harry Crosby purchased the building in 1992, and converted it to a luxury hotel. The new Clarence presents an atmosphere both spare and sumptuous. Its spacious rooms, appointed with angular Bauhaus-inspired furniture, feature an assortment of subtle conveniences only a much-traveled rock star would think to include: generous closets, comfortable reading chairs, powerful showers, good reading lights, and a room service menu that far outclasses the average inn's dreaded club-sandwich-and-pizza fare. You want Thai coconut soup or cappuccino tiramisu at 4 a.m.? Book a room here.

According to Edge, the heart of his and Bono's interest in the Clarence has nothing to do with personal nostalgia, or the wish to have a nice spot to put up Christy Turlington when she comes to town. It's all about what lurks in the hotel's basement. There, the singer and guitarist have established a club that's become the center of Dublin's post-rock underground.

As U2 consume their spiced pies at Hanover one Thursday night, the Kitchen rapidly fills with kids in pajama-ish rave gear, dancing and chatting and making out to the sounds of visiting London DJ Justin Roberts. Behind a heavy curtain guarded by a weathered, Hell's Angel type lies the club's exclusive back bar. Tonight, it's filled with legends of Dublin's night life, including noir cabaret singer Gavin Friday, who's widely acknowledged as Bono's right-hand man; actress Veronica Quilligan, who starred in Neil Jordan's first film when she was only 16; Peter Rowan, U2's *War* boy, now a handsome tough embarking on an acting career; and Guggi, along with Friday, a former member of the legendary punk band the Virgin Prunes, whose quiet, mystical drawings adorn many of the Clarence's rooms.

A little after 2 a.m., the mood in the room warps and expands as Bono, Edge, Flood, Howie, and several other studio rats wind in and toward the bar. Bono sits down next to me and begins, as he is wont to do, to chat about temptation. We're discussing what rock 'n' roll meant to us as teens, how it can feel like the only religion that matters. "There's something about that adolescent state when you're really open that's worth hanging on to," he reflects. I ask him how his sense of spirituality has changed since he was bowled over by faith as a boy. "In faith, there's different elements," he replies. "There's karma, living right, but then you've got grace. And grace comes out of nowhere. It can come from any corner."

He continues to wax philosophical, but we're distracted by a pouty blonde who's taken the seat beside us. "Excuse me," apologizes Bono. "I have to talk to her. She's been waiting." At first the woman seems angry that Bono doesn't place her. Soon enough, though, she's forgiven the slight, and is deep in discussion with the singer. Then he gets her laughing. "Let's rescue him," motions a longtime Principle employee. We do, handing him a fresh drink. The woman wanders off, satisfied.

Bono is famous for such people skills. Here in Dublin, he and his bandmates walk a line between notoriety and warm welcome—they're international stars, and deal with the adulation and enmity fame always brings, but they're also bloody determined to remain locals. Rather than violating his privacy, he considers his ability to move through Dublin like a normal person a part of that privacy—a right the city offers him in return for the generosity he displays toward its citizens.

"There are seven women who work in that pub, and they're all named Angela," he informs me one afternoon when we've stopped for a pint. One of the seven Angelas has just walked by and enjoyed a brief conversation with him. It's a sunny day, so we've taken our Guinness across the street to the river's edge, and Bono waves and yells whenever a passing car gives him a honk. He never seems to tire of the attention. "I'm not very inhibited," he says, stating the obvious. "My strongest trait is curiosity. I'm just lifting stones, you know, opening doors. Looking out windows, around corners, up skirts."

This mischievous Bono is a recent incarnation. For years his fans thought Bono a saint, and critics accused him of playing that role falsely even when he was just trying to be himself. "I used to think that my image was something to live up to," he says. "Now I feel it's almost a duty to let people down." The only way Bono could dodge his own shadow was by assuming its cartoonish opposite—becoming MacPhisto or The Fly, modern devils as degraded as his previous public self was holy. "One thing I might regret from early times was just showing that one side of me," he says. "The egomaniac was always there, too. And some people have always seen me with horns."

In Dublin, Bono surrounds himself with people who see him with neither horns or halo, friends he's had for 20 years and workmates who understand his regular side. Like Edge and Mullen, he also keeps his family here. Ali and Bono have been together since high school, a shocking fact considering the average length of most marriages, let alone relationships cultivated by rock stars. "It's beyond love, marriage, death, friendship," he says. "We're onto some other thing. We're closer than most people are, and yet capable of being at a great distance physically. It's amazing how it works out."

Family is a crucial aspect of U2's Dublin life. Larry, Ann, and their new baby have a home here; Edge maintains strong ties to the city because of his three children, who still live with their mother. At 12, his oldest daughter, Holly, is a rock 'n' roll kid. "I *think* I've heard her say good things about us," says Edge a little nervously. "But we haven't actually released a record other than *Passengers* since she got into music. When *Zooropa* came out, she was nine."

He pauses to reflect, the picture of the nervous dad trying not to fall into the generation gap. "It will be interesting to see what she thinks of this record." Fractured dance-rock not her usual fare? "Actually, she seems to be into Oasis. But they're not her favorite group."

Who is, then?

Consternation fills Edge's normally placid face. "I'm trying to remember," he laughs. "I actually wouldn't like to say, because if I get it wrong, I'm dead."

Summer is long gone when I hear from Bono again; *Pop* has broken all of U2's deadlines, but the singer has shed the anxiety that sometimes crept into his voice during the album's making. Instead, when he calls me from Miami one Thursday night, he's positively joyful, enjoying a particularly sweet seduction—the thrill of falling in love with something of your creation.

"We finished the album yesterday at about seven in the morning," he tells me. "We'd tried to finish in six months, but we couldn't. Somewhere along the line we realized we'd never made a record in six months. We were trying to put together such disparate elements. Flood was, in the end, the man. We bought him a spiky helmet from the World War I era, to help him rein us all in."

Bono's eager to describe *Pop* in detail, every cut, every groove. "When the record opens, it's full tilt—it starts out like a party and then it turns mean on you. The intro to 'Discotheque' is beyond, it's very dizzy. Then 'Do You Feel Loved'—that's a bit yahoo—and 'Mofo.' Then 'If God Will Send His Angels.' That's sci-fi gospel, it's air, and it leads right into 'Staring at the Sun.'

" 'The Last Night on Earth' doesn't know what it is. With 'Gone,' the record peaks a bit. 'Miami' is followed by 'Playboy Mansion,' which is a hymn to trash. 'If You Wear That Velvet Dress'—I don't want to talk about that song too much, but let's just say it's haunted. It's all tangled up in ultraviolet.

"Finally there's 'Please' and 'Wake Up Dead Man.' We didn't really want to end with that, but you can't help it. It's an ending song."

Bono pauses for breath, but not for long. "Right up to the last month of making this record I had this feeling that it could go any way," he admits. "It could be extraordinary, or such crap. We had the sense that we were trying to make the impossible happen. Can we be this? And we can."

U2

U2's Crash: Why *Pop* Flops

Dave Marsh
***The Nation*, August 25, 1997**

For any rock music fan opposed to cultural hegemony or self-righteous sanctimony, it is difficult to resist gloating over the fact that U2's *Pop* album and its ongoing U.S. tour have bombed. The tour's most noteworthy emblem is a gigantic stage prop in the shape of a lemon, and that could not be more perfect. *Billboard's* most recent album chart places *Pop* at No. 124. After the long-anticipated *Pop* premiered in the No. 1 slot in March, U2 was outperformed on the charts by the Spice Girls, Aerosmith, Squirrel Nut Zippers, and Matchbox 20. The singles from *Pop* have tanked. The tour canceled shows or played to half-houses from South Carolina to San Diego. The ABC-TV special that was supposed to kick off the Irish quartet's current foray into Bonomania was the lowest-rated TV show in major network history. The PR rejoinder was that "the album is selling well outside the U.S." But when Bono and company announced their tour in February with an absurdist press conference at a K Mart in New York City, "big in Japan" wasn't what the band members had in mind.

That pop stars suffer from hubris is hardly news. But the U2 crash may carry a broader and more encouraging message than that. Rock is basically a supply-side game, but the flop of *Pop* suggests that rock, though increasingly dominated by corporate decision-making, is not a supply-side-only affair. Unlike your average consumers, the most committed rock fans, who are both numerous and tend to create the trends, feel empowered by the very rhetoric of the music to make judgments—sometimes punitive judgments—about their heroes. Furthermore, they not only expect to be entertained but expect to have certain "needs" met in the process. Rock stars carry a heavier load of symbolism than any other contemporary performers. It is impossible to imagine Clint Eastwood's audience rejecting *The Bridges of Madison County* because of Eastwood's marital strife—but that's just what happened to Bruce Springsteen, who had drawn an audience to his romantic view of relationships, after his divorce.

Concert-biz spin-doctors now proclaim that the U2 tour has grossed almost $50 million and has sold a greater number of tickets than any other tour this year. Neither category, however, implies sold-out shows or profitability. Few professionals doubt that U2 did miscalculate, and their miscalculation has many sources. One may have been revealed at that K Mart press conference. Bono openly sneered at a reporter who dared ask a real question: Why was the band, by its appearance, promoting K Mart, a chain that censors recordings, as does Wal-Mart? Bono called the guy a snob.

I doubt that one U2 fan in a thousand even knows about that specific incident But the attitude—you're a snob, and out of line, if you question U2 shilling for K Mart—violates U2's image as a "progressive" rock band. This image developed as the band toured for Amnesty International, dared to challenge the violence on both sides in Ireland, provoked L.A. cops in its movie *Rattle and Hum*, and hung out with Bill Clinton and George Stephanopoulos when Clinton still seemed to be some kind of stealth-MTV presidential candidate. To put it in the kind of terms a rock fan might use, U2 now seems out of touch, alienated from its roots: consumers who turn to rock bands precisely for what they cannot find at K Mart. It's not that rock fans automatically reject crass commercialism— millions of Kiss and Bon Jovi fans prove otherwise—but at least the music is supposed to be self-generated crass commercialism, not the prefab bargain-store crap provided at K Mart.

U2 and other rock commodities are clearly out of touch as they buy into corporate pop's obsession with spectacle for its own sake. More outrageous and shocking spectacle still works, because it's oppositional. That's why local bureaucrats across the nation have busied themselves trying to ban Marilyn Manson. The members of Manson would be lucky if K Mart let them through the door to shop, and, certainly, if Manson wants a golden arch for its onstage golden showers, it will not find McDonald's giving the go-ahead as easily as it did for the golden arch that dominates U2's stage set. The current U2 tour is like one of those "big box" department stores that come into town and shove smaller retailers out of business, a behemoth of a production that takes days to set up and move out of stadiums—and all to support an album full of the weakest material of the band's career. *Pop*, the album, is too prefab to deserve to be called daring, as it was in the pre-release hype because of its use of the latest dance beat, "electronica"—what used to be called techno before British pros lifted it from Detroit black kids. In a classic bait-and-switch, there's not even much electronica here; most of the recording is an unremarkable rehash of what the band has done in the past.

From the Frankfurt School to the Situationists, cultural theoreticians have argued that this should pose no real problem: a mass audience is too crass and preoccupied to notice subtle deterioration in quality. Corporate commodification, the theorists would say, has weaned the masses from being put off by the kind of hypocrisy expressed in Bono's "snob" remark (and a dozen other condescending devices in the stage show). In Guy Debord's *Society of the Spectacle*, the mass audience wants more, bigger, louder, faster, flashier, brighter, ratcheting up the circus every time out, and if you simply drown out the few critical voices, all will be well.

Why doesn't this always work? Why have the record sales and tour grosses of just about every superstar and supergroup of the past decade—U2, Springsteen, R.E.M., Sting, Prince, Public Enemy, Madonna—fallen so precipitately? The music industry panic of 1997 is supposed to be about the failure to develop new stars; but the real music industry crisis has existed for most of this decade, and it's about the failure of the system to sustain the stars it's created. The media corporations made huge investments in each of the artists named here, and yet none of the music companies seem to have a clue how to exploit them effectively.

Well, the system of corporate commodification doesn't function smoothly. Even celebrities like Schwarzenegger and Seinfeld have half-lives. Media corporations don't enjoy having to stumble around in the dark searching for the next set of superstars as the ratings and profits of the current bunch dwindle. They would prefer to establish a handful of brand names and tinker with packaging periodically (ideally, bigger and better packaging—like the *Pop* tour). But that doesn't work. It's not just the charges of pedophilia against Michael Jackson, or Springsteen becoming a folkie, or U2 miscalculating how much marketing people are willing to have rubbed in their faces, or Madonna deciding to make a film about a fascist concubine with music by the world's worst composer. Nothing seems to work. R.E.M.'s first flop, *Monster*, was in many respects the most musically daring record it ever made.

To say that this descent of stars reflects a mere generational shift doesn't explain much. The fact is that, even with sophisticated marketing and surveying, corporations still cannot readily identify market preferences in music, let alone control them. Electronica has so far produced few chartbusters. And the music that the industry most loathes and fears—

rap—remains its commercial powerhouse. (U2 got headlines for selling about 350,000 copies of *Pop* its first week in the racks. Wu-Tang Clan's *Wu-Tang Forever* sold almost twice that many its first week.)

A more likely explanation is that today's rock, with its roots in and continuing links to society's most dispossessed, somehow effectively does promote resistance, even critical thinking—even if this operates at a pretty shallow level. Rather than lapsing into cynicism, newer rock performers already show signs of recognizing these links. Rage Against the Machine, chosen as U2's opening act early in the tour because it's probably the biggest new concert act in rock, used the stadium shows to talk about, among other things, the injustice of Mumia Abu-Jamal being on death row. And R.A.T.M. made this work because its members don't talk about such issues coldly but with real rage. They project a sense of conviction that speaking out will make a difference—a sense of conviction you can't buy at K Mart, but that has been indispensable to the success of most acts mentioned in this article. (Immediately upon R.A.T.M.'s departure, a spokesman for U2 announced that U2 itself would most certainly not waste any of its time defending "this accused cop killer," although its friends at Amnesty International continue to do so.) Of course, by agreeing to appear with U2, just as by recording for Sony, R.A.T.M. also chose to become part of the spectacle. It's too soon to say that eventually such involvements will tranquilize them—but it's worth worrying that it might. For instance, the sponsorship agreement between the successful women's tour, Lilith Fair, and Borders— which Lilith Fair founder Sarah McLachlan says she made in full awareness of the book chain's involvement in a major labor dispute—is a more concrete piece of bad news.

Other artists—Ani DiFranco comes to mind—have rejected spectacle altogether. DiFranco has done so in ways more crucial than the noisy pronouncements made by lingering sixties vets like Neil Young, a major California landowner who moans about the price of tickets to the Rock and Roll Hall of Fame dinner. The popular anarchist DiFranco has refused to accept a major-label record deal. She has also shoved hip-hop beats into the face of her folkie audience. That has a lot to do with her insistence on personal freedom, of course, but it also reflects a different concept of how to liberate listeners. Rage Against the Machine pulls off a similar aesthetic coup by tying agitprop, like its supportive comments on Mumia and Leonard Peltier, to the kind of dense metallic noise that lefties have always frowned upon. Is this effective? Well, it certainly hasn't damaged either R.A.T.M. or its subjects. And R.A.T.M. has raised the profile of Mumia and Peltier (and Noam Chomsky and the radical groups cited in R.A.T.M.'s album notes) among rock fans.

Watching pop culture bombast on the U2 scale collapse beneath its own pretension and arrogance is indeed rewarding. But vengeance doesn't get you very far, in either politics or culture. Young performers like DiFranco and R.A.T.M. create their own forms of resistance. That they have found listeners who respond and that they have inspired others to emulate them suggests that the celebrity system that obscures so much of contemporary reality can be undermined. Corporate rock has already proven that it cannot learn. The few stars who seem to have teamed something in the process of being commodified—Springsteen, R.E.M.—have been utterly unable to marshal the corporate forces and regain their mass audience. Given the way the game is rigged, it's impossible to imagine a music *business* free of corporate control—to believe otherwise is to whistle "Won't Get Fooled Again" past the graveyard. But as DiFranco has been none-too-subtly pointing out, one can imagine *music* free of corporate control. Once you do that, you don't need to grab 'em with spectacle because you've got 'em by the heart. Rock's best performers keep looking. That's one of the best reasons for the rest of us to keep listening.

CHAPTER

5

THE MOST IMPORTANT BAND ON EARTH

At a dinner honoring his former booking agent, Frank Barselona, Bono recalled the agency's reaction to the proposed PopMart tour. "They couldn't see it," he noted. After a beat, he conceded, "They were probably right, and they were probably the only people honest enough to tell us about it beforehand."

He could make this concession easily, as earlier that month Bono and the band had picked up half of the eight Grammy awards they had been up for, including Record of the Year. This made good a statement he had made the previous year when they picked up three Grammys for the song "Beautiful Day": he had quipped that U2 were reapplying for the position of World's Best Rock Band. With the success of the Elevation Tour and the three million copies of *All That You Can't Leave Behind* sold in the U.S. alone, it seemed they had been picked for the job.

With the September 11th terrorist attacks on New York City and the Pentagon, U2's music had become something of a salve. Rock fans turned in droves to the messages of songs like "One" and the band added a scrolling list to their show, naming people lost in the attack.

By the new millennium, the group became so popular and mainstream that they were invited to play the National Basketball Association's All-star game and halftime at the Super Bowl.

And the group just keeps on growing…

Raw Power: Never Mind the Bollocks, Here's U2—and They Want Their Rock and Roll Crown Back.

Anthony DeCurtis
***Revolver* magazine, December 2000**

"I did make some changes to the bed," Bono announces as he leads Larry Mullen and me on an impromptu tour of his newly purchased New York City apartment. "It had all these bits around the top"—he gestures towards what obviously used to be a canopy— "and it kind of looked like where Elvis used to sleep." He pauses a beat, as if a light suddenly switched on in his head. He turns, looks at us, smiles and says, "As opposed to where Elvis *will* be sleeping."

Bono's longstanding Elvis obsession aside, his new digs on Central Park West could not bear less of a resemblance to Graceland, the King's monument to kitsch in Memphis, Tennessee. For one thing, the word "Spartan" does not begin to describe the apartment's practically desolate décor. Each room contains only enough furniture to define itself—a table and chairs in the dining room, a small coffee table in the living room, a bed in the bedroom—and all of it left by the previous owner. "That table cost more than the whole rest of the apartment," Bono says dryly as we move through the dining room and into the kitchen. "Pretty Japanese," is Mullen's bemused summary of his lead singer's bare-to-the-bone lifestyle.

Bono, who with his wife and children still maintains his primary residence in Dublin, would scarcely be himself if he didn't have a full-blown theory to validate the way he's living now in his New York pied-a-terre. "So many rockers were destroyed by furniture removals, trying to choose a Chinese rug, and deciding on the right taps for the bathroom," he explains, evidently only half joking. "Most rock and roll people come from very little and are nervous with their nouveau-riche status. They're anxious to buy just the right piece of art and the right carpet, so they spend all their time and money on that. And their next album's crap!

"You think of some artist who set fire to your imagination when you were a youngster," he continues, "and then you think, what the fuck happened? I guarantee you: It was not divorce. It was not drugs. It was buying furniture. Taste is the enemy of art!"

Not coincidentally, perhaps, Bono and U2 lately have been applying the same less-is-more approach to their music. The artwork for the band's new album is lying on Bono's coffee table, and the title sums up their sentiments perfectly: *All That You Can't Leave Behind*. It's all about paring down to essentials, building songs on the elements of a band's sound that are crucial to its identity. After the self-conscious excess of U2's 1997 album *Pop*, the garish confusion of the PopMart tour that followed, and the logic-defying interviews that accompanied both (Bono prattling on about "jewels amid the trash" or some such), this refocusing is much welcome.

"Has rock and roll bequeathed the charts to R&B and pop?" Bono asks, in discussing the ideas that informed the making of the new album. "Is rock music now afraid to bite the arse of the pop charts? It shouldn't be. And if it has lost some ground in the last years it's because it's forgotten the discipline of the 45 and the shock therapy that Nirvana brought to the pop charts, that the Sex Pistols had and the Stones and the Beatles. We're in a new era of progressive rock—and we should be very afraid!

"So that was it—a pretty simple brief for a U2 album. No polemic. Just 'Is that a good tune? No? Well, fuck off then with your big ideas.'"

"We just went into a room and played," Mullen explains, "which was really kind of odd, because we hadn't done it for a long time. If you weren't happy with something, the band could just replay it as opposed to having to get things programmed up. It was good fun to feel like a musician again! When we get into a room together, something really happens. I mean, if you set up the gear now, we could play all the songs on the record in this room.

"That's why U2 started. That's why I wanted to be in a band in the first place. I mean, technology makes me sound great. Give me a drum machine to play and I'll sound great. But there is another thing, and that's playing with the other guys. It was a good record, then, from the band point of view. We had all the chances to make things right; we have no excuses. And I haven't felt like that since our first record."

It is in the spirit of U2's new ethic of discipline that Bono makes a truly shocking announcement shortly after I arrive at the apartment. As I re-enter the living room from the terrace, where I marveled at the spectacular view, from 16 stories up, of the Central Park Reservoir, Bono says a bit sheepishly, "I've stopped drinking." He clearly notices my surprise—and in the interest of full disclosure, my disappointment. "Only for a few months," he hastens to add, then laughs nervously. "I want to get in shape—but it's driving me mad! I want to go out and celebrate and tell everybody how proud I am of the new album. But sober, I'm much more modest!"

For me, the prospect of interviewing a sober Bono is, well, a bit sobering, if only by virtue of its strangeness. My 13 years of reporting on U2 is a merry—if somewhat blurry—memory soaked in rivers of red wine and whiskey. But Bono's plan is working, at least. Clad in a green T-shirt and black trousers, he looks fit and firm—in impressive fighting shape. He's turned 40 this year and seems set to confront middle-age head on. As for Mullen, who is now 39, there simply is no question that a portrait of him is miserably decaying in an attic somewhere, like Oscar Wilde's *Picture of Dorian Gray*. In his black T-shirt and shiny black workout pants, Mullen looks no different from the way he did when I first met him in 1987.

"What else are you going to do in your late thirties," Bono asks rhetorically, as he continues to describe U2's no-nonsense approach to creating *All That You Can't Leave Behind*. "You're not going to be harder. It's hard to be funkier. You just better have some tunes, and something to say. You stop thinking about who's hip and you start thinking about 'Bridge over Troubled Water'—and the sick feeling you get in your stomach every time you hear it.

"You can dial up a groove and you can call down an atmosphere from any $100 Casio," he goes on, "but, for us, we've got to get to another level with the songs. The arrangements can get as fucked-up as the album in questions requires, and this one didn't require that. But that's where we're going now—with the songs. They're the eternal things. That's what we're looking for—the essentials."

Heralded by its luminous first single, "Beautiful Day," *All That You Can't Leave Behind* is a back-to-basics U2 album. But as with, for example, the music of the post-psychedelic Beatles, the album's simplicity is earned. It's a conscious aesthetic strategy, a choice, not a retreat from ambition. Songs like "Beautiful Day," "Walk On," "Stuck in a Moment," and "Kite" are elegantly constructed and ring with the spiritual yearning in U2's music that has spoken to so many millions of people over the past two decades. In a whirling, unsettled time, the album is an encouraging statement, a declaration in both its music and its message that some things remain true, whatever else might change. "What you don't have/You don't need it now," Bono sings at the end of "Beautiful Day," and it's a freeing idea: Let go, and live fully in the moment.

Still, at the end of "Kite," the album's most moving song, Bono describes himself as "The last of the rock stars/When hip-hop drove the big cars." At such moments, you realize that all the uplift and encouragement of the album are meant as much for the band as for its listeners. For all their bravado, U2 must be uncertain about their commercial prospects at this time in their career. "Who's to say where the wind will take you/Who's to say what it is will break you/I don't know which way the wind will blow," Bono sings on the soaring chorus of "Kite," and, coming from a singer and a band that have never made any bones about their lust for a huge audience, such a yielding to forces beyond their control is no small matter.

Bono and Larry settle in on the green leather banquet that provides seating at the sleek silver table in the breakfast nook of Bono's kitchen. They're sipping tea, and Bono has put out some orange slices. They occasionally pull cigarettes from Larry's pack of American Spirits, the smoke of choice for enlightened rock stars these past few years. Larry combs the cabinets and finds some oyster-shaped ashtrays. "I did not buy those things," Bono says emphatically.

In part, Bono and Larry are in New York, where Larry has for the past eight years also maintained an apartment, because bandmembers attended MTV's Video Music Awards show. Despite whatever questions they may harbor about their place in the pop firmament—and despite their relatively advanced years—U2 have no interest in ceding MTV to Britney and the boy bands. Bono and Larry served as presenters at the show, and Bono, at least, seemed fully in his element. On his way into Radio City Music Hall, he snuggled up to Jennifer Lopez and, backstage, he greeted actress Kate Hudson by crooning Macy Gray's "I Try."

It's all part of the plan. "We make pop music, we're in the pop business," Mullen says bluntly. "We want to be on the radio. We want to compete on that level, and we're not embarrassed about that. Pop music is what's happening, and we're competing for that space. There doesn't seem to be a lot of rock music right now. What would you call Korn and Limp Bizkit? What is that? I appreciate some of it, but I don't know what it is. It's not rock and roll."

"There's a visceral side to that music, which is something you could call rock," Bono counters. "It's that physical thing that Jimi Hendrix and Led Zeppelin did—like a boxing match on your ear. The scream that everybody holds inside is released in music like that. I'll tell you, if it gets the groove, if it gets hips, it's powerful. Without the hips, it's Cookie Monster."

He laughs, and continues, "There is, though, a huge difference in the end between pop and rock. It's something to do with pop telling you that everything is okay, and rock telling you it isn't. Rock music says you can change the world—the world inside your head, the world inside the room, and even the world outside the room. Pop music says, 'Why bother? Everything's okay.'

"That's why I hope there are radio programmers out there who will take a chance with putting a rock band in a pop format. And that's why I like MTV. Everything is not in its ghetto there. MTV has a younger audience now, but I was 11 years old when John Lennon blew my mind. Music meant everything to me then. So I want us to be on MTV."

That will to battle for an audience is very reminiscent of the U2 of the early eighties, when the band came rocketing out of Dublin. So much post-punk music from the U.K. at that time seemed anemic and vitiated, and so many of those bands viewed popularity in America with a smug contempt. U2, on the other hand, pursued it wholeheartedly. The band seemed intent on conquering America, one club show at a time. By the time Bono was climbing the scaffolding high above the stage at Live Aid in 1985 [*actually, that moment occurred at the US Fest in 1983*]—electrifying a worldwide audience estimated at one billion—the band was on its way to the superstardom it would enjoy well into the nineties.

But that stature for the band is no longer guaranteed, if, in fact, it still exists at all. The conceptually muddled *Pop* album did not sell well by U2's multi-platinum standards, and by the end of the PopMart tour, the band was failing to fill the stadiums that had, for better or worse, become its accustomed live setting. U2 had never shown any instincts for moderation—pushing further and getting bigger had always been the group's guiding principles. But the *Pop* album foundered on half-digested concepts drawn from dance-club culture, and the PopMart tour—with its huge hydraulic lemon, gigantic vidi-walls, and gleaming golden arches—may have set out to comment subversively on commerce and show business, but ultimately seemed only to be particularly depressing symptoms of the problem.

Audiences in general had already begun to grow more fickle, and the possibility loomed that even U2 fans—the loyalest of the loyal—might be losing interest. After nearly 20 years of mad ambition—and extraordinary achievements—it seemed like U2 had finally overreached.

"*Pop* hurt us here, in the U.S.," Bono admits. "It was difficult with the tour and the hoopla. I'm not sure all our fans knew or cared about Andy Warhol and what we were trying to do—all our concepts, and pop as the death of God, and whatever. It was 'Phoooo! Let's hear the songs, Bono.' And the songs were special, but we didn't bring home every arrangement. People had to work at it a bit too much. And some of the sneakers-and-short-pants crowd didn't see the bright colors of what we were doing with PopMart as vivid. They saw it as lurid."

"We made some fundamental errors in our planning," adds Mullen. "We'd planned to go on the road before we finished the album, so we went straight out of the studio and onto the road. We were using a lot of technology, and we didn't have the time to get it together. It took us a while to figure it out. That didn't help."

"And there was the other thing of having that quiet little gig to start up with—in Las Vegas," Bono says, laughing, about the PopMart tour's wildly publicized opening date. "I wasn't singing well. Everyone turned up, and they heard the sound of a balloon being burst. And I remember Los Angeles, a place where we had never played a bad show: It was the first time I could feel, 'They're eating popcorn out there.' It's weird being a performer—you can sense stuff. Like, 'They're buying T-shirts during *this* song?' And yet, beneath all that pomp and color, there was humor and heart and soul, but it was not coming through.

"I think people were on irony patrol, and it wasn't at all ironic," Bono insists. "We'd come in through the crowd and come walking up to the stage, and 'Mofo' would kick off. The band stops, and the opening lines go, 'Looking for to save my, save my soul/Looking in the places where no flowers grow/Looking to fill that God-shaped hole/Mother, mother-sucking rock and roll.' I mean—that's hardcore. Not at all effete or smart-ass. But it maybe *looked* smart-ass. So there you have it."

Yes, there you have it, indeed. And here you have the new U2 working hard to undo the damage that was done. The band will not be hitting the road until the spring this time, and there are no plans for any stadium shows. "This time we want to go indoors," says Bono, "play for like four months and see if we want to go on from there. We're really going to rock the house. We're going in for lift-off, and our band in full flight is something to see."

"I'm so looking forward to playing indoors," says Mullen, "to be able to look at people and see the whites of their eyes."

Intriguingly, U2's move towards simplicity began during the PopMart tour, inspired by an unlikely figure. "It was a DJ that may have sent us down this road," Bono says. "When we weren't tight enough at the start of the last tour, we had to find time to rehearse. So we ended up at one point in the basement of a hotel in Washington, D.C. Howie B., whom we'd worked with on *Pop* was DJing on the tour, and also helping out front during the show with effects and mixing with our own sound guy. Howie was at the rehearsal, acting as a kind of producer.

"We couldn't get all the gear in," Bono goes on, "because it was all in the trucks on the road. So we just had a rented bass guitar, drums, a Vox AC30, and a PA at this rehearsal—nothing else. Howie walks into the room as we're playing, a three-piece and a singer, and he just starts going, 'What's going on here? *What is that sound that you're making?'* And we just go, ahem, 'Howie, this is rock music.' And he's like, 'Wow, the sound of the drums and the bass is incredible.' So he started removing effects at the live shows, and by the end of the tour there were very few loops and treatments. He said, 'It's really odd. The more I'm taking out, the bigger the sound is getting.' And then he said, 'That's the kind of record you should be making next.'"

Talk about getting back to all that you can't leave behind—or maybe, more appropriately, "Tonight a DJ Saved My Life." Whichever, U2 are back at full strength—and we can sure use them.

Anthony DeCurtis is a contributing editor at Rolling Stone and teaches in the creative writing program at the University of Pennsylvania.

Keeping the Peace

Erik Philbrook
***ASCAP Playback*, October 2001**

The world has changed, but not U2's mission. In the wake of the terrorist attacks on America, Bono speaks about the importance of music in uncertain times and how his band creates the songs that have come to mean so much to so many.

It's wild, man," says U2 singer/songwriter Bono when asked about the photograph on the cover of the band's latest album, *All That You Can't Leave Behind*. It shows the band members, four dark figures, standing in an airport waiting to board a plane. In the wake of the terrorist attacks of September 11, the image holds chilling connotations. But if in art context is everything, then the symbolism of one of the world's greatest, most beloved rock bands preparing for flight is a welcome sight. Upon closer inspection of the album artwork, however, you can find an even more symbolic image: in one photo, behind the band on the flight announcement board, shines an icon of a heart in a suitcase.

U2 are Irish, but they are really citizens of the world. And for two decades, several albums, and umpteen world tours, they have given the world their all, both musically and spiritually. From creating soul-searching, inspirational rock—best-represented on their 1980's masterpiece, *The Joshua Tree*—to actively supporting a host of causes from Greenpeace, War Child, and Jubilee 2000, the world debt reduction campaign, they have expanded the notion of what a rock band can be...and do.

After a decade of experimentation in which they purposefully and playfully messed with their image and their sound, last year they released *All That You Can't Leave Behind*, produced by the band's longtime producers Daniel Lanois and Brian Eno. A return of sorts to their classic "live" sound, featuring Bono, guitarist The Edge, drummer Larry Mullen, and bassist Adam Clayton playing passionately together, the album was released into a fickle marketplace, where teen pop and angry rock predominated. However, their first single, "Beautiful Day," got a foot in the door, rising up the charts and winning a Grammy. Unsure of the band's relevance in his new era, Bono jokingly announced at the 2000 Grammy Awards that U2 was applying for the job of Best Rock and Roll Band in the World.

After their highly successful Elevation 2000 tour, U2 got the job. But ticket and record sales, Grammys, and chart position aside, what was more important was that U2's well-crafted rock songs with a message mattered. Now, they matter more than ever. The album is the perfect collection of songs for this dark moment in our history. In songs of yearning, reflection, remorse, and hope, U2 has unwittingly provided a musical salve for a world stricken by fear and uncertainty. From "Walk On," "Stuck in a Moment You Can't Get out Of," and "In a Little While" to "Kite," "When I Look at the World," and "Grace," the titles alone speak to our time. A Las Vegas radio station began playing another song from the album, "Peace on Earth," immediately after the attack on the World Trade Center, splicing in disaster news commentary. It quickly became one of the most requested songs on the station and on stations in other cities as well.

As U2 prepared to take to the skies again for another round of concert dates, Bono spoke to *Playback's* Erik Philbrook about music and the world now.

Playback: Often in times of crisis, people turn to the arts for different reasons. What do you think music is providing for people in the wake of these horrific acts?

Bono: The musical climate has immediately changed. Sugar-coated pop doesn't seem to matter much right now. Likewise, the metallic fugue and breast-beating of the hormonal kind. That too has paled. Sex and violence, as an entertainment, is the first thing that suffers when lives are lost. After something like this, we see everything out of the moment. And pop music usually lives in the moment. So the music that we stray to tends to be more eternal.

For pop music, that is a contradiction a lot of the time. But great pop music is eternal. I like to hear the Supremes in church (laughs). I actually do turn to pop music. It is hard to define what is ephemeral, as we all know now, and what is not.

In the '70's and the '80's, the music that we were told was important and progressive, turned out to be the great lurgy. However, some of the stuff that we couldn't own up to in our record collections has turned out to be timeless. One of the things I love about music is that it is still magic. And part of that magic is its ability to turn into something else in a given moment.

Like so many other people, I watched the performances on the Tribute to Heroes telethon on television and was tremendously moved by it. It was a very powerful two hours. So many artists, like yourself, Bruce Springsteen, Billy Joel, and Stevie Wonder played songs with real depth and meaning. And it really showed the importance that songs have in our culture.

I wasn't around for it, but I have studied the pop charts around the time of the Vietnam War. And you see this incredible array of music, across all different genres. It does seem that in a time of a bull market, when people have their eyes on the pink pages, the pop music seems to suffer. It just reflects, in a prophetic way, the state of the culture. It's like the idea that, in a democracy, you get the government that you deserve. It might be true with pop music too. It is not there by accident. It is what people want to hear.

I know that people in New York and in the United States are asking themselves very hard questions. That is going to be reflected in the music. And they are hard questions. They are important questions.

The President of the World Bank, Jim Wolfensohn, is somebody that I've had a lot of dealings with on Jubilee 2000, concerning debt cancellation. I like him, even if I've been across the table from him in the debate. A few days after September 11, he said the roots of this problem are in abject poverty. Of course, it isn't what people want to hear. It isn't what people want to hear in London, or in New York, or Madrid, or Berlin. Because globalization doesn't work for most of the people whose lives it impacts, and poverty fuels fanaticism. So those thinking people are left with nagging questions. And I hope that that will be reflected in the pop music of the day.

Of course, this was a wake-up call, not just politically but culturally as well. Do you think there is an opportunity now, with the world so sharply focused on one thing, that some good can come out of this?

Yeah. America has always worked because of the notion of an expanding middle class. More and more people have access to its prosperity. And it is the same in Europe. If only 4 percent of Americans had 40 percent of the wealth, there would be trouble. It is the same in Europe. We are sitting here asking ourselves, how can people loathe us so? But they see greed. They don't see that the United States had intervened in Kosovo on behalf of Muslim people. They don't see that. They see trade barriers, not a level playing field, a sort of bullish attitude to the environment, and to the world's resources. That's what they feel when they see us. My prayer is that, after the desire for justice, comes the desire to sort out our own house, because it needs some sorting.

You support a lot of causes, and you travel so much in support of them. Do you feel that your own music is also a cause? By that I mean, do you feel a sense of mission in spreading your music around the world, because it does carry a message, and it does mean something to so many people?

You have to avoid polemics. People have asked me why aren't I writing songs about the work that I'm doing for Africa regarding debt cancellation. I rather tritely reply, "statistics just don't rhyme." This is really dull and boring subject matter. When you are younger, man, you throw stones at the obvious targets. As I've gotten older, I've turned more on myself, and the hypocrisy that I've found in my own heart. There is plenty of subject matter there. The artists that inspire me the most have all done the same thing: the Marvin Gayes, the Bob Marleys, the Bob Dylans, the Leonard Cohens; there's always enough to write about there. Your politics are forged by the way you see the world, and at a deeper level, the way you see yourself. That is what has inspired us over the while.

How do you achieve writing lyrics that are personal and yet are also universal?

At times, it has been humbling for me as a lyricist. In the '80's, often there were no re-writes. The very first lines that were written to accompany the melody were the ones that went on record. And looking back, I see a lot of unfinished songs. It annoys me sometimes that I look back and see a sort of inane couplet. I have to live with it. But they can also be very deep and powerful. Like the opening of "Where the Streets Have No Name." It is an extraordinary throw-down to an audience. If you see us in front of 100,000 people, and you ask, do you want to go on a journey to somewhere that none of us have ever been before, to that place where you forget yourself, and who you are, and where you can imagine something better? It's a spine-chilling moment for you as a singer, and for anyone in the audience. It is a real challenge. But it comes out on *The Joshua Tree*, as "I want to run, I want to hide, I want to tear down these walls that hold me inside." That is so sophomoric (laughs). But that is the way it came out.

The lesson for me from the '80's was that sometimes the first words communicate the best. You realize, especially after the events of September 11, how unimportant it is to be smart. Or worse, smart-ass. To be true is all in pop music. Some of my favorite writers are clever with words. But the ones I go back to are the ones that are clever with ideas.

In the past, your lyrics have reached for the sky in a grandiose way. On the new record, I find that your lyrics are much more organic and earthbound, and yet still hold that sense of spirituality that has always characterized your songs.

I just wanted them to be quite basic. It is interesting. I try to put into words what I felt from the music. We spend most of our time working on the arrangements and the melodies, and then at the last minute, I try to articulate the feeling we found while we were improvising.

With U2, it's songwriting by accident. That is really how we work. We find a mood. We find a moment. And then I've got to put it into words. If I'm singing, if I'm using my full vocal range, all I'm left with are vowel sounds to play with. And with vowel sounds, you don't get much information. That's where the airborne aspect of U2 comes in. The words that come to you are just the words in all the vowel sounds, like "love."

Then, in the nineties, when I wanted to expand my vocabulary, I brought my voice down. I treated it. I sort of distorted it, and I got a whole new vocabulary. The natural distortion box of Bob Dylan's voice gives him access to a vocabulary that most people can't get to. In the '80's, corn flakes vox was never going to make it when you're singing up there with the B-flats, and all the other hot air balloons.

But in the nineties, I went after more bass. At that time, I was lifting stones. I was exploring the creepy crawlies, psychologically speaking, and it was all about what I was discovering in the dark recesses of my mind as someone who has high ideals. And I knew I wanted a bottom to match the top.

So going into this record, I asked myself, "can we have both on the same album? Can we have both in the same song? In fact, can we have both in the same line? Can we reach that high and admit to being that low in the same bar?"

When you say that you write by accident, where does it start? Does it start with a chord progression that The Edge has provided?

Usually myself or Edge provides the chord progression. But it can be Adam. And it can also start from a rhythm, or a groove. And we start improvising as a band. Our producers will tell you that's where we do our most magic work.

Are [U2 producers] Brian Eno and Daniel Lanois usually there at that early stage in the process?

That's right. One of their great gifts, actually, as producers, is their ability to be a catalyst for these things. Brian will sometimes come up with an atmosphere for us to jump off of. Because, as a three-piece, you can run out of colors. So having someone like Daniel Lanois and Brian Eno to provide you with something to jump off of, is really valuable.

Brian or Dan would say that the best work comes from improvisation. I think also some of the best work comes from preparing in the old-fashioned way, where Edge and myself work in a traditional fashion. Edge will come up with a chord sequence and I'll come up with a vocal melody for it. And then I'll get to a lyric. Now, Edge has become a great contributor on that front, and is more than an editor. In the way that I would always be on the lookout for the hook and the melodic opportunities, he's also there for me with a backup lyric or a title.

You have collaborated for so long as a band, do you instinctively know when you've stumbled across something interesting, inspired, or have discovered a new color?

The new color is a good analogy, because if you think of painters, there are painters who you think own certain colors. Like, Van Gogh owns the color yellow, that kind of suicide yellow, and those flowers. You are very lucky if you get to own a couple of colors. I think that in U2, there are moods or feelings that no one else has done before. And I think that finally, that is the most important thing, which is to find something that's your own color, and unique.

A criticism of our recent work is that, in a way, we have learned the craft, and it nearly ruined us. Because, in the end it is magic. The magician pulls a rabbit from the hat, and he is as surprised as the audience (laughs). And God has to walk through the room, as I think Quincy Jones describes it. All your best work you can't claim, but all the average work you can.

No one is as smart as the best pop song. To go to back to the Supremes [sic], "Baby, I Love You," is the best song you could have heard on September 11th. And the pop versus rock debate just disappears. You look for a moment of truth. That would be a strong point of ours. It is our ability to find those moments.

I remember as a child, growing up in Ireland. We were taught the poetry of William Butler Yeats. I must have been ten years old. The teacher said, "and then Yeats went through his dry period. He had a writing block and he couldn't write about anything." I remember putting up my hand, and saying "Well, why didn't he write about that?" And the teacher just looked at me and said, "Oh, be quiet." But that is exactly the answer to the writing block. You write about your own emptiness, and we've done that for years now.

In a way, the success of this record is due to the fact that it is a return to the "classic" U2 sound and themes. A lot of passion, a lot of Edge's guitar. People really love those familiar elements. Do you still get a charge out of it yourself?

Well, you've got to keep it fresh for yourself. As it happens, returning to the sound of a three-piece and a singer was very fresh for us, because we hadn't done it for so long. We also returned to a more live arrangement of the songs. It was a thrill, actually. Suddenly, the drummer goes from the high hat to the ride cymbal and it sounds like an orchestra. Now, you hear a sound of a band playing on the radio, and it sounds futuristic. It is an odd thing. Suddenly, the machines sound old-fashioned.

We will always work with technology, and technology has driven rock and roll from the start, from overloading the circuits in a fuzz-box through to the drum machine. You should never be purist about what you use. But, right now, in a digital age, hearing musicians thinking for each other, sounds radical.

I remember in an interview once, someone asked you what you thought the music of the future would sound like. And you said it would be the sound of a guy sitting by himself singing and playing a guitar, which I thought was a great response.

In our densely populated airwaves, space is the most valuable real estate. The final mark of greatness, I think, is emptiness. The least you need. That is true of music, painting, of anything. The less you can do it with, the more powerful you are. It is true of combat.

How much more touring will you be doing for the record?

Well, actually this tour that is coming up was supposed to be a lap of honor. We had such a great time the first time around. But I have a funny feeling that this album is just coming into itself. There are songs on it, like "When I Look at the World" and "Kite" and "Grace," that are suddenly right in the middle of what people are listening to now. And they weren't three weeks ago. I've never been as excited to go on tour.

It is the perfect album for the moment we're living in. When you originally made the record, you made it for the reasons you did, but I think for a lot of people, it is really providing a voice for what they are feeling now.

Interscope's Jimmy Iovine rang me up, and he was just devastated by what happened. But he said, "you know you've been swimming against the tide for the last nine months, and suddenly you're not." I'm deeply humbled by that thought. And I hope we can live up to people's expectations in the next few months.

U2

Assessment: U2, Their Vague Majesties of Rock

David Plotz
***Slate*, January 25, 2002**

For the past two years, U2 has been enjoying a miraculous run. After its disastrous '90s flirtation with irony, the Irish quartet returned to the swaddling comfort of earnestness at just the right moment. U2's 2000 album *All That You Can't Leave Behind*—a throwback to the sweeping righteous love of *The Joshua Tree* and *The Unforgettable Fire*—was raved by critics, hit No. 1 in more than 30 countries, and continues to throw off huge singles. Since Sept. 11, their super-sincerity has been in particularly high demand. Bono orchestrated the all-star remake of Marvin Gaye's "What's Going On," proceeds going for Sept. 11th relief. And both "Walk On," off *All That You Can't Leave Behind*, and the old hit "One" have become Sept. 11th anthems.

In December, U2 finished one of the most profitable concert tours in rock history, was named *Spin's* Band of the Year and *Rolling Stone* readers' Artist of the Year. Next month promises more glory. The band is nominated for eight Grammys—more than any artist—and will almost certainly win a handful at the February 27 ceremony. And next weekend, U2 headlines the Super Bowl halftime show, a gig for 800 million viewers.

U2 has now been good longer than any other important band in history. The Rolling Stones have been around forever, but their creative period lasted only 15 years. The Beatles imploded after a decade. U2—the same lineup of Bono, The Edge, Adam Clayton, and Larry Mullen—has been making acclaimed albums since 1980's *Boy*.

The band's achievements depend on two neat tricks. First, Bono—the public face of U2—has a genius for cognitive dissonance. He is the upstairs, downstairs king of rock: he simultaneously inflates himself into the most grandiose, arrogant, self-righteous rock star and deflates himself with self-mockery and modesty. He describes U2 as reapplying for the position of "best band in the world"; calls the band "magic" and "extraordinary"; announces on *Rattle and Hum* that "All I have is a red guitar, three chords, and the truth"; and insists that "We've always been about more than music. We're about spirituality. We're about the world we live in."

But Bono counters every claim of godliness by throwing a pie in his own face. Asked by an interviewer if he is a pioneer, he declares that he is "one of the inventors of the mullet." The band mocked themselves on *The Simpsons*. Bono cheerfully disses his own political activism: "The only thing worse than a rock star is a rock star with a conscience."

Both stances are sincere, and it is a very winning combination. The worshipful fans adore the earnest grandiosity and sing along as Bono claims transcendence. A U2 concert is one of the few places on the planet where intelligent people wave cigarette lighters without irony. In those moments when you want to believe that rock music is something bigger than entertainment—and who doesn't haven't such moments?—U2 offers exalted nourishment. *They're about more than music, man. They're about spirituality. They are the unforgettable fire!*

But U2's self-consciousness inoculates them against critics, who can find no point of attack. If you ridicule Bono for his pomposity, he will not only laugh at the joke, but will twist the knife deeper in his own chest. They are grand spectacle, but with a wink for those who are looking for one. The combination of self-important grandeur and self-deprecating humor is exceptionally rare, especially among celebrities. Many popular musicians have one or the other (almost always the self-important grandeur). The few that have both—the Rolling Stones, the Beatles, and Elton John are at the top of the short list—can survive greatness and don't get destroyed by their pretensions (as did humorless sorts such as the Doors, Guns N' Roses, Led Zeppelin ...).

U2's other trick is to pretend that it is a political rock band. It's true that U2 is politically promiscuous. The liner notes for *All That You Can't Leave Behind*, for example, endorse Amnesty International, Greenpeace, the charity War Child, the Jubilee 2000 debt-relief campaign, freedom for Burma, and justice in Sierra Leone. And that's just one album. U2's roster of cause songs includes: "Sunday Bloody Sunday" (one of many about Ireland's troubles); "Seconds" (nuclear war); "The Unforgettable Fire" (also nuclear war); "Pride (In the Name of Love)" (Martin Luther King, Jr.); "MLK" (also Martin Luther King, Jr.); "Bullet the Blue Sky" (U.S. Central America policy); and so on.

It's also true that Bono is exceptionally political offstage, like his admirable debt-relief campaign. But U2 has duped their fans into believing their music is political. Bono declares that his songs are about this or that cause, but no fan could ever know that from listening. Consider a typical passage from "Walk On," supposedly about Burmese democracy activist Aung San Suu Kyi. What has it to do with Burma? I adore "Pride (In the Name of Love)" as much as anyone, but I defy anyone to explain what it teaches about Martin Luther King, Jr.

U2 is perhaps the world's vaguest band. If a U2 song isn't written in the first person, it is penned to an unnamed, indistinct "you." Instead of stories or wordplay, they rely solely on fuzzy imagery. I opened the liner notes to *All That You...*and wrote down the first three lines I read: "See the canyons broken by clouds"; "I and I in the sky"; "A man takes a rocket ship into the skies." Classic U2 haze—skies, rockets, clouds, canyons. Doesn't anyone have a name? There are never any actual people in U2 songs, never any characters. (Compare U2 to the narrative specificity of Bob Dylan or Bruce Springsteen.) This vagueness drains U2's lyrics of any content: it is impossible to think about a U2 song. "One" includes depressing lines like "We hurt each other/Then we do it again" and "You say love is a temple/You ask me to enter/But then you make me crawl"—yet this hasn't stopped fans from turning it into a Sept. 11 anthem. If it is political music, it is for the Bob Kerreys of the world, for folks who seem full of great, but totally inchoate, ideas.

U2's music—especially The Edge's soaring guitars—supports this lyrical vagueness. Their songs are gorgeous and majestic, but they produce only a single (though wonderful) emotion: a kind of lovely swelling of the soul.

This is the U2 paradox. Bono and Co. are constantly dedicating songs to specific causes, exhorting their fans to think and act in the world. Yet their music does exactly the opposite of what it intends. Politics is the process of channeling the heart into thought and action. U2's music declares that the heart is all that matters.

U2

Bono's World: Part Rocker, Part Policy Wonk, U2's Singer Calls Himself 'The Thinking Man's Perry Como'

Tom Gliatto; Eileen Finan, in Dublin; Pete Norman, in London; Rachel Felder, in New York City; Lyndon Stambler, in Los Angeles and Jen Chaney, in Washington, D.C.
***People* magazine, March 4, 2002**

Bono, lead singer of the Irish supergroup U2, is at Finnegan's, a pub just up the road from his white Georgian home in Killiney, south of Dublin. Sipping a pint of Guinness, he is explaining how a person can be nominated for eight Grammys, attend a global economic conference with Bill Gates, move the irascible Sen. Jesse Helms to tears, and still feel—especially when in Dublin—like an Everyman. You just have to be Irish. "We are taught not to court success here," says Bono. "There's an old story about an American and an Irishman looking up at a mansion. The American looks at it and says, 'One day I'm going to live in that place.' The Irishman looks at it and says, 'One day I'm going to get the bastard who lives in that place.'"

Others are less reticent about giving Bono his due. The 41-year-old singer, along with guitarist The Edge, 40, drummer Larry Mullen, 40, and bassist Adam Clayton, 41, are "unquestionably the greatest rock band in the world at the moment," says their friend and fellow rocker Elvis Costello. This year's Grammy Awards, which will be handed out in L.A. Feb. 27, will likely second that. U2's eight nominations include the biggies: record of the year ("Walk On"), album (*All That You Can't Leave Behind*) and song ("Stuck in a Moment You Can't Get out Of"). "Artistically," says Bono, who already has 10 Grammys with U2, "it's been my best year ever."

Last year, too, there was more to U2 than music. Many found the band's keening, anthemic sound an effective balm in the aftermath of the Sept. 11 terrorist attacks; some of the songs on *All That You Can't Leave Behind*, released in October 2000, even seemed eerily prescient. (One, "Kite," begins, "Something is about to give/I can feel it coming.") After U2 performed Sept. 21 on the nationally televised memorial concert America, A Tribute to Heroes, they returned to their sold-out concert tour, where Bono cradled the flag and the names of the Sept. 11 dead were projected on a massive screen. When U2 sang "Where the Streets Have No Name" at the Super Bowl Feb. 3, "it was like taking a big bite out of a giant apple pie," Bono says. "To feel the full embrace of America was the pinnacle."

It had been an unusual week, to say the least. Two days before the halftime show, Bono appeared at the World Economic Forum in Manhattan, where he sat on panels with South African Archbishop Desmond Tutu and U.S. Treasury Secretary Paul O'Neill. An activist for nearly as long as he has been a performer, Bono has earned a reputation as a detail-oriented wonk who stays with a cause—be it Third World debt relief or aid for AIDS-ravaged Africa—for the long haul. At the forum, the singer self-deprecatingly introduced himself as "the poor man's James Joyce or the thinking man's Perry Como." But he's no dilettante, not "some leprechaun," says O'Neill, who plans to visit Africa with Bono later this year. "He's a lot more than that." Says Sen. Patrick Leahy (D-VT): "A lot of celebrities lend their names to something for the moment. But Bono cares." Adds a friend, producer Hal Willner: "It's amazing that Bono can read and understand all those economics books."

Still, John Maynard Keynes never had the option of indulging in a little rock-star swagger to make a point. Seldom without his trademark fly-eyed sunglasses, Bono startled conference attendees with a foul-mouthed anticapitalist plea. Nor is Bono always patient. "He will knock down a lazy thought," says the band's manager, Paul McGuinness, "whether it is a bad political argument or a mundane lyric."

Yet even as he meets with heads of state, including Pope John Paul II, he remains on solid and equal footing with his bandmates, all friends since high school. "They call it the politburo," says Bono's friend, rocker Bob Geldof, who drafted Bono into famine relief with the all-star benefit single "Do They Know It's Christmas?" in 1984. "They often say no to him, and he defers."

Managing his personal life also can require delicate negotiating. He made it home in the midst of the band's year-long, 109-concert Elevation tour in May, when his wife of 20 years, Ali, 40, gave birth to their son John. Even before the new baby, Ali—who also has two daughters, Jordan, 12, and Eve, 10, and another son, Eli, 2, with Bono—preferred to be left behind in Killiney (their home for 13 years) and away from the media scrum when U2 hit the road. Although she has had her own causes, including an Irish charity to help children of Chernobyl, "she doesn't want to be part of any entourage," says Bono. "But I spend a lot of time with my kids—more than most other dads. I took my girls to California on tour. I took Eli to Venice." Bono isn't likely to have to worry about making time for any more deliveries: Ali recently told the Irish Independent, "We are very happy [but] definitely no more kids—we are overrun as it is."

There have been heartaches. Three months after John's birth, Bono's father, Bob Hewson, a retired postal worker, died of cancer at 75. Bono went almost directly from his father's deathbed in Dublin to a U2 concert in London, where he dedicated the song "Kite" to him. "The show must go on," says screenwriter Simon Carmody, one of Bono's circle of old Dublin friends. "That is Bono's real political philosophy."

The roots of that philosophy were sown in the North Dublin neighborhood of Glasnevin, where Bono—born Paul Hewson and raised Protestant in the overwhelmingly Catholic Irish Republic—lived with his dad, mother Iris, and brother Norman, 48, now proprietor of a Dublin health-food cafe. "They would save hard, and they didn't drink much at all," says Bono pal Guggi, a Dublin artist. But normal family life changed dramatically for Bono at 14, when Iris, who had worked in the offices of a local dairy, died of a stroke. Bono had already shown his friends that same passion for resolving trouble that he would later put to use in world issues. "If I fell out with some other kid," says Guggi, "Bono would work very hard to bring us together." With his mother's death he became markedly more serious in all his interests, particularly music. That was always a strong presence in the Hewson household, says Guggi. "There were records—classical, opera, Sinatra. His dad had an incredible voice."

But the future star's biggest inspiration, says Geldof, was England's powerful punk band the Clash. After hearing them, says Geldof, "a band was what he decided to do." At 14, he'd already been dubbed by Guggi with what would come to be a perfect rock moniker: Bono (pronounced BAH-no). "The word suggests his shape, his vibe," says Guggi (whose own real name is Derek Rowen). "There was a hearing aid shop, Bonovox of O'Connell Street. I thought he looked like the place."

A restless student, Bono was tossed out of one high school, St. Patrick's, for flinging dog manure at a teacher "who'd been giving him a hard time," says Guggi. He transferred to Mount Temple, where fellow student Mullen posted a bulletin board notice looking for bandmates. The quartet of Mullen, Bono, The Edge (full name: Dave Evans), and Clayton came together in 1976 as a band, Feedback.

Bono was making other friends at school too. When the fledgling rocker first introduced Guggi to classmate Alison Stewart, he recalls, "she just looked like the straightest girl, wearing this gingham dress and a little cardigan. I didn't get it. But he adored her." Wed in 1982, "they are a bit similar in their spirit," says Simon Carmody. "They both have a bit of 'go' about them."

Bono definitely had it. Changing their name to U2 in 1978 at a friend's off-the-cuff suggestion, the band quickly established itself on the Dublin rock scene. Their first album, *Boy*, made a minor splash in the U.S. By the time of their fifth album, 1987's *The Joshua Tree*, which yielded two No. 1 singles, critics regarded them as the band of the decade. "I was kind of getting in my stride by that time," says Elvis Costello. "Then they came roaring past at 100 mph."

Ten albums and 15 Top 40 singles later, Bono is rich enough to own a Dublin hotel, the Clarence (The Edge is co-proprietor), and a villa in the south of France. And yet, if he has it all, he has remained committed to the have-nots. In 1999 Bono approached his friend, music and movie producer Bobby Shriver (son of Eunice Kennedy and Sargent Shriver), about working on the Jubilee 2000 campaign, urging wealthy nations to forgive billions of dollars owed by the world's poorest countries. "Ireland has a tradition of famine and wanting and suffering," says Shriver, 47.

Shriver calculates that Bono made at least 12 trips to Washington, D.C., meeting everyone from President Bill Clinton to the Senate's most adamant conservative, North Carolina's Republican Helms, who choked up when Bono told him stories of dying children in Africa. "I went in there thinking he was going to spit on me," Bono later told Gene Sperling, then Clinton's chief economic adviser. Instead, "we bonded." In October 2000 Congress passed a $435 million debt relief bill. "It's tremendous," says Shriver, "to see a guy accomplish a thing he has no business accomplishing."

Back in Finnegan's, Bono is enough of a regular that no one looks his way. "I'm happy to be in Dublin," he says, "and a noncelebrity." But he concedes he'll likely be back in the thick of things soon, lending his high profile to public debate. "I love the din of argument," he says. "We Irish go insane if there is accord."

U2

CHAPTER

6

POLITICS

Bob Geldof is probably partly to blame if you find Bono politically insufferable. A fellow Irishman and once lead singer of The Boomtown Rats, in the early '80s Geldof devised the idea for a televised concert to raise funds for famine-stricken children in Ethiopia. Recruiting U2 as one of the acts to be featured on the "Do They Know It's Christmas" single, Geldof also included them on the bill of the bicontinental, sixteen-hour concert extravaganza and television broadcast that reached 1.5 billion people worldwide—Live Aid.

Fueled by the success of Live Aid and wanting to do more, Bono and his wife Ali spent three weeks working in Ethiopia, seeing firsthand its poverty and devastation. Fifteen years later, this experience led to Bono's full-scale political assault on behalf of Jubilee 2000, an effort to get the major industrial countries of the world to forgive the debt that was crippling many developing Third World nations.

It wasn't Bono's first cause and it won't be his last. While the rest of the group gives their tacit approval, Bono is U2's activist. Not only has he worked on behalf of developing nations, but he has also rallied against nuclear reactors, raised awareness of Amnesty International, brought attention to the plight of the Bosnian people, and hobnobbed with such strange political bedfellows as Jesse Helms, Bill Clinton, Paul O'Neill, and the Pope, who traded rosary beads for a pair of Bono sunglasses.

The Onion

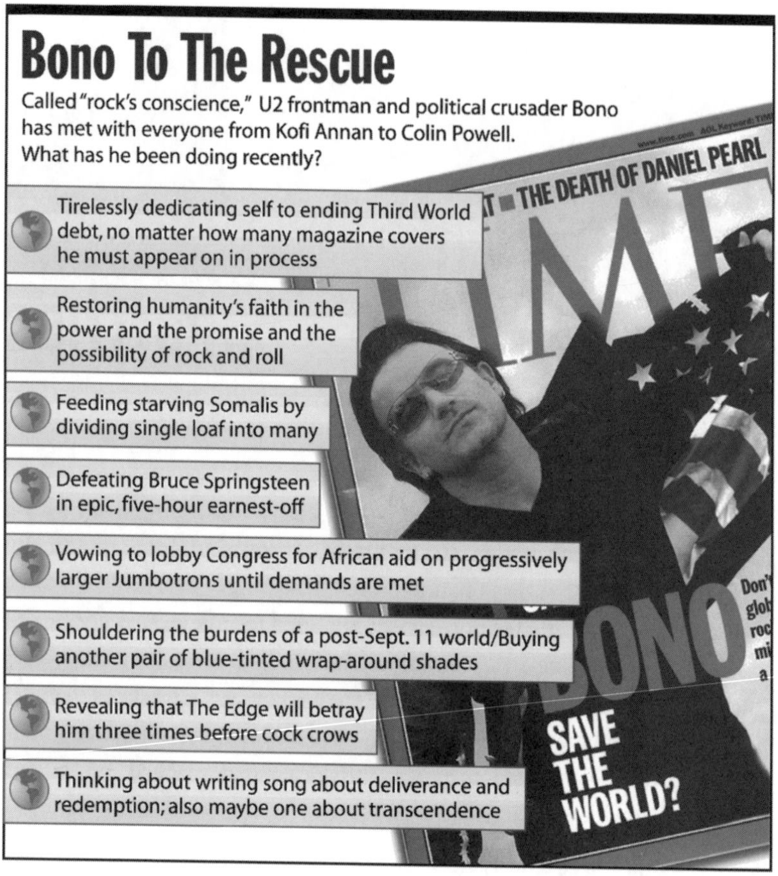

Bono To The Rescue
Called "rock's conscience," U2 frontman and political crusader Bono has met with everyone from Kofi Annan to Colin Powell. What has he been doing recently?
Tirelessly dedicating self to ending Third World debt, no matter how many magazine covers he must appear on in process
Restoring humanity's faith in the power and the promise and the possibility of rock and roll
Feeding starving Somalis by dividing single loaf into many
Defeating Bruce Springsteen in epic, five-hour earnest-off
Vowing to lobby Congress for African aid on progressively larger Jumbotrons until demands are met
Shouldering the burdens of a post-Sept. 11 world/Buying another pair of blue-tinted wrap-around shades
Revealing that The Edge will betray him three times before cock crows
Thinking about writing song about deliverance and redemption; also maybe one about transcendence
THE DEATH OF DANIEL PEARL
BONO
SAVE THE WORLD?

This graphic appears courtesy of *The Onion*.

Washington Diarist: Actually (excerpt)

Andrew Sullivan
***The New Republic*, October 26, 1987**

I got into pop music late: about 1983 to be exact. But now that I've mastered the artful charms of nodding sagely whenever anybody mentions the Bronsky Beat, I'm thinking of getting out again. "What Bono revealed beneath his well-defined and carefully controlled surface was an enthusiast in the grips of reason; a wishful idealist stimulated and confused by his own contradictions; and a young man who quite honestly has not found what he's looking for—and may never," writes David Breskin in the latest issue of *Rolling Stone.*

Bono, in case you didn't know, is the lead singer in the U2 pop band, the latest heartthrob of the under-16s and ersatz Gandhi to all those happily married 35-year-olds who still miss John Lennon. He also leads his fans in antiwar chants, supports Amnesty International, and has a friend called Edge. In other words, it's serious, Camus-serious: "Who is it—Camus?—who said, 'Wealth, my dear friend, is not exactly acquittal, just reprieve...,'" is how Bono described the spiritual agonies of being a multimillionaire. But moral compromise, it seems, is the burden every artist has to bear: "It would be a trap for me to spend my whole life fighting a battle about something—my knuckles would be bleeding from beating on the walls of the music business." Not that he's self-righteous, you understand. Dipping momentarily beneath his well-defused and carefully controlled surfaces, Bono is cheerfully frank about commercial exploitation:

"Without being precious about U2, let me say I'm learning to accept T-shirts; what I'm not willing to accept is bad T-shirts." An enthusiast, as they say, in the grips of reason.

U2 Flips Zoo TV Channel to the Horrors of Bosnia (excerpt)

Thom Duffy
***Billboard*, September 4, 1993**

During the first show of U2's recent four night stand at London's Wembley Stadium, the aural and visual blitz of the *Zooropa* show paused as one of the massive video screens picked up a live Zoo TV feed from Sarajevo. A documentary filmmaker had gathered three women—one Croat, one Serb, one Muslim. "We want to live together," one of the women said. "We *shall* live together." But this was not a war, the fans filling the stadium were told, it was a massacre.

Was this an exploitative use of the horror of Bosnia, cheapened in the context of a rock 'n' roll show? Some critics later suggested as much.

U2 manager Paul McGuinness says the Sarajevo segment was added to the *Zooropa* show earlier in the tour as "a genuine attempt to draw the attention of 50,000 people a night" to Bosnia at a time when the war had dropped off the nightly news. And with press attention again peaking, U2 has since dropped the TV exchange from the show. Yes, McGuinness conceded, the band risked criticism of its motives and methods.

Whatever financial aid U2 has contributed to victims of the war has not been publicized. But as the politicians struggle with the complexities of the conflict, artists are left with the rather simpler task of raising awareness—and cash. It is worth asking why the music industry worldwide, for all its social consciousness, has yet to respond on a scale to match the need.

For a fan who has watched U2 from its earliest wide-eyed tours of America through the idealism of its 1986 Amnesty International tour, it was striking at the Wembley show to note how world-weary Bono sounded as he replied to the Sarajevo women: "Nobody knows what the fuck is going on; we have no answers." He remarked how ludicrous it was for someone living in the "fantasy" of a mega-rock tour to try to connect with the misery of a war zone.

"We're doing what artists throughout the ages have done in exposing contradictions," says McGuinness.

That does not mean, he adds, the artist can always offer answers.

No one is dancing on the edges of rock 'n' roll's contradictions as effectively these days as U2. The Sarajevo segment of the *Zooropa* show reflected how easy it has become for a hi-tech society to confront, then twist and turn away from, tragedy with the ease of TV channel-hopping. And that realization, ironically, could not help making you feel that tragedy deeper still, if you were at all wide awake.

Transcript of Bono's Class Day Speech at Harvard

Bono
***Harvard* magazine, June 10, 2001**

I suppose I should say a few words about who I am and what on earth I'm doing up here.

My name is Bono, and I am a rock star.

Now, I tell you this, not as a boast but as a kind of confession. Because in my view the only thing worse than a rock star is a rock star with a conscience—a celebrity with a cause...oh, dear!

Worse yet, is a singer with a conscience—a placard-waving, knee-jerking, fellow-traveling activist with a Lexus and a swimming pool shaped like his head.

I'm a singer. You know what a singer is? Someone with a hole in his heart as big as his ego. When you need 20,000 people screaming your name in order to feel good about your day, you know you're a singer.

I am a singer and a songwriter but I am also a father, four times over. I am a friend to dogs. I am a sworn enemy of the saccharine; and a believer in grace over karma. I talk too much when I'm drunk and sometimes even when I'm not.

I am not drunk right now. These are not sunglasses, these are protection.

But I must tell you. I owe more than my spoiled lifestyle to rock music. I owe my worldview. Music was like an alarm clock for me as a teenager and still keeps me from falling asleep in the comfort of my freedom.

Rock music to me is rebel music. But rebelling against what? In the fifties it was sexual mores and double standards. In the sixties it was the Vietnam War and racial and social inequality. What are we rebelling against now?

If I am honest, I'm rebelling against my own indifference. I am rebelling against the idea that the world is the way the world is and there's not a damned thing I can do about it. So I'm trying to do some damned thing.

But fighting my indifference is my own problem. What's your problem? What's the hole in your heart? I needed the noise, the applause. You needed the grades. Why are you here in Harvard Square?

Why do you have to listen to me? What have you given up to get here? Is success your drug of choice or are you driven by another curiosity? Your potential. The potential of a given situation. Is missing the moment unacceptable to you? Is wasting inspiration a crime? It is for a musician.

If this is where we find our lives rhyme, if this is our common ground, well, then I can be inspired as well as humbled to be on this great campus. Because that's where I come from. Music.

But I've seen the other side of music—the Business. I've seen success as a drug of choice. I've seen great minds and prolific imaginations disappear up their own ass, strung out on their own self-importance. I'm one of them.

The misery of having it all your own way, the loneliness of sitting at a table where everyone works for you, the emptiness of arriving at Aspen on a Gulfstream to stay in your winter palace. Eh, sorry, different speech...

You know what I'm talking about—you've got to keep asking yourself why are you doing this? You've got to keep checking your motives.

Success for my group U2 has been a lot easier to conjure than, say...relevance. RELEVANCE...in the world, in the culture.

And of course, failure is not such a bad thing...It's not a word that many of you know. I'm sure it's what you fear the most. But from an artist's point of view, failure is where you get your best material.

So fighting indifference versus making a difference. Let me tell you a few things you haven't heard about me, even on the Internet.

Let me tell you how I enrolled at Harvard and slept with an economics professor.

That's right—I became a student at Harvard recently, and came to work with Professor Jeffrey Sachs at CID—to study the lack of development in third-world economies due to the crushing weight of old debts those economies were carrying for generations.

It turns out that the normal rules of bankruptcy don't apply to sovereign states. Listen, it would be harder for you to get a student loan than it was for President Mobutu to stream billions of dollars into his Swiss bank account while his people starved on the side of the road. Two generations later, the Congolese are still paying. The debts of the fathers are now the debts of the sons and the daughters.

So I was here representing a group that believed that all such debts should be cancelled in the year 2000. We called it Jubilee 2000. A fresh start for a new millennium.

It was headed up by Anne Pettifor, based out of London—huge support from Africa. With Muhammad Ali, Sir Bob Geldof, and myself, acting at first just as mouthpieces. It was taking off. But we were way behind in the U.S.

We had the melody line, so to speak. But in order to get it on the radio over here, we needed a lot of help. My friend Bobby Shriver suggested I knock on the good professor's door. And a funny thing happened. Jeffrey Sachs not only let me into his office, he let me into his Rolodex, his head, and his life for the last few years. So in a sense he let me in to your life here at Harvard.

Then Sachs and I, with my friend Bobby Shriver, hit the road like some kind of surreal crossover act. A rock star, a Kennedy, and a noted economist crisscrossing the globe like the Partridge Family on psychotropic drugs. With the POPE acting as our...well...agent. And the blessing of various rabbis, evangelists, mothers, unions, trade unions, and PTAs.

It was a new level of "unhip" for me, but it was really cool. It was in that capacity that I slept with Jeff Sachs, each of us in our own seat on an economy flight to somewhere, passed out like a couple of drunks from sheer exhaustion.

It was confusing for everyone—I looked up with one eye to see your hero—stubble in all the wrong places...His tie looked more like a headband. An airhostess asked if he were a member of the Grateful Dead.

I have enormous respect for Jeff Sachs but it's really true what they say. "Students shouldn't sleep with their professors..."

While I'm handing out trade secrets, I also want to tell you that Larry Summers, your incoming President, the man whose signature is on every American dollar, is a nutcase—and a freak.

Look, U2 made it big out of Boston, not New York or L.A., so I thought if anyone would know about our existence it would be a treasury secretary from Harvard [and M.I.T.]. Alas, no. When I said I was from U2, he had a flashback from Cuba 1962.

How can I put this? And don't hold it against him—Mr. Summers is, as former President Clinton confirmed to me last week in Dublin, "culturally challenged."

But when I asked him to look up from "the numbers" to see what we were talking about, he did more than that. He did—the hardest thing of all for an economist—he saw through the numbers.

And if it was hard for me to enlist Larry Summers in our efforts, imagine how hard it was for Larry Summers to get the rest of Washington to cough up the cash. To really make a difference for the third of the world that lives on less than a dollar a day.

He more than tried. He was passionate. He turned up in the offices of his adversaries. He turned up in restaurants with me to meet the concerns of his Republican counterparts. There is a posh restaurant in Washington they won't let us in now. Such was the heat of his debate—blood on the walls, wine in the vinegar.

If you're called up before the new president of Harvard and he gives you the hairy eyeball, drums his fingers, and generally acts disinterested; it could be the beginning of a great adventure.

It's a good thing that I got invited up here before President Rudenstine hands over the throne.

Well, it's at this point that I have to ask—if your family doesn't do it first—why am I telling you these stories? It's certainly not because I'm running for role model.

I'm telling you these stories because all that fun I had with Jeff Sachs and Larry Summers was in the service of something deadly serious. When people around the world heard about the burden of debt that crushes the poorest countries, when they heard that for every dollar of government aid we sent to developing nations, nine dollars came back in debt service payments, when they heard all that, people got angry.

They took to the streets—in what was, without doubt, the largest grass roots movement since the campaign to end apartheid. Politics is, as you know, normally the art of the possible but this was something more interesting. This was becoming the art of the impossible. We had priests going into pulpits, pop stars into parliaments. The Pope put on my sunglasses.

The religious right started acting like student protesters. And finally, after a floor fight in the House of Representatives, we got the money—four-three-five million. That four-three-five—which is starting to be a lot of money—leveraged billions more from other rich countries.

So where does that money go? Well, so far, 23 of the poorest countries have managed to meet the sometimes over-stringent conditions to get their debt payments reduced—and to spend the money on the people who need it most. In Uganda, twice as many kids are now going to school. That's good. In Mozambique, debt payments are down 42 percent, allowing health spending to increase by $14 million. That's good, too. $14 million goes a long way in Mozambique.

If I could tell you about one remarkable man in rural Uganda named Dr. Kabira. In 1999, measles—a disease that's almost unheard of in the U.S.—killed hundreds of kids in Dr. Kabira's district. Now, thanks to debt relief, he's got an additional $6,000 from the state, enough for him to employ two new nurses and buy two new bicycles so they can get around the district and immunize children. Last year, measles was a killer. This year, Dr. Kabira saw less than ten cases.

I just wanted you to know what we pulled [it] off with the help of Harvard—with the help of people like Jeffrey Sachs.

But I'm not here to brag, or to take credit, or even to share it. Why am I here? Well, again I think to just say "thanks." But also, I think I've come here to ask you for your help. This is a big problem. We need some smart people working on it. I think this will be the defining moment of our age. When the history books (that some of you will write) make a record of our times, this moment will be remembered for two things: the Internet, and the everyday holocaust that is Africa. Twenty-five million HIV positives who will leave behind 40 million AIDS orphans by 2010. This is the biggest health threat since the Bubonic Plague wiped out a third of Europe.

It's an unsustainable problem for Africa and, unless we hermetically seal the continent and close our conscience, it's an unsustainable problem for the world; but it's hard to make this a popular cause because it's hard to make it pop, you know? That, I guess, is what I'm trying to do. Pop is often the oxygen of politics.

Didn't John and Robert Kennedy come to Harvard? Isn't equality a son of a bitch to follow through on? Isn't "Love thy neighbor" in the global village so inconvenient? God writes us these lines but we have to sing them...take them to the top of the charts, but its not what the radio is playing—is it? I know.

But we've got to follow through on our ideals or we betray something at the heart of who we are. Outside these gates, and even within them, the culture of idealism is under siege, beset by materialism and narcissism and all the other "isms" of indifference. And their defense mechanism—knowingness, the smirk, the joke. Worse still, it's a marketing tool. They've got Martin Luther King selling phones now. Have you seen that?

Civil rights in America and Europe are bound to human rights in the rest of the world. The right to live like a human. But these thoughts are expensive—they're going to cost us. Are we ready to pay the price? Is America still a great idea as well as a great country?

When I was a kid in Dublin, I watched in awe as America put a man on the moon and I thought, wow—this is mad! Nothing is impossible in America! America, they can do anything over there! Nothing was impossible; only human nature and it followed because it was led.

Is that still true? Tell me it's true. It is true isn't it? And if it isn't, you, of all people, can make it true again.

U2

Bono

Brian Libby
Salon.com (www.salon.com), October 2, 2001

Over two decades, U2's leader has evolved from heart-on-his-sleeve idealist to irony-drenched rock 'n' roll Liberace to hopeful pragmatist.

In June, Bono of U2 delivered the commencement address to graduating students at Harvard. Before sharing his thoughts about AIDS, Africa and Third World debt, the legendary singer began with an Alcoholics Anonymous-style confession: "My name is Bono, and I am a rock star."

At 41, Bono is at an age when many rock musicians start exploiting bygone successes to keep feeding at the trough of fame. But with Bono, it's more than a rock 'n' roll career. Behind the black leather togs and wraparound shades, there has always been an earnest social crusader. Embarrassingly earnest? Perhaps. But, oddly, that's part of his charm. In a business where people sell their souls for success, he has constantly risked celebrity-cause cliché—and he knows it. "The only thing worse than a rock star," he told the starry-eyed Harvard grads, "is a rock star with a conscience. I've seen great minds and prolific imaginations disappear up their own ass, strung out on their own self-importance. I'm one of them."

But as we accept the notion that the horrific attacks on the Pentagon and World Trade Center on Sept. 11 have changed our world irrevocably, Bono looks better than ever; his earnestness suddenly feels a lot less corny. It's not to say that he has all the answers, but once again, celebrities who crusade have less reason to fear ridicule. The great thing about Bono, though, is that he probably doesn't care whether he looks cool along the way.

Bono's humanitarianism has always been purchased on the credit line of U2's fame, which is precisely why it has made a noticeable return in the last year. Many U2 fans (and rumor has it, even Bono and his band mates) had speculated that the band's best days were behind them. But now U2 have suddenly made their best album in a decade. *All That You Can't Leave Behind*, released in fall of 2000, has received nearly unanimous critical acclaim and sold millions. The accompanying Elevation 2001 Tour has sold out arenas throughout the world, and U2 have racked up a slew of honors. Suddenly, it's as if they never stopped being the biggest band in the world.

"It's hard for rock 'n' roll artists to grow and mature and find ways to have long careers," says *New York Times* rock critic Ann Powers, an avowed fan of the band. "U2 figured out how to break out of that, and a lot of bands don't."

In the wake of *All That You Can't Leave Behind*, Bono and U2 have been praised for coming back to the kind of guileless art-rock that originally gained the band acclaim before Ronald Reagan had even unpacked his bags in Washington. But like his band mates, Bono is not the same man he was 20 years ago. In U2's first several albums, Bono's lyrics exhibited uncommon faith in an era full of anger and gloom. But after the darker introspection of the band's albums from the last decade, *All That You Can't Leave Behind* is particularly notable because Bono has again come to see the glass as half full.

Yet when he sings "It's a beautiful day, don't let it get away," it's not youthful pie-in-the-sky optimism, but a faith that's been redeemed over time. That's something altogether more meaningful. And while that was already true before Sept. 11, it's even more relevant now. This is no time for idealism, but rather one in which defiant, profound hope is desperately needed. And that's what *All That You Can't Leave Behind* is all about.

As Bono has become a prominent spokesman for Third World debt relief and the related African AIDS epidemic, there's no doubt it recalls countless pet causes of years past. In the mid '80s, as *War* (1983) and *The Unforgettable Fire* (1984) first carried U2 toward multi-platinum success, they were fixtures in the Band Aid and Live Aid campaigns to end famine in Africa. When *The Joshua Tree* (1987) was about to make them the biggest rock band in the world, U2 joined Sting and Peter Gabriel, belting out hits for Amnesty International. Around the same time, Bono joined the chorus of artists singing "I ain't gonna play Sun City," in an effort to end South African apartheid. Because it's easy to be cynical about high-profile celebrity causes, it's to his credit that such a high-profile star managed to maintain credibility while so actively utilizing the spotlight, however nobly, for his own objectives.

Remember back in the late '80s when Arizona dragged its feet establishing a Martin Luther King holiday? Soon after, a lot of famous acts (Stevie Wonder, the Doobie Brothers) canceled their concerts there. Not U2. Playing a sold-out arena in Tempe, they instead prepared a statement of protest for the crowd, played a rollicking show, and afterward invested thousands of their own dollars in the grass-roots campaign against Gov. Evan Mecham, the MLK holiday's chief opponent. "Who are they to tell Arizona what to do?" raged one of Mecham's aides. And really, he was right. U2 should probably have canceled the show, which Bono later confessed to biographer Carter Alan. But, however clumsily they came off, or how much they exposed themselves to justifiable criticism, U2 were willing to risk themselves, to use music as ammunition in a larger struggle regardless of the consequences. How many corporate rockers can you say that about?

Yet compared to Bono's meeting this summer with North Carolina Sen. Jesse Helms to discuss the African AIDS crisis, all that past activism seems like child's play. In recent times he has brought his crusade to the likes of President Bill Clinton, British Prime Minister Tony Blair, and Pope John Paul II, the last of whom famously donned the singer's trademark shades in a surreal photo op. But Bono's summit with Helms was much more noteworthy, because it marked a leap over the ideological divide.

For millions the North Carolina senator symbolizes American conservatism at its ugliest. And yet here was Bono breaking bread with Helms at the Capitol as if the two were old chums. "You'll always be a friend here," Helms told Bono that day.

"U2 has always been about bringing ideas to a larger audience, and crossing boundaries," says Powers. "I think that Bono's wise enough at this stage of his life to see that sometimes the right connection can come from a surprising place."

Bono's meeting with Helms reflects a rite of passage most of us experience sooner or later. Maybe his more idealistic days seemed a more appropriately romantic rock star stance, but Bono has learned that all the posturing in the world won't make cohesive progress without cooperation across the political boundaries. Why wave protest signs outside when you can waltz through the corridors of power?

"He's very articulate," says *Rolling Stone* contributing editor Anthony DeCurtis, who has written about U2 frequently over the last 15 years. "In a great tradition of Irish rhetoric, Bono has a way of just leaping over contradictions, and through sheer eloquence and charm managing to bridge otherwise completely unbridgeable gaps."

Whether it's our friends or our idols, the people who capture our imagination are always changing. Bono has evolved over two decades from heart-on-his-sleeve idealist, to irony-ensconced rock 'n' roll Liberace, and finally to a sort of hopeful pragmatist. Regardless of the actual effectiveness of his crusades, his more practical political acumen is something Bono has been working toward—in and out of music—for most of his life.

What originally transported U2 from Dublin clubs to the world stage was a combination of punk rock aggression and a defiantly purposeful attitude. Mere months before U2's band mates first met, the Sex Pistols's Johnny Rotten famously sang that there was "no future for you." Growing up just across the water in Ireland at a time of near-revolutionary civil strife, nobody could have blamed Bono for feeling the same kind of bitter angst.

As the child of a Catholic father and Protestant mother, however, Bono saw beyond the polarized religious rhetoric, his lyrics demanding a more promising future. As U2 gained notoriety in songs like "Sunday Bloody Sunday," with Bono singing, "I can't believe the news today, I can't close my eyes and make it go away," the band pleaded for peace with 11th-hour urgency. We loved them for it, even if deep down we knew it wouldn't change the world.

Various strains of this idealistic persona remained all the way to the album and concert film *Rattle and Hum* (1988), but by that point in U2's career something had to change. Whether it was their derivative rendering of American roots music, or how their overexposed politicking simply grew tiresome, by 1991's *Achtung Baby,* a complete reinvention was not only advisable, but downright essential.

In the changed musical landscape of the post-Nirvana early '90s, a lot of famous acts lost their way. But the masterly *Achtung Baby* suddenly made U2 more vital than ever. And after bristling for so long at the notion of rock 'n' roll stardom, their embrace of the crazy burlesque pageant that is rock was oddly refreshing. While U2's stage persona took a turn toward the bombastic with the Zoo TV Tour in 1992, Bono largely took leave from high-profile social activism as his lyrics entered a sort of blue period, exploring the doubt and desperation we've all felt at times.

"For all of the theatrics of Zoo TV and *Achtung Baby*, there still is a core of belief in U2 that has remained constant," notes DeCurtis. "There's a kind of skepticism, or questioning side of them, that's come to the surface, but also there's a kind of yearning that real ironists never admit to." Looking back with the hindsight of history, the darkness of *Achtung Baby* is precisely what gives the optimism in *All That You Can't Leave Behind* its legitimacy.

Great artists also have an intrinsic sense of timing, and U2 are no different. Just as *Achtung Baby* perfectly reflected the irony-obsessed early-'90s zeitgeist, *All That You Can't Leave Behind* embodies our renewed taste for the genuine, which has only increased following the events of Sept. 11. "It reminds me of that aphorism by William Blake: Enough or too much," says DeCurtis. "That's pretty much U2's guiding principle. Whether it's their total reinvention on *Achtung Baby* after *Rattle and Hum* or *All That You Can't Leave Behind's* return to essentials, the connection is that they've always bounced back from something beyond its usefulness."

And so a man who just a few short years ago was parading the concert stages of Europe dressed as MacPhisto, an absurd combination of Faust's Mephistopheles and Liberace, can go on to share the stage with the most powerful men and women in the world. That Bono has so often looked absurd and bounced back gives every one of us who has embarrassed ourselves at a party, or pontificated far too long at a podium, or created art that disappointed, hope that the future is indeed unlimited. Bono reminds us that time makes everything possible.

Not only is that timing useful when it comes to making rock records, but it's equally important in politics. That's why we see Bono out there now with Jesse Helms and John Paul II. As the age of irony wanes, and the world unites against an uncannily elusive enemy, a rock star like Bono can speak matter-of-factly about social causes again and actually be taken seriously. Whether it's in the studio or on the steps of the U.S. Capitol, Bono knows he's got to ride the wave while it lasts.

U2

Bono Turns up the Political Heat

Richard Blow
***George* magazine, April 2000**

One would not expect to find U2's Bono, dressed simply in black pants, an olive shirt and a military-style cap, at Café des Artistes. The rarefied European-style restaurant, just off Manhattan's tony Central Park West, caters more to affluent retirees than to rock stars, and the conversations are so hushed that the place feels like a library reading room. But Bono, who arrives by foot from a borrowed apartment 10 blocks away, is at home amid the old-world atmosphere. "I love this place," he says, and the restaurant staff discreetly nod and welcome him as a regular with a penchant for privacy. Scanning a menu, Bono orders a beet salad, steak fries, and a bottle of Cote de Beaune. "I have a place in France," he says. "I'm learning a bit about wine."

Talk soon turns to world politics. "I'm not saying I know a lot about these subjects," he insists, though he clearly does. That isn't the rock star in Bono speaking, but the figure he is evolving into: a political leader for the new century.

How did you get involved with your organization for Third World debt relief, Jubilee 2000? It's not exactly a household topic.

It's a hard sell. That's why you need to get pop stars in a photograph with a pontiff before people will pay it any attention. You have to create drama some other way.

For me this goes back to Live Aid and the song "Do They Know It's Christmas." That whole thing affected me on a very profound level, that this little piece of plastic, vinyl, could affect the lives of millions. And raise $200 million for Africa. Later, I found out that Africa spends $200 million a month on its debt repayments.

So you bought a month?

Yeah. But I was really carried away with it, and my wife, Ali, and I went to Africa. We worked there for a month, just following through. Walking in the camps. We swore to each other that we would never forget our experiences there. And in the background we were always thinking that we've got to get beyond just putting your hand in your pocket—it's the structure, the relationship between the West and the economies that, for our own spiritual well-being, we'd better come to deal with. And when this idea came up, I thought, "Here it is; this is it."

How much progress has been made?

A lot. In the United States, very few people are aware that the government has canceled the debts of 36 countries. That's an extraordinary step. It has forever changed the relationship between the developing and the developed world. Once the president of the United States said that it is immoral for a man to repay loans rather than feed his starving children, everything changed.

President Clinton has mentioned you in speeches at least twice. Does that make you at all uncomfortable—the President of the United States citing a rock star about a policy that involves billions of dollars?

Part of the smartness of this administration is their openness to new ideas, no matter how you're dressed. So I walk into the Oval Office in my khakis. They offered me an audience because they're not looking at me, they're listening to the idea. And that's smart.

In Ireland, we have a history of poets and painters involving themselves in politics. Poets and politicians conspired to create a mythology, a vision of Ireland that probably wasn't true. The poets created this kind of mythical Ireland that sheltered us from the sleet and hailstones of colonialism.

When you're meeting with these young White House aides, how do you know they don't just want to be able to say they've met Bono?

That might be the start of it. But on this issue, that hasn't been the end of it. And I've been surprised. Not just in Bill Clinton's White House, but in Wall Street, in the Treasury department; with some Republicans, there's been an openness I really wasn't expecting. I arrived with lock picks, and they were opening the door.

You didn't expect such good treatment from the establishment.

We love this idea, especially in rock 'n' roll, of good guys and bad guys. We're the good guys; they that wear the suits are the bad guys. But in fact they're just the busy guys. [*Laughs*] They don't have the time to see the bigger picture. Which is inexcusable, by the way, if you're in the seat of power.

And if you don't make the time, you get [the riots at December's World Trade Organization meetings in] Seattle.

So they were smart to listen.

Yes. We have a constituency.

When you're onstage and you've got 75,000 people hanging on your words, there's a power that's about more than rock music. It's almost fascistic.

Sure.

Did you ever stand onstage and think, "What if I told these people to go jump off a bridge?"

You know what they would do? Just go home. Look, we have our share of assholes that come see us. Onstage as well. [Laughs]. I'm one of them at times. But our audiences are very smart, and if we abuse that relationship it would simply end. If I told people how to vote, they would tell me, "Go fuck yourself."

What do rock stars and politicians have in common?

They're both performers. Both, if they're any good, have a sense of occasion. But politicians are more like pop stars than rock stars.

What's the difference?

Their audience has a short memory.

Which are you?

I am both. But U2 is a rock band.

Are you a politician?

Jim Morrison called himself an erotic politician, didn't he? [Laughs] I have a respect for the word politician that is unusual in my world. It comes from having met them, and seeing how hard they work. I have actually sat down with people in bands who describe politicians as the anti-Christ and are sure that the Capitol is the domain for all anti-Christs. And I'm saying, "You don't understand. These people get home really late. If they went into business, they'd be a lot wealthier. We should pay them more and expect more from them." I have to confess, I've got a respect for them that I really didn't expect.

Do politicians respect you?

I don't care. I really don't. I care for Jubilee 2000, or Amnesty International, or whatever. I want them to get respect. People can get confused and think that because your issue is worthy, therefore you are. To be in a position where people expect a lot from you personally, rather than from your work, is dangerous.

But people do expect that. I don't think U2 could behave badly and not have that behavior undermine your politics.

I thought we did a very good job of trashing our public image. After Zoo TV, people thought, "Well, there they go, they've embraced the cliché." And, partly, that's true. But we did it in a smart way, because we just didn't like wearing the righteous shoes. They really slowed us down.

Politicians do get [judged by their behavior], but musicians, we don't. And we mustn't. We're judged for the songs, or the work.

It seemed a delicate balancing act to change your old image without rejecting the passionate politics of U2 in the 1980s.

And we never did reject that. Because as a person, as a performer, you're looking for wholeness. On a spiritual level, I think that's God's design for us. Wholeness. And that often amounts to embracing contradictions. So we started to mine our own hypocrisy, rather than throwing stones at the political system, as we did in the '80s. In the '90s, we started to have a go at ourselves. Some people preferred the other way, which was like, rebel throws rock through the glass case of some obvious evil. But it's the same thing in the end. Outside of the songs, we continued on the same path of protest, politically, that we'd always been on.

But the songs did become less explicitly political.

They did. The songs definitely changed.

And that was conscious?

It is now. [*Laughs*] I mean, I don't write songs about things I could write an essay about.

Did the fact that songs can be misunderstood cause you to write less explicitly political songs? You were obviously uncomfortable with the way some people interpreted 'Sunday Bloody Sunday' as a pro-IRA song.

Right. That was a religious outburst, contrasting the idea of Easter Sunday with the Easter Sunday when British paratroopers shot dead 13 protesters. It was naive. A lot of our work in the '80s was very naive. But I like that now. It's ecstatic music. It has a sense of wonder and a joy about it. And joy is the hardest thing. You can create anger. You can achieve drama easily. But joy...

Do you feel the same way about your politics in the '80s?

Pretty much, yeah. I can't remember anything that I regret.

Because you're spending so much time with politicians now, there must be things that you can't say now that you could have said then.

I have a kind of Tourette's syndrome, though, where the very thing I'm not supposed to say just forces its way out of me gob. The foot is destined for the mouth. So in that sense I'm probably not a good politician.

At least you never said U2 is bigger than Jesus.

No. Jesus has made us big.

Isn't there a risk of being co-opted by politicians? By someone who wants to be seen with you, to associate themselves with your fame or moral authority, but they're not necessarily going to come through for you?

I can't worry too much about that. In Guyana people have a life expectancy of 47 years. And they're spending as much on repaying their loans to the West as they are on educating their people. So I don't think I can be too worried about who I'm sitting down with. Conservative Republicans—they want to talk the scriptures, I can talk the scriptures.

How long have you known Clinton?

We met him when he was campaigning in 1992. Politicians and rock stars have similar touring schedule—they travel at night and then they work through the day. So we would cross paths. And there was an incident in Chicago where we were in the same hotel. At, like, three o'clock in the morning, we were all eating pizza and drinking wine, and somebody said, "Where's Bill Clinton? Ask him if he wants some pizza." We were being cheeky.

It was a reasonable question.

[*Laughs*] For some reason, we were politely turned away. But the next morning, he came up to our room and wanted to talk about Ireland. That's his curiosity for new ideas and new people. But the relationship between politicians and musicians is always going to be amusing. I can walk out of the White House and praise the president for what he's done in Ireland or with debt relief. But the next year I might be chaining myself to the railings.

That seems particularly important with Bill Clinton. There are a lot of people who have felt that they knew where they stood with him and later felt betrayed by him.

I have a different point of view. I'm a European; I see an America that's rehabilitated in a way that was unimaginable to me 10 years ago. Back then the U.S. was the neighborhood bully, inept in foreign policy, beating up on the wrong guy everywhere. With *The Joshua Tree*, we were writing about Central America and the dark side of the United States. Now America looks smart and, dare I say it, sexy again. During [the war in] Bosnia, when this Muslim population was living with genocide and a united Europe couldn't agree on anything, it was the Americans who came to rescue them.

Is it tougher, in a way, to have somebody like Clinton as president, rather than someone who had clear differences with you?

It's a lot different, especially in musical terms. Rebel rock has a certain romance. Arriving with your statistics and bowler hat is never going to ring the same.

Have your own politics changed much over the last 20 years?

I'm what you call a champagne socialist. My father was from the left; I grew up on labor ideas. Simple adages: housing, health, education. I thought having a family would actually take a lot of my energies away from such passions. I'm surprised that it did rather the opposite. My children have made me more aggressive about the world that they're about to inhabit.

Has your political work infused the record you're making?

The record is in no way a political record. It's a very personal record. But it has a certain fire to it that you get when you're all where you're supposed to be. I would go off to America and come back and I'd have songs in my head.

How is the album coming?

We've got all the songs now. And we've just got to put them into arrangements. I mean, we have the songs, and we just haven't quite finished them. Some great songs in there.

Can you characterize the album?

If we had only one record to make, this would be it. That's the way we're looking at it.

Are you a role model for younger musicians?

[*Groans*] Oh, don't I think a lot of people out there just think, "Oh, yeah, weren't they the band that had all those ideals in the '80s and then they started dressing up in shiny suits and got all artsy?" I don't think people see us as a role model, and I rather like that they don't. We're going after the soul music now. That's where the battle is won and lost for me politically—in the deep waters of the soul.

CHAPTER 7

SPIRITUALITY

"That's where the battle is won and lost for me politically—in the deep waters of the soul."

The soul, the spirit has been the one truly consistent thread in U2's existence. A unifying element for Bono, Larry, and The Edge in their very early days was a religious fellowship called Shalom. Shalom nearly broke up U2 by questioning whether a person could be both a "believer" and a rock musician at the same time. Ultimately, after a time of crisis, the band decided they could indeed be both.

While the Shalom experience left them leery of "organized religion," the three never shed their spiritual nature. As much as any self-proclaimed "Christian Rock Band"—a genre and appellation U2 resists—U2's music is rife with Judeo-Christian metaphor and symbolism, as evidenced in such songs as "If God Should Send His Angels" and "40," their rewrite of the 40th Psalm.

This frequently mentioned facet of the band, a fascinating piece of the whole that makes up U2, has been explored in Steve Stockman's *Walk On: The Spiritual Journey of U2*. Certainly prominent in their lyrics, this spirituality is part of the source of Bono's passion. It is reflected in the way the band live and it is a part of what allows them to remain "one of us" at home in Dublin.

It is not only his innate spirituality, but his early biblical indoctrination that allows Bono to quote scripture to Jesse Helms and relate to the Pope. More importantly, it creates a strong context for the band—a lingua franca of Western culture that nearly everyone understands. With the Bible's contents referred to by word or theme, U2's music is a touchstone of human values in the industrial world.

U2

Stop in the Name of Love

Jim Miller
***Newsweek*, December 31, 1984**

It's not often that one of the world's most popular—and exciting—young rock bands is attacked in the press for promoting "the hocus-pocus of Christian enlightenment." But then the group called U2 is no ordinary rock band. All four members hail from Dublin, Ireland—hardly a rock hot spot. Three of them are Christians who make no secret of their convictions. Opponents of violence, they made a point of launching their stirring pacifist anthem "Sunday Bloody Sunday" in war-torn Belfast, Northern Ireland. The band's unusual public stature was confirmed last year by Ireland's prime minister, Garret FitzGerald, who asked the lead singer, Paul (Bono) Hewson, 21, to join a government committee investigating the problem of unemployed youth.

To many fans, of course, U2 is simply a rock band of rare passion. Earlier this month in Worcester, Mass., in the second concert of a whirlwind American tour—they will return for a two-month visit next February—U2 showed off the bravura style that has won it a fervent following. As usual, the spotlight was on Bono, a lyrical singer, and Dave (The Edge) Evans, 22, the band's brilliant lead guitarist. Playing droning clusters of notes and using chiming, bell-like timbres, as well as abrasive, buzz-saw textures, The Edge creates an electronic wall of sound that has an elemental power—it is, as he describes it, "Emotionally saturated." For all the nervous jangle of the music, its sheer scale and Celtic overtones create a weird, primordial resonance: the Worcester concert may have taken place in a vast indoor arena, but it was easy to imagine yourself watching the sunrise at Stonehenge.

"The message, if there is a message in our music, is the hope that it communicates," says Bono, whose intensity and seriousness are rare for a rock musician. His religious faith, he adds, is "a very personal one. I'm very wary of people who bring 'the message' to the masses. Sure, belief gets us out of bed in the morning and gets us onstage at night. But the way it affects our audience is that we feel a responsibility to give everything we have onstage."

The band members' interest in politics grew out of their first trip to America. "People were throwing money on the stage during the Bobby Sands hunger strike," recalls Bono. "But what was that money for? Those dollars were arriving in the streets of Belfast and Derry as weapons and bombs. Some things are black and white—but the troubles in Northern Ireland are not. I know: I'm the son of a Protestant mother and a Catholic father." The song "Sunday Bloody Sunday," says Bono, was meant "to take the image of Northern Ireland out of the black and white and into the gray, where it truly belongs."

The band's ambitions have never been modest. Several years ago, Bono predicted that U2 would become a great rock group, on a par with the Beatles and Rolling Stones. The band's latest bid to join the pantheon is the Island album *The Unforgettable Fire*. Co-produced by Brian Eno, champion of free-form composition, the record defiantly ignores most of the clichés of hard rock—even those coined by U2. On one side are textured electronics and resident imagery, climaxed by "Elvis Presley and America," an all-too-effective evocation of Presley's stupor in his last days. On the other side are three great pieces of numinous hard rock. "A Sort of Homecoming" is a hymn for patriotic mystics. "Pride (In the Name of Love)" is a clanging elegy to the Rev. Martin Luther King, Jr. And "Wire," with The Edge playing eerie harmonics on slide guitar is one of the best examples yet of the band's unique brand of raw, wind-swept rock. Some critics have poked fun at the lyrics of the songs. But even on "Pride," the most earnest one, the words matter in large part because Bono sings them with such fierceness and fervor.

By 1983, when "Sunday Bloody Sunday" was released, it was clear that U2 had become one of the most influential new acts of the decade. Its sense of idealism and minimalist approach to guitar-based rock have already inspired the British bands Simple Minds, The Alarm and, above all, Big Country. "We've taken the love that was a part of '60s rock and the anger that was a part of punk," says Bono. "We want a spiritual side to our music as well as a raucous and rowdy side. I think we have never achieved the balance we're looking for, and perhaps we never will. But that's what we want from our music—freedom, I suppose. And a little bit of humanity."

In Sight

***America*, June 6, 1987**

Archbishop Enlists Rock Lyrics for Justice: Archbishop Roger M. Mahony of Los Angeles, in the baccalaureate address at the University of Southern California, used the words of the rock group U2 to urge graduates to work for peace through justice. Saying that, "in our nuclear age, peace means the survival of the world," the Archbishop quoted from the song "Bullet the [Blue] Sky" to emphasize his point: "In the howling wind comes stinging rain. See it driving nails into souls on the tree of pain. From the firefly, a red orange glow. See the face of fear running scared in the valley below." The Archbishop urged the graduates to "hear the heartbeat of every human being who is lonely, poor, a victim of injustice or unjust systems: the addict, AIDS victims, the migrant laborer, the garment factory worker. Never be afraid to stand for the good of those who suffer, those in need."

The Scripture According to Bono

Terry Mattingly
Scripps-Howard News Service, June 20, 2001

As lunch ended in the ornate U.S. Senate Foreign Relations Committee conference room, Sen. Jesse Helms struggled to stand and bid farewell to the guest of honor.

Bono stayed at the conservative patriarch's right hand, doing what he could to help. For the photographers, it would have been hard to imagine a stranger image than this delicate dance between aging senator and rock superstar.

"You know, I love you," Helms said softly.

The singer gave the 79-year-old North Carolina Republican a hug. This private session with a circle of senators during U2's recent Washington stop wasn't the first time Bono and Helms have discussed poverty, plagues, charity, and faith. Nor will it be the last. Blessed be the ties that bind.

"What can I say? It's good to be loved—especially by Jesse Helms," Bono said two days later, as his campaign for Third World debt relief continued on Capitol Hill.

The key to this scene is that Bono can quote the Book of Leviticus as well as the works of John Lennon. While his star power opens doors, it is his sincere, if often unconventional, Christian faith that creates bonds with cultural conservatives—in the Vatican and inside the Beltway. Bono has shared prayers and his sunglasses with Pope John Paul II. Don't be surprised if he trades boots and Bible verses with President Bush.

The hot issues right now are red ink and AIDS in Africa. An entire continent is "in flames," said Bono, and millions of lives are at stake. God is watching.

The bottom line is that the Bible contains 2,000 verses about justice and compassion. While it's crucial to answer political and economic questions linked to forgiving $200 billion in Third World debt, Bono said this also must be seen as a crisis of faith. The road into the heart of America runs through its sanctuaries.

"What will really wake people up," he said, "is when Sunday schools start making flags and getting out in the streets...Forget about the judgment of history. For those of you who are religious people, you have to think about the judgment of God."

Bono knows that this bleak, even melodramatic, message sounds bizarre coming from a rock 'n' roll fat cat. In a recent Harvard University commencement address, he said the only thing worse than an egotistical rock star is a rock star "with a conscience—a placard-waving, knee-jerking, fellow-traveling activist with a Lexus and a swimming pool shaped like his own head."

This is old news to Bono, who has had a love-hate relationship with stardom for two decades. In U2's early days, other Christians said the band should break up or flee into "Christian rock," arguing that fame always corrupts. Bono and his band mates decided otherwise, but the singer soon began speaking out about his faith and his doubts, his joys and his failures.

"I don't believe in preaching at people," he told me back in 1982. A constant theme in his music, he added, is the soul-spinning confusion that results when spirituality, sensuality, ego, and sin form a potion that is both intoxicating and toxic. "The truth is that we are all sinners. I always include myself in the 'we.' I'm not telling everybody that I have the answers. I'm trying to get across the difficulty that I have being what I am."

Eventually, Bono acted out this internal debate on stage. In the 1990s, he celebrated and attacked fame through a sleazy, macho, leather-bound alter ego called The Fly. After that came Mister MacPhisto, a devilishly theatrical take on mass-media temptation. The motto for the decade was, "Mock Satan and he will flee thee."

Today, U2 has all but dropped its ironic posturing and the soaring music of this tour covers sin and redemption, heaven and hell, mercy and grace. Bono is quoting from the Psalms and the first Washington concert ended with him shouting: "Praise! Unto the Almighty!" It wasn't subtle and it wasn't perfect. Crusades rarely are.

"I do believe that the Kingdom of Heaven is taken by force," said Bono, paraphrasing the Gospel of Matthew, chapter 11. "God doesn't mind if we bang on the door to heaven sometimes, asking him to listen to what we have to say...At least, that's the kind of religion I believe in."

U2

The Spiritual Journey of U2

Jason White
Religion News Service, February 12, 2002

More taboo than drugs or sex, God is a most unwelcome guest in the world of rock 'n' roll. But that's precisely why Bono, lead singer of U2, finds God to be such a powerful subject for the band's songs. "You're in a rock band—what can't you talk about? God? OK, here we go," he once said. "You're supposed to write songs about sex and drugs. Well, no, I won't."

From the band's origins as four dreaming teenagers in Dublin, Ireland in the 1970s to its current status as among the greatest rock bands on the planet, U2 has written and performed music shot through with a religiosity that defies easy categorization.

On its 2001 Elevation Tour, U2 sold out arenas and stadiums around the world, using in the process a surprising amount of religious imagery. The band usually closed with "Walk On," a song from its newest album, *All That You Can't Leave Behind.* Toward the end of the song, Bono would shout "Unto the Almighty, thank you!" and lead the crowd in a chorus of hallelujahs.

Bono and the rest of U2 would seem to fit comfortably with evangelicalism and contemporary Christian music. That placement, however, is resisted by both the evangelical establishment and the band itself. U2's members—Bono, guitarist The Edge, drummer Larry Mullen, Jr., and bassist Adam Clayton—drink and smoke and swear, causing some pietistic Christians to question the band's beliefs.

U2 doesn't seem to care whether churches accept the band. Over 20 years, U2 has grown uncomfortable with organized religion, calling church life "claustrophobic" and blaming Christianity, at least in part, for dividing Ireland. "I have this hunger in me... Everywhere I look, I see evidence of a Creator," Bono has said. "But I don't see it as religion, which has cut my people in two."

The question of U2's religious beliefs, and the ways band members have expressed them, is the subject of a 2001 book, *Walk On—The Spiritual Journey of U2* (Relevant Books), by Steve Stockman, a Presbyterian minister in Ireland. Stockman mines U2 interviews and books about the band and its music to write a spiritual companion to the band's career.

Stockman wrote that in U2's early days in Dublin, Bono, The Edge, and Mullen embraced a charismatic evangelical form of Christianity unusual then for Ireland. They found like-minded believers in a small group called the Shalom Fellowship. In the early 1980s, one of Shalom's leaders declared that U2 would have to give up rock 'n' roll to please God.

It was a crossroads for the band, and after deciding that God would rather have them play rock music than stay in the fellowship, Bono, The Edge, and Mullen left. Never again would any members of U2 be formally aligned with a religious group. "For Bono, The Edge, and Larry, the God that they met and have pilgrimaged with down the amazing road is a God who is bigger than church or religious boundaries," wrote Stockman.

U2's Hi-Tech Tent Revival

Steve Braden
***America*, January 7, 2002**

God is in the room—even more than Elvis," quipped the lead singer Bono in reference to U2's concert performances last summer. The third and final leg of their world tour, called "Elevation," opened on Oct. 10 in Notre Dame's Joyce Athletic Convocation Center to a sold-out crowd of approximately 10,000 fans. It was loud, ridiculously fun, and the closest thing to a tent revival this Catholic boy has ever experienced.

To begin to understand the mystique of the Irish rock band U2, one needs only to experience the presence of Bono: the leather-clad, Scripture-quoting, wraparound-sunglasses-wearing lobbyist for Third World debt relief whose larger than life personality effortlessly lights up a room. Or a stadium. A tireless performer on the concert stage, Bono pursues an assortment of social causes around the world as well. A rock star who hangs out with Senator Jesse Helms and Pope John Paul II, Bono also gave the commencement speech at Harvard University's graduation in 2000.

As the band struck the opening chords of "Beautiful Day," the J.A.C.C. erupted with screams. Bono's first words were, "This is holy ground." Unlike Moses in Exodus, however, the singer elected to keep his shoes on. On the very next song, "Until the End of the World," the lead guitarist, known as The Edge, and Bono walked out to the tip of the giant, heart-shaped stage for a slightly bizarre piece of performance art, acting out the tension between Jesus and Judas at the Last Supper. I quickly realized this was not your ordinary rock concert.

But then again, this band has always puzzled me. The idealism of their early rock records gave way to mid-1990's experiments of electronica with dark lyrics that were barely accessible to many fans. For some concerts, Bono would actually parade around onstage wearing a pair of devil horns. But I guess it is the privilege of great artists to lose their minds eventually.

The Judeo-Christian story reminds us of the cyclic pattern of sin-grace-redemption, and great art has always reflected those themes. The songs of U2's first public performance in a post-Sept. 11 world tended to concentrate on the later elements of that pattern. During the gradually building introduction to "Where the Streets Have No Name," Bono quoted a few verses from Psalm 116 before tearing around the perimeter of the stage at breakneck speed. By the time he started singing, the valley of the J.A.C.C. was shaking like a small earthquake. No longer a mere witness to a performance, I had been transported to that mythical place in "Brother Love's Traveling Salvation Show" where Neil Diamond captures perfectly the feeling of a Southern Gospel tent revival in his famous song.

Ah, but Brother Love never had the level of technical support at his tent show that U2 has. Nitrogen smoke rose like incense from the stage prior to the band's arrival. Dazzling lights, video screens, and visuals were projected around the arena's walls. Images of star charts, candles entwined in barbed wire, symbolic doves of peace, suitcases decorated with a heart and other signs that point to spiritual realities flashed everywhere. While much of U2's stage show may be evangelical, the special effects were evidence of their sacramental imagination.

At one point in the gospel-flavored "Still Haven't Found What I'm Looking For," Bono, leading the sing-along, said "Take it to church; that's right, you're in church." People never seem to tire of singing about the search for grace. And what tent revival would be complete without a sermon? During the encore song, "One," Bono spoke for several minutes about the Sept. 11 disaster and creative ways to respond. He mentioned that his friend, the president of the World Bank, believes the roots of terrorism lie in the abject poverty of much of the Middle East and how dealing with it will take bravery—bravery much like what was shown by the New York City Fire and Police Departments on that fateful day in September. And so for the altar call and final song, "Walk On," U2 brought onstage about a dozen members from the N.Y.P.D. and N.Y.F.D., who had flown in just for the concert, to take a bow and receive some appreciation from Notre Dame's audience.

Grace, she takes the blame,
She covers the shame
Removes the stain.
Grace, it's the name for a girl, it's also a thought
that changed the world.
Grace finds goodness in everything,
Grace finds beauty in everything
Because Grace makes beauty out of ugly things.
—from "Grace," on U2's album
All That You Can't Leave Behind

Although the band never returned for a second encore, the arena sound system played the CD version of the final song, "Grace," as the crowd filed out into the autumn breeze.

The theology of the piece appears to mix together Augustinian and Thomistic concepts. Bono can't seem to decide if the depravity of the fallen world is too deep to clean, or if we live in the graced universe defined by St. Thomas Aquinas, where all of creation is redeemed. But then again, on some days, neither can I.

Just as pilgrims in medieval Europe would travel great distances to experience something transcendent, I felt a sense of solidarity among the fans milling about in the parking lot before and after the show. Some had traveled from other schools in Indiana; some were visiting from halfway across the country, no doubt staying with current Notre Dame students in their dorm rooms. Several mentioned that the concert was a religious experience that would keep them aglow for days. U2's performance at Notre Dame was the only college stop on their tour and in their smallest arena to date since the mid-1980s. Perhaps the band was intrigued by the chance to see the "Catholic Disneyland" outpost that Irish-Americans have helped build. Bono admitted during the show that he was impressed with the beautiful campus, which he had toured on a borrowed bike that afternoon. He also commended Notre Dame's ethos of service, mentioning how our teacher-volunteer program was a way of changing the world.

In this postmodern world, there are fewer events that bring people together. For much of history, the church was the only show in town. It provided surreal cathedral architecture, dazzling stained-glass light shows, the clergy in elaborate costumes and stories of sinners who became heroic saints depicted in art. Yet with the dwindling numbers of young people who identify with "organized religion," I must admit there is something we could learn from a band whose fans wait in line for several hours to buy tickets for $46 or $86 apiece. Days before the show, tickets were being bid up to $400 a pair on E-bay. But hey, nobody ever said salvation was cheap.

Even though part of me tries to deny it, I believe that contemporary cultural attitudes are influenced more by the people who write popular songs, movies, and television programs than all the classrooms and pulpits in this country put together. But even this most thoughtful band has a fair amount of contradictions. In a global environment, where most people live day to day, this group enjoys the high life in penthouse suites at the finest hotels around the country while it is on tour. Maybe there is still room for God in the decadent world of rock and roll, as U2's song lyrics are among the most socially aware, compassionate, and hope-filled on the radio today. The realms of the sacred and the profane have never been so blurred.

U2

The New U2

John Smith
***On Being* (Australia), November 1993**

To write an analysis of U2 for the Christian public is akin to doing a film review of Martin Scorsese's *Last Temptation of Christ*: no matter how balanced, insightful, careful, or even courageous the effort, inevitable protest, denial, and misinterpretation will result. It is symptomatic of the situation that the most vitriolic letter I have received in the last few years is a savage personal attack on me for my apparent admiration or even acceptance of U2's art performance.

The real problem is we still haven't found what we are looking for! In this Hollywoodified age, the Christian public subtly craves idols who conform to our image, yet which are also acceptable to our secular mates. We don't have a good record, wildly acclaiming the conversion stories of everyone from Little Richard to Van Morrison, from Bob Dylan to U2.

Someone has said that the problem with idols is that you must either be an unqualified worshipper or an unmitigated iconoclast in their presence—uncritical adoration or untempered hostility!

Of course, in our desperately hasty attempts to prove that our Christianity is valid and relevant in this media age, we have hitched our wagons to many fallen stars; and, once they have disillusioned us, our inarticulate hostility and unjust criticisms give them valid reason to dismiss their genuine flirtations with faith in earlier days.

To this must be added the problem of general Christian—and secular—ignorance of art forms, symbolism, and media techniques. So without a serious look at us there is little use looking at them.

Why do we have such morbid necessity for Christianized mega-stars in the first place?

Earlier this year, Bono expressed it to me in these terms. What does it matter what U2 think of Jesus? (For those who miss the point—the guys have not discarded Jesus or their faith.) So what if U2 do or don't believe! Surely, the point is whether Christ Himself is believable.

For U2, a conflict has arisen between the enormous expectations of Christians to perform predictably and their obvious innovative and creative genius. We don't choose a medical doctor according to the number of Bible texts displayed on the surgery walls but we do judge professional performers on a "how-many-Christian-references" scale.

An article on U2 raises enormous issues of missiology, ethics, comparative value systems, public persona, and the entire gamut of perplexities regarding the moral culpability of media and market forces manipulating the performers for public consumption. I fear the trivialising of it all in an insultingly brief resume of extraordinarily complex issues surrounding a uniquely complex rock group.

If we are disillusioned with U2 we must ask ourselves what were our illusions in the first place.

Simplistically the story goes like this: A backyard garage ensemble of unlikely Irish punk rockers resulted from Larry Mullen's scruffy note pinned to a notice board. Paul Hewson, Dave Evans, and Adam Clayton respond, with nothing in common. Crude, doubtful abilities were fired by

Paul Hewson's odd mixture of Catholic/Protestant parentage, Irish temperament, mercurial intelligence, and a genuine, rebellious, newfound spirituality.

The chemistry was there and the pilgrimage was forged by predictable fundamentalist opposition, mind-shattering experiences, and the exposure of the group to the mega-issues of human rights via Central American Mission Partners' guided tours amid the wreckage of El Salvador.

The unforgettable fire remains kindled by firsthand experience of the Bosnian disaster. But the group's responses are an enigma to those who neither understand the nature of artistic pilgrimage nor the forces of demonic Western politics and the manipulations of the media age ingeniously exposed by the cynicism and satirical brilliance of the Zoo [TV] Tour.

The problem for many Christians is their ignorance of modern art forms. This leads to a literal interpretation of symbolism and U2's satire is perceived as embracing rather than exposing the demonic. All was quiet on the Christian front during the days of "Sunday Bloody Sunday," when U2 sermonized "We must finish the work Christ began on that Sunday, bloody Sunday."

For thoughtful evangelicals—who had a rightful place in their hearts for Martin Luther King and Archbishop Oscar Romero's self-giving martyrdoms—"In the Name of Love" rang the right bells.

Shallow souls on Christian and secular fronts totally missed the point of "I Still Haven't Found What I'm Looking For." For the shallow opponents of Christianity it served as a departure from sermonizing faith. For fundamentalists, who neither understood nor empathized with the Lord's Prayer (Thy Kingdom Come, Thy will be done on earth as it is in Heaven!), they had betrayed the simplistic slogan of "Jesus is the answer," failing to enter into the Christ-like agony of a world so racked with Divinely rejected injustice, loneliness, and corruption. That the song reaffirmed Christ's vicarious embracing of our guilt and sin and reasserted the declaration of faith ("You know I believe it") was overlooked in a frenzy of Sunday school responses.

Rattle and Hum maintained the tradition. "When Love Comes to Town," to the insightful, was reminiscent of the old gospel Salvationist song "Love lifted me when no one but Christ could help, Love lifted me." It may not have named Him but the images were inescapable.

It was during the period of the recording of *The Joshua Tree* that I spent in-depth time with three of the four musicians in Dublin and became aware of both the genius and the evolution of U2 from soulful, visceral, passionate performers to technically and artistically avant-garde innovators in both style and content. The open relationship with both their Irish, biblically conservative pastor and a few other pastorally caring "ad hoc" Christian contacts around the world remains intact.

The public images of cigar smoking, performance paraphernalia (notably, the devil's horns of the *Zooropa* [tour] innovation) and the enigmatic and bewildering array of symbolism have sounded the death knell for much Christian support. Though I am not prepared to betray personal conversations in the interest of prurient, ignorant, and critical Christian public curiosity about U2, I am prepared to say that the Bono et al of 1993 on stage are both authentic and utterly misleading as to the genuine passion, faith, and even humility of the private personae.

That is not to say that I concur with either the philosophical interpretations of all the art or the total methodology of their rock genre...But then the safe, predictable expression of the Christian evangelical performers gets up my nose for its lack of prophetic pain and Biblical protest.

Three personal influences of thought lay behind the radical departures of U2's recent shows.

Firstly, Bono's view of art and prophecy are virtually synonymous. He reminded me earlier this year that Jesus declared that His parables were not to make the meaning easy but inaccessible to the idly curious who "having ears, do not hear..." For Bono, in order for art to be legitimate as a prophetic form, it must be iconoclastic, unpredictable, outrageous—even at times offensive.

This is not an uncommon view in avant-garde Christian art circles. Frankly, I believe it oversimplifies several issues, given that the self- and media-driven nature of modern music is dangerously open to a self-deluded anarchy of the soul.

Oversimplified, too, is the understanding of the audience. At 51, I question how many adoring teens have the depth of experience of the dual developments of the technopsyche and rock and roll's subliminal power to interpret the imagery. But for all that, what I am convinced of is the basic integrity and, at times, somewhat obscure genius of their present journey.

Second, the elevation of U2 as icons of rock 'n' roll for believers placed upon them an intolerable unreality. As one of them said, "We are no different from anyone else. We struggle from day to day to keep alive our faith and understanding like anyone else" (paraphrased).

If people are to believe, it can't be in U2. In one sense Bono declares the darker side of U2, and of all of us, to explode all the idolatrous tendencies of our age, which are extraordinarily exemplified in the televangelist superstardom myth.

Third, U2 has an intellectual (if undisciplined) native drive to reflect on culture in innovative and outrageous ways. While we may not feel comfortable with all the images or reported statements and rumors (who takes them seriously anyway!), a community supposedly based on grace should surely struggle in prayer and hope for its children in an age of chaos and abandonment.

Well, what of the Zooropa tour? Having not seen it yet I am limited to the copious media reports, snatched conversations with Bono and Larry in an Irish café, and the severely limiting audio base of my CD. One thing is for sure—U2 have innovated to the point where the medium is substantially the message.

Line by line analysis of lyrics—the this-is-subtly-a-spiritual-statement-about-that type of analysis—totally misses the point. The *Zooropa* tour is a pantomime of farce; a mocking extravaganza of absurdity "impudently sending up technology and the video age," turning their silver suits and shades into self-mockery and the blaspheming of the pop star world.

The problem for many bewildered good folk is that they take it all too literally and too seriously. As Jackie Hayden said in *Select*, "There are two Bonos—one is the...saint with all the problems of the world on his shoulders and some answers in his heart. The other Bono knows that Bono is not to be taken too seriously."

One of the best descriptions of the tour is in the September edition of *Juice* which, describing the new U2 in an "environment of mega video screens, computerized graphics, and interactive technologies ... slogans ... psychobabble and truisms," says that the band demonstrates "that it was all fatuous AND profound." As the report said, some of the absurd send-ups and deliberately inept music moments bring crazed audience responses indicating that, if U2 burp three times into a microphone, people still go wild.

How overdue is a response to cyberspace absurdity in the face of such a contrived and ludicrous world? The sudden projection on superscreen of past rock superstars interactive with the live band—in all a visual mockery of the deadly seriousness surrounding the electronic rock idolatry—is a daring extravaganza of self-ridicule reminiscent of Jeremiah's bizarre behavior, only in the form of modern sardonic epicurean humor.

Zooropa, according to Adam Clayton, extends the friendship with irony. "It is like a critique of Europe. It is like okay, yeah, a real united Europe... so what? What is a united Europe? And has anything changed? Shouldn't you be questioning that?" *(Juice)*. *Juice* asserts: "...on Zoo TV is history meaningless. Strangely all that's left is music."

If art is the nerve ends of the sensual, suffering soul of humanity, U2 may currently be an authentic form of prophetic utterance, albeit for some, in an art form bewildering and disorientating. But then, without unfamiliarity who ever knows they're lost?

For U2, privately the passions for human rights, for Amnesty International, and for reality remain intact. The inextinguishable fire of protest burns on.

But two things trouble my frequent prayers for the unique pilgrimage that is U2. Will they survive the soul-destroying trilogy of power, praise, and possessions in spite of their very tweaking of its serious nose? And will the community of faith go outside the confines of the virtuous village to welcome the apparent prodigals, while they may appear to be "still a great way off"?

As one critic observed, just at the time when everybody else is getting unplugged and escaping to the nostalgia at the '60s and '70s, U2 have plugged into the madness of the '80s and '90s. Escapist nostalgia is certainly no challenge to the techno-urban society. Maybe, just maybe, U2-driven cyber-cynicism may spark revelation and resistance.

U2

CHAPTER

8

ON THE ROAD

The US Festival was a combination commercial media event and Woodstock for the '80s, televised to millions in 1983. One of the true standout images from that telecast is the young lead singer from this Irish punk band called U2 climbing up a lighting tower.

More than so many bands that fall by the hard shoulder of the music business, U2 made their reputation and won over their earliest supporters with their live shows. Remarkably, they manage to keep their performances exciting, vibrant, and relevant even after twenty years. U2 is a band that can, within a stadium of 60,000 strangers, encourage a feeling of intimacy.

They manage this both with personalities large enough to project across a football field to the people in the upper boxes or behind the stage and with technology that amplifies these personalities to the extent necessary to achieve that reach.

In the '90s such endeavors took the form of theatricality and artifice: U2 seemed in competition with showman rockers like David Bowie on the one hand, and Parliament on the other, creating a set that was both high-tech and bizarre. The lemon that turned into a mirror ball took P-Funk's mother ship to another dimension. The tongue-in-cheek depravity of 100-foot-tall swizzle sticks spoke again of Bowie's staging. Yet U2 pulled it off as something unique.

And then there's the U2 community; a syndicate of the loyal and faithful who meet six nights a week in hundreds of different venues over the course of a touring year.

These elements, along with their enthusiasm and spirit that has not lessened in over two decades, are perhaps the key to their continued success. Where for the Rolling Stones going on tour and trotting out the old hits at $300 a ticket smacks of cynicism, U2 makes you believe their show is all about you. They direct this energy directly at you, the concert-goer. They did this for 3,000 in 1980 and they did it for 60,000 in 2002.

U2

Honesty Goes out of Control

David McCullough
***Sounds* magazine, December 8, 1979**

U2's lead singer Bono is tense and anxious about the band's first gig outside their native Ireland. While the gear is set up he stands with the rest of the band around the side of the stage. Guitarist Edge's hand is in plaster following a car crash, and they don't know how he'll cope. U2's feeling of tension comes, it seems, through no straining from the notion that they're already a touted commodity with two significant front covers under their belts, but from a feeling close to bursting with an urgent need to get their music across.

"We'll show them, we've got to show them, you know..." The floodgates spread wonderfully open as the band sweep elegantly into "Concentration." Everything pours out, the sound soars with a kind of majestic relief. U2 are at least where they belong, progressing their fresh, vigorous r 'n' r sensibility to the perimeters of a wider audience.

It was good seeing a band taking the stage by the throat once again. U2 has so much to say and so little space to say it in, as support to the Dolly Mixture. The space they had was stuffed brilliantly with a smart sampling of their potential.

U2 are about four people. Their music has minimum distortion and, free of fad or image associations, their songs reflect the strength of the four individuals. Imagine that strange quality that everybody used to aimlessly tag to Penetration, that weird thing called "honesty," and you come close to the U2 vibe. There's a kind of naïve, young, rushing feeling about their music, flickering at times between the Skids, Penetration, Doors, the Fall, and Swell Maps.

The guitar sound is a tackier, rawer Adamson breed: the overall noise sprawls about as decadently and as exotically as Penetration at times did: in singer and spokesman Bono they already have a focal point as engaging and charismatic as a Mark Smith, somebody who can pull all the various band attitudes together, somebody who gives new and disarming angles of parody to the Heavy Lead Singer role (at one point he excitedly asked for a fag from the audience, and heroically receiving it, spent the rest of the song coolly trying to light it and failing).

Bono is U2's fall guy. He gives the kind of warmly instructive performance that's at the root of the band's music. Bono is the archetypical mixed-up, fucked-up teenager who doesn't know where or how to ask for direction. He says, "I've heard a lot about all your lovely fads and fashions over here. Well U2 aren't either of those..." and the music reflects the unaffected, honestly searching character of Bono's frantic, obsessive performance.

You see, I've this strange notion that you shouldn't have to leave a gig feeling deflated, that you shouldn't be let down because you've seen something that's saying it's better than you or that somebody has told you is better. U2 seem to possess the ability to instruct a wide, immediate audience about myths and lies and dark areas of modern living, particularly relevant to the young, male individual. The sugarcoating for these bitter pills you're invited to swallow is the most refreshing new pop music I've heard all year, powerfully pointing along a scintillating guitar sound, a flexible rhythm base, and Bono's ever-improving, identifying vocals.

The effect is, three or four times in 20 minutes, having the hairs on the back of your neck stand on end, startled by an elegant guitar or bass flourish or moved by the collective, climactic inner tension of songs like "The Dream Is Over," "Inside Out," or "Shadows and Tall Trees." The unifying, centrifugal force of the music on something like the first recent Irish CBS release "Out of Control" (available here on import—try Rough Trade) is simply remarkable.

Small chinks linger; the exaggerated pap spoof of "Boy/Girl" and the line "I open doors for you so I can shut your face" meaning the only reason men open doors for women is to assert their male superiority, which in itself is far more effective than any self-righteous sexist histrionics.

All the way there's a lot of soul on display, a lot of laying things and ideas right on the line. Really, I can only recommend you go far out of your way to catch them before they return home at Christmas. Bono, like some r 'n' r evangelist says, "We'll need your support." I'd say U2 give the lie to a lot of current youth-rebelling masturbation.

Irish U2, a Young Quartet, Plays at the Ritz

Stephen Holden
***The New York Times*, March 9, 1981**

The Irish rock quartet U2, which has received extravagant critical praise in the British press, made a strong showing at the Ritz on Saturday. For such an accomplished band, U2 is unusually young. Ranging in age from 18 to 20, its members met three years ago at a Dublin secondary school. Yet their sound, and eclectic hard rock with a mystically romantic strain, makes them one of the most harmonically sophisticated rock bands to emerge in recent years.

U2's musical focus is its gifted guitarist, "The Edge" Evans, whose extended lyrical guitar flights have a muscularity and an exotic flavor similar to Tom Verlaine. Mr. Evans knows exactly how far to push his mysticism without its turning sickly, and his best solos have a passionate emotionality that is rare in rock these days.

Bono Hewson, U2's lead singer, has a moderately strong voice that was partially drowned out at the Ritz. This was a shame, since the band's material is of considerable interest. Most of the songs on its debut album, *Boy*, are visionary reflections of adolescence, with lyrics that have a consciously poetical ring. Their stark imagery is well served by extended modal melodies. Where poetically ambitious rock bands tend to get mired in their visions, U2 brings to its purpose a healthy balance between energy and lyricism.

U2: Peace with Honor

Jeff Nesin
***The Village Voice,* May 24, 1983**

As the ecstatic young coed crowd cheering U2's second encore swarmed over the front of the Palladium stage last Wednesday night. I watched with pleasure, feeling older though not particularly wiser. Touring sold-out halls on the crest of *War*, their third album, and the sales amid airplay phenomenon of the year, the young Irish band has forged a coalition that center-left politicos would sell their mamas for: millions of young people like themselves, frightened and frustrated by escalating nuclear eschatology, searching earnestly for an activist though (and this is essential) nonviolent resolution. If you haven't watched the evening news lately you may not realize that the actual political arms of this new coalition are themselves the airplay phenom of the early '80s.

Though I was born one week after the atomic bomb was dropped on people, I have always expected to live out my appointed days. But recently it's been evident that large numbers of teenagers, adolescents, even children now fully expect that their appointments will be cancelled by person or persona unknown, so a vast anti-militarist ground swell isn't much of a surprise. In years past, as a foot soldier in many similar sorties, I came to believe, at least theoretically, in the efficacy of armed combat; clearly, the Vietcong didn't shoot down helicopters with their karma. So I watched across a distance that I'm embarrassed to call wisdom as Bono, U2's lead singer and frontman, stormed around the stage brandishing a huge white flag, obviously feeling as he sang, "too right to be wrong." There again, my personal experience indicates that right and wrong have had little to do with history, though they have been marshaled effectively by surviving historians, Still, as a vision shared, undeniable righteousness is thrilling. U2 was thrilled, their audience was thrilled and, truth be told, I was, too.

I don't mean to dwell on issues that are no larger a part of what U2 do than any of the elements of the band's Cinerama sound. The Edge (if his mother doesn't mind, why should I?) has become a very self-effacing guitar hero. Laboring as long and hard on the furious rhythm tracks as on the leads, moving deftly from lap steel to old hollow-body to snazzy Gibson to get the perfect line or fill, he plays—like young Steve Cropper—only what is necessary. And Bono sounds and moves like Paul Rodgers did when he was Free, but with a smoother, more powerful top and no blues rasp—in fact, no blues at all. Massive echo makes them almost Zeppy, but with a crucial difference: Bono's genuine warmth and the band's overwhelming desire to give something to their fans.

So it comes back to attitude after all. In the pop coliseum of the '70s and '80s (sworn to fun, loyal to none), content of any sort, much less urgent content from a commercially successful act is in itself thrilling. Still, my exhilaration and their popularity derive principally from the fact that they write fine songs (that they mean) and, with producer Steve Lilywhite—the right man for the job— make great records of them, beacons in the FM fog. *War* has already yielded two impressive radio hits. "New Year's Day," a steadfast affirmation of Solidarity's struggle, showcases imaginative playing wholly in the service of the song—now a U2 trademark. In concert the Edge showed himself a master of the appropriate, taking the critical guitar solo from the piano stool in typically low-key fashion.

The follow-up, "Sunday Bloody Sunday," with more of their striking, echoed choir-loft backing vocals, is about the ravage and contradictions of the "troubles" in Ulster. Again, not your usual pop fare. The obvious—perhaps only—antecedent in this tough territory is the Clash, and in interviews U2 proudly call themselves "a garage band from garageland." Nonetheless, though a noisy, ash-can-lid drum mix may fool the casual listener, their recorded (and live) sound is precise, compelling, and attractive and *War* offers substantial variety and range as well. The next single, "'Two Hearts Beat as One," is just what it seems, a heartbeat love song with gusto and a high danceability quotient. Then there's my current fave, "The Refugee," a politically acute chant (and it's hard to be politically acute in rock and roll—or anywhere—without nihilism) that reminds me of pygmy hocketing. And "Had Light," with its sweetly soulful vocal. And "Like a Song," a renovated "Street Fighting Man" that doesn't settle for ambivalence: "A new heart is what I need/Oh God, make it bleed." And finally the lovely, soothing "40," loosely extrapolated from the 40th Psalm (cf. "Chapter 27," "Tomorrow Never Knows," "By the Rivers of Babylon," etc.). Three of the four band members are practicing Christians, not exactly a grotesque anomaly, but not that commonplace in rock and roll, either. Though ambient spirituality suffuses some of their lyrics, Spirit in Flesh they ain't, and they're never so benighted as to suggest that prayer changes things. Not that different from Richard Thompson, actually, though the iconography is more familiar and familiarity often breeds just what you'd expect. Wherever their personal grace derives, I was certainly amazed at how *haimisher* and non-manipulative the band—as stars—were on stage, making abundantly clear that there was no human distance or difference between them and their fans.

Early in last Wednesday's show Bono declared, "We're not just another English fashion band passing through. We're an Irish band and we're here to stay," and I can only hope he's right. I have slowly come to feel that U2 is as important as any band I have ever cared about. And why should you care? Because, Mr. and Ms. America, U2 sure sound good. And to these ears they sound like they believe what they say. You can believe what you like. All you need to do is turn it up and say "amen" to no more happy wars and sad love songs.

U2 Starts National Tour on a Political Note

Robert Palmer
***The New York Times*, April 4, 1987**

TEMPE, Ariz., April 3—A national tour by the Irish rock band U2 got off to a controversial start Thursday night at Arizona State University in Tempe. The group issued a statement before the show deploring Gov. Evan Mecham's recent rescission of a state holiday on the Rev. Dr. Martin Luther King, Jr.'s birthday, and announcing that they had made a financial contribution to a committee for the Governor's recall.

The rock quartet's singer and lyricist, Paul Hewson, who goes by the name Bono Vox, added further complications when he partly lost his voice shortly before the concert. "I must have stayed out in the sun too long," he told the capacity crowd at Arizona State's Activity Center. "I'm glad you're singing with me tonight."

The crowd of about 14,300 did sing the choruses to U2's songs, offering the band sufficient encouragement to turn what could have been a disastrous show into an affirmation that the bond between U2 and its audience is a special one.

Feedback from the Audience

"I've heard people say this, but tonight the fans really were the stars of the show," said Dave (The Edge) Evans, U2's guitarist, afterward. "The songs that we play often deal with belief in something, whether it's our support for Amnesty International, or Martin Luther King, or just having some spiritual ideals and some dignity. I think people relate to that, and we get this feedback from the audience. That's what makes our shows so special. If we aren't feeling that buoyant when we go onstage, we're just taken up by the crowd and carried along"

U2 arrived in the Phoenix-Tempe area a week ago to begin final rehearsals for their 13-city, 30-concert spring tour of the United States, which concludes with six nights at New Jersey's Brendan Byrne Arena May 11–13 and May 15–17. With the band's new album, *The Joshua Tree* (Island Records), No. 1 in Britain and No. 3 in America, the demand for tickets has been exceptional. Front row seats for Thursday's show, which cost $15.50 at the box office, were reportedly changing hands for $150 or more. Ticket brokers said they had seen nothing like the demand since Bruce Springsteen's last tour.

"Shortly after we arrived," Mr. Evans recalled, "I was sitting by the pool at the hotel reading the paper, and I read that the Doobie Brothers, who were planning to do a benefit reunion concert at Arizona's Gus River Indian Reservation, had moved the event out of state because of the Governor's rescission of the Martin Luther King holiday. I was just shocked.

"The band got together and we were all appalled, but it was just too late to cancel the shows. If we had known about this earlier, we would have canceled. As it was, we decided we had to issue a statement, to let the fans and the press know how we felt." U2 has written and recorded two songs in praise of Dr. King, "Pride (In the Name of Love)" and "MLK."

Let's Return to the '60s

After the Los Angeles band Lone Justice opened Thursday's concert with a rousing set, the show's promoter, Barry Fey, read U2's statement to the audience. "We were outraged when we arrived in Arizona last weekend and discovered the climate created by Governor Mecham's rescission of the holiday honoring Dr. Martin Luther King, Jr.," the statement said. Each sentence of the statement was greeted by thunderous cheers and applause.

After the reaction had begun to die down at the end, Mr. Fey added a thought of his own. "Let's return to the '60's," he said, "and let the music lead the way to justice."

The Governor's press secretary, Ron Bellus, called the entire issue "a legal-technical matter." The holiday had been established through an executive order by Governor Mecham's predecessor, Bruce Babbitt, without the consent of the Legislature. Governor Mecham reviewed the executive order and declared it invalid. "U2 is not familiar with the laws of the state of Arizona," Mr. Bellus told the press. "They should have lobbied against Governor Babbitt for creating an illegal holiday."

U2 hit the stage at 9:15 P.M. and in the charged atmosphere established an immediate rapport with the audience. Mr. Vox, normally an emotional, open-throated singer, was hoarse and missing notes almost from the first, but Mr. Evans and U2's bassist, Adam Clayton, helped him out on the songs' choruses, while the drummer Larry Mullen, Jr. laid down a brisk backbeat. On songs like the group's early hit "I Will Follow" and "Pride! (In the Name of Love)," the audience's singing seemed as loud as the band's.

The group might not have been able to carry off the concert without the audience's good will. But it was a tribute to the ensemble's musicianship as well. Mr. Evans played with clarity and an incisive rhythmic momentum, filling out the band's sound, with the judicious use of finger-picking patterns and resonant drones. His harmonies often bounced off Mr. Clayton's full-bottomed bass lines in a manner that suggested the presence of additional instruments.

After the show, Mr. Evans noted that his formative influences included two guitarists associated with New York's late '70's punk rock scene—Tom Verlaine of Television and Robert Qulne of Richard Hell and the Voidoids—along with earlier favorites such as Led Zeppelin's Jimmy Page and Keith Richards of the Rolling Stones.

Grand Gestures Work in Concert

"I've been trying to delve more into blues and country music lately," Mr. Evans said, "going back to the originals, like Robert Johnson and Hank Williams. What we're trying to do musically is to combine or bridge what I would call the post-blues approach of the punk rock period with some of the better aspects of the earlier, more blues-oriented rock. As for the use I make of drones, that comes, I think, from being Irish; it's like the sound of the pipes."

The grand gestures of Bono Vox's lyrics—the concern with victims of economic inequities and political repression, the appeals to spiritual aspirations, the desire to function as what he calls "a conspiracy of hope"—can sometimes seem overly earnest on records, but they worked well in concert, getting the songs' points across in spite of the lyricist's ragged singing. In rock and roll, it's the feeling that counts in the end, and the feeling was there. At times, the concert was moving in a way a more polished performance could not have been.

After the show, Bono Vox whispered hoarsely that the group could and would do better at subsequent performances. But the crowd, which left peaceably without the vociferous demand for multiple encores that become such a rock concert ritual, seemed well satisfied.

A band spokesman said tonight that Saturday night's concert had been canceled on the suggestion of Mr. Vox's doctor, but that unless complications developed, the remainder of the tour would be carried out as planned.

Achtung Baby, It's U2 in Paris

Alice Rawsthorn
***Financial Times* (London), May 9, 1992**

In his goodie-goodie old days, Bono used to sweep on stage clad in black leather and swathed in shades to treat his audience to a prayer. These days U2's lead singer is still in leathers and shades, but he welcomes himself to Paris in the bad-boy rocker tradition with "The only problem with this city is you never get to bed."

U2 kicked off the European leg of their Zoo TV tour at the Omnisport, Bercy on Thursday night. Zoo TV, so-called in deference to Zoo Station in Berlin where the band made most of *Achtung Baby.* Its latest album is both a set-piece for the album itself and a video extravaganza on the TV-addicted, inner urban angst of the 1990s. The show started with a sequence of songs from *Achtung Baby*—all shrieking electronic emotion and dark, despairing themes. The set, an electronic playpen of giant video screens and clapped-out cars in fluorescent colors, was a perfect backdrop.

U2 was at its best when taking *Achtung Baby's* angst to extremis. "The Fly" was a wonderful whirl of raw electronics accompanied by a staccato sequence of words—"Luxury," "Chaos," "Condom," "Flower"—thumping on and off the videos. The pathos of Bono's voice thrusting through the electronics in "One" and "Tryin to Throw Your Arms Around the World" was eerily evocative of the individual's struggle to surface through the clutter of everyday life.

The only hitch was that there was little attempt to adapt *Achtung Baby* for a live performance. Most of the time this was fine. But one song, "Mysterious Ways," fell flat, sounding as though it sorely needed the support of the techno-toys in the studio.

This is ironic given that it was only when all the electronic paraphernalia was stripped away and band abandoned the electronic playpen main stage for a small podium—and in the second part of the show, when it rattled through its old rocker numbers—that you realized how talented U2 really is. The crowd, which had howled its appreciation throughout, went wild, as if with relief, whenever the strobes were switched off and it could see the band clearly on the stage.

The real appeal of Zoo TV was how neatly it illustrated its own message. A rock concert is, after all, the perfect platform to illustrate how individualism can be crushed by the mechanics of modern media, marketing, and merchandising. At times U2 looked like victims of their own plot—as the cameras chased them around the stage to video them against their own videos, and Bono, the singer who used to start his shows with prayer, splayed himself crucifixion-style across one of the biggest screens of all.

Reluctant Rock Star: How U2's Adam Clayton Learned to Play—and Conquer the World Onstage

Gregory Isola
***Bass Player*, November 11, 2000**

Somewhere between Bono (the world's biggest rock star), The Edge (the world's coolest rock guitarist), and Larry Mullen, Jr. (the world's baddest rock drummer) stands U2 bassist Adam Clayton. "I just keep the bottom end moving," shrugs the affable 40-year-old. "I'm right on a good day, but there are so many great cats out there. Really I'm just glad to be in the club."

The release of *All That You Can't Leave Behind* marks two decades that U2 has been in the bona fide rock star club. But while other top-drawer rockers learned to play in bedrooms and dank bars—before friends and forgivable fans—Clayton's evolution as a player took place on the world's biggest stages. Of course, superstardom was never the point. The three Dublin schoolboys who answered Mullen's ad for bandmates really just wanted to see what it was like to stand onstage and bash out three-minute songs—and they were terrible. That is, until they started writing their own songs. "Even up through our first few records we got by on very little, at least musically," Clayton grimaces. "But we were always able to make something of it, just in the way we played together."

U2 created an unprecedented blend of stark, post-punk instrumental textures, spiritual lyrics, and over-the-top bombast that resulted in some of the most majestic rock music of the 1980s and '90s. Along the way, Clayton went from struggling to hold together simple eighth-note grooves to incorporating bass influences from Motown to reggae into his ever-evolving style. As elemental riffs like "With or Without You" and "New Year's Day" gave way to the Jamerson-style bounce of "Angel of Harlem" and "Sweetest Thing," Clayton quietly became one of rock's reigning bass heroes—whether he knows it or not.

BP: Many see 1983's* War *as a breakthrough for U2. You in particular became a distinct musical voice.

> *AC*: On the early records, it was really just a case of Edge and Larry struggling to keep the whole thing together. We were all surviving on

minimal technique, and the formula in those early days was 4/4 bass over a relatively complex beat from Larry, with Edge doing his arpeggios over the top. But by the time we got to *War*, the songs were more structured, and the bass sound was featured more. Also, I suppose by then I could actually play things in time—and in tune—so I was able to be a bit more melodic.

BP: "New Year's Day" remains your most famous riff.

AC: That actually grew out of me trying to work out the chords to the Visage tune "Fade to Grey." It was a kind of Euro-disco dance hit, and somehow it turned into "New Year's Day."

BP: What else were you listening to during those formative years?

AC: I was drawn to things I thought were either sexy or aggressive—or both. I really liked the violence of what Jean Jacques Burnel was doing on the first couple of Stranglers records. He had this mighty sound of his own, but it was also mixed with their keyboard player's Hammond organ bass for a very interesting effect. And there was Bruce Foxton of the Jam and Joy Division's Peter Hook, and of course Paul Simonon of the Clash. His playing was more sexy than violent, plus it was a bit more dubby, which I wasn't fully tuned into at the time.

Later on I got into the classic Bob Marley records with Aston Barrett. I always liked the position the bass took on those records, as opposed to the position the bass is usually given. Same with John Entwistle—he plays remarkable stuff that can be hard to follow, but I love that he refuses to be put in the background.

BP: Is it true you were U2's musical leader in the beginning, back in the late '70s?

AC: Perhaps—but that's only because punk rock had just happened, so it wasn't really important that you knew how to play so long as you had some equipment [laughs]. I'd simply decided I was going to be a musician, so I got this Ibanez copy of a Gibson EB-3 and a Marshall head, and I guess those crucial ingredients made the others figure I knew a bit more about music. I did know a thing or two about my equipment, but I certainly didn't know anything about playing.

BP: What were the band's goals in those days?

AC: The ambition was just to end the song together! We had these interminable rehearsals where we would never actually get to the end of the song. But we also wanted to be part of what we felt was going on. In terms of musical values, it was a time of throwing off the idea that people who played guitars in bands were these rock gods who were to be obeyed and saluted. We got off on the idea that you could play a three-minute song with a few basic chords as fast as you possible could, and that was a good enough reason to be onstage. It meant that you had a life right now—that you didn't have to spend three years in your bedroom trying to figure out how to play "Stairway to Heaven."

***BP: Your playing got a lot groovier later on, starting with 1988's* Rattle and Hum.**

AC: That may have been me getting lucky in a way. It's always depended on the tune with us, so as our songwriting became more developed and there were better chord progressions, I found I would fall into more interesting things. I wouldn't literally know where I was headed when I started out, but Larry's drums have always told me what to play, and then the chords tell me where to go. Because of this, my parts are very much created as the song is evolving.

BP: Does the whole band compose this way?

AC: We do write in an unconventional way, I suppose. If we try to arrange a song that's already been worked out on acoustic guitar, it's hard for us. But if we start with a few bits and then work around each other to develop the song, we seem to go to more interesting places. "Bullet the Blue Sky" is a great example; it's really just one musical moment, extended in time. Larry started playing that beat, and I started to play across it—as opposed to with it—while Edge was playing something else entirely. Bono said, "Whatever you guys are doing, don't stop!" So we kept playing, and he improvised that melody. "Please" [*Pop*] was another happy accident. One of our producers, Howie B., was playing a record in the studio, and I started to play a bass part over the recording. It created these strange grooves and keys, and my line really began to work only after Howie stopped the record.

BP: How important is your three-piece lineup to this free-form approach?

AC: Three pieces can be limiting, but there's something to be said for learning your chops as a three-piece. If you can hang together that way, it becomes easy to know if the instruments and people you're adding on top are right or not. I'm grateful this was never a band with a keyboard player and another guitar player, because then what chops would I have ever needed?

Still, we've almost always augmented our records with keyboards and other things. We got a lot of attention with the *Pop* record, since we'd all become very interested in club music and computer-generated loops. But those were things we'd been using pretty much from *Unforgettable Fire* onward. Lots of bands in the late '90's were saying, "We use the studio as an instrument"—but we were doing that with Brian Eno as early as 1984. It's not that we don't like what U2 does naturally; it's just that we sometimes want to stretch what U2 can be, and where it can go.

BP: Unlike much of U2's '90s work, the new record is quite stripped-down.

AC: We came to *All That You Can't Leave Behind* feeling that the unique thing about U2 is the very thing we do when we get together. That sounds vague, but the idea with this record was to look at the band itself, and to realize that is our strength—that's what nobody else has. So as a consequence the songs on this record are very stripped down. Everyone simply contributed the essence of what they've always done. For my part, it was about finding what was necessary to get the song right, and not consciously looking for any "Wow!" moments. In fact, in several cases we simply kept performances that began as demos from when we began writing for this record, almost two years ago.

BP: Does past U2 music ever get in the way of new U2 music?

AC: For us there's U2 music, and then there's everything else. And between records, we listen to the stuff that interests us; we really don't listen to much U2. We're always re-establishing the fact that we share musical tastes in the same way we did 20 years ago. The music we like now may be different from what it was then, but our shared tastes give us a way of judging things we can still trust. So if everyone in the band is saying they don't like something, you know why, since you know their frame of reference. And every time we make a new U2 record, we bring along that frame of reference.

BP: What has it been like to play with Larry for over 20 years?

AC: After we'd been together a couple of years and we were doing our first record, people were talking about Bill Wyman and Charlie Watts having played together for 20 years. Everyone was saying they must really have it down—but I remember thinking, what are you talking about? At that time I didn't appreciate what they did at all. Now I appreciate it much more. When you've been playing with the same group—and particularly the same drummer—for that amount of time, you don't really need to talk too much about it; you just do it. So in some ways it's gotten simpler over time, and in some ways I'm less reverent about my parts. You don't worry as much; you just know you don't have to overplay.

BP: You still have a way with a simple part. The eighth-note line in "Beautiful Day" changes feel throughout.

AC: I'm sure it does! That's probably Larry making me sound good. When we put that track down I was actually intentionally not thinking too much about it. I wanted to just go with it, because it is really a basic eighth-note part. Sometimes when I'm playing, I get to a place where the bass seems to find its own rhythm, and then it becomes just a matter of which notes to push and which ones to hold back on. It's a discipline, really.

I once read an interview with Tony Levin where he said, "I'm a bass player—I like doing the same thing over and over again." And that's exactly it, you know? For me, that discipline comes from years and years of playing with Larry, and knowing he has a certain rhythm, and certain ways of producing his sound. Our two approaches just get mixed up into one.

BP: Are you still playing your '72 Precision?

AC: I am. It's got a bit less varnish than it once had, but it's still around. I see photographs of it from different tours, and I can see the varnish gradually wearing off. It's a really light instrument, which is fantastic, because it's got this nice brightness without losing any bottom end. I'm always changing something on it, but it's still pretty much the same instrument I've always played. I did put a Jazz neck on it very early on; I find the Jazz neck suits my left hand better. The Precision is a painful, physical thing to do battle with. The Jazz is a bit more ladylike.

BP: You've also played some odd custom basses over the years. What do you listen for in a bass?

AC: I like a clean top end that can cut through, but I also like a big, air-moving bottom. The Precision has always given me that, so the custom basses I've used have always been selected because they complement my Precision. That big yellow thing—the banana bass—that I played on the *Pop* tour is a great-sounding example. It was made by Auerswald, the German guy who makes Prince's guitars.

Recently I've actually been playing Jazz basses, though, because I've been using my fingers a lot more, and I've been after a bit more definition. I recorded the new album with two Jazz basses—a '61 and a '72. I also used my old Gibson Les Paul Recording bass. It's a short-scale thing with this great, round bottom that just moves air. It's great in the studio.

BP: You've always blended a direct line with a miked SVT rig, but this record sounds different.

AC: This time around I was after something that sounded good at really low volume. I'd like to say it's about tone, but it might just be age [*laughs*]. So I recorded with an Ashdown 800 head and the matching cab with two 12s and one 15. Also, we moved around a lot in the studio this time, trying different rooms and all, so I used an Ashdown 400 4x10 combo, too. Occasionally we'd add extra bottom end with a dbx 120XP Subharmonic Synthesizer—but these days I don't much. I've come to prefer the pure, clean sound of the bass. I like the physical effect of a good bass sound; that's really what it's all about. And that's why the best place to stand when you see a band is always in front of the bass rig!

BP: Which lines on the new record have this effect?

AC: "In a Little While" and "Elevation" both have that physical bass punch. I always think the bass should be much, much louder on songs like that. They're both fairly simple in terms of structure and chords, but the bottom end is moving, and that's what's beautiful. "Kite" is another line that, although it's basic, seems to really talk.

BP: After all these years, what are the best and worst things about being U2's bassist?

AC: Sometimes we get photographed a bit too much, and for the wrong kinds of papers [*laughs*]. You feel like saying, "I just play bass! You don't need me in your paper!" But it's a celebrity culture, and we don't suffer for it too much. We're good at hiding behind music, but sometimes people do get excited for the wrong reasons.

As for the good parts, we've got great fans. They follow us through all sorts of changes, and in many ways they encourage us to continue pursuing music that excites us. But the best thing really is that I get to hang out with three friends and musicians. And if I get stuck, in whatever way, I've got three guys who are willing and able to help. That's a great thing.

CHAPTER

9

ON THE RECORD

Most people know U2 from their recorded music—heard over the radio, brought home on CDs (and vinyl and cassettes in the early days), and even downloaded off the Internet. Concerts, while powerful, are ephemeral. Recordings last (virtually) forever.

U2 have sold over one hundred million recordings worldwide. *The Joshua Tree* has gone diamond (ten million sold in the U.S.), and *Achtung Baby* is not far behind.

U2's songs are a staple on "classic rock" stations—even their newer ones like "One," which became a balm for wounded psyches during the days, weeks, and months after the September 11th terrorist attacks. This music spoke to us; helped soothe us. U2 records became an important part of what got many through this trying time.

Critically, U2 records are often loved, but not necessarily unconditionally or universally. These reviews reflect the way people who wrote them felt at the time. Most critics have reviews they wish they could retract. When Bob Christgau puts out his decade-wide consumer guides, he reserves the right to do just that. For good or bad or ugly, these are the opinions of people who are paid to have opinions on popular music.

Critical Discography

Perusing the U2 Catalog
Jim DeRogatis
***Chicago Sun-Times*, May 6, 2001**

With a quarter-century's history behind it, U2 has actually been three or four very different bands over the course of its long and storied career. The quartet's development can be charted via its recordings, which comprise of one of the most rewarding discographies in rock.

U2-3 EP, 1979 [2.5 stars]

At first, the band trampled its way through standard late '70s punk fare, including material by the Pistols and the Ramones, but its own sound was beginning to emerge on its first recording, a three-song EP that won a following in Ireland but made little or no impact in the U.S. The disc is a collector's item now, of course, but its embryonic sound isn't all that exciting.

Boy, 1980 [3.5 stars]

On the strength of its Irish success, the band signed to Island and recorded its debut album with Steve Lillywhite, a staff producer known for the booming drums and ringing guitars that he gave to new wave artists like Ultravox, Siouxsie and the Banshees, XTC, and the Psychedelic Furs. In retrospect, the relatively stripped-down if echo-laden sound of U2's debut has aged well: it doesn't seem nearly as dated as the work of other enigmatic guitar bands from this era—say, Echo and the Bunnymen, or Big Country, which appeared as a blatant U2 clone in 1983.

The disc yielded two underground hits with "I Will Follow" and "Stories for Boys," but the track that stands as most representative of the early sound is probably "An Cat Dubh," with its massive drums, tinkling bells, minimalist Edge guitar licks, and anthemic Bono chorus. All together now: "Whoa-oh-oh! Whoa-oh-oh!"

October, 1981 [3 stars]

More confident and self-assured, U2 opens its second Lillywhite-produced disc with the classic "Gloria," which builds on the sonic hallmarks of *Boy* while introducing the spiritual themes so important to the musicians in their personal lives (everyone but Clayton is a devout Christian). It's a cheeky move for any rock band to pen a tune called "Gloria" in the wake of Van Morrison's classic, but U2 pulls it off with a song that's almost as great, building to a transcendent choral sing-along ending.

The Christian concerns continue on "Fire," "Rejoice," and "With a Shout," but "Gloria" aside, the disc isn't quite as strong as its predecessor. (The music has aged better than the moody glamour-puss photo of the band on the cover, however. Check those floppy new wave hairdos!)

War, 1983 [3 stars]

Having gotten religion, the quartet from Dublin now gets political. Many fans consider this U2's first great album, but I disagree: While the Lillywhite-produced music is probably the best example of the early U2 sound, with more imaginative arrangements and Edge's stately piano coming on strong, the lyrics of tunes like "Sunday Bloody Sunday," "New Year's Day," and "Seconds" are often heavy-handed, clumsy, and strident. "Gold is the reason for the wars we wage!" Ugh.

The Unforgettable Fire, 1984 [2.5 stars]

Enter U2, Mach Two. Lillywhite is out, and the "ambient atmospheres our specialty" team of Daniel Lanois and Brian Eno is in. Unfortunately, their impact wouldn't really be felt for a while, and this remains a problematic and transitional effort. Lyrically, Bono is becoming increasingly obsessed with the U.S.— witness "4th of July," "Elvis Presley and America," and of course "Pride," a ham-fisted tribute to Martin Luther King, Jr. The singer was never more preachy, more self-righteous, or more insufferable.

The Joshua Tree, 1987 [3.5 stars]

The best example of the band's second incarnation still finds Bono crooning about America, but this time, the critiques and observations in songs like "Bullet the Blue Sky" (about U.S. involvement in El Salvador) and "In God's Country" are much more artful and poetic. Meanwhile, the music on tunes such as "Where the Streets Have No Name" and "With or Without You" finds the band moving into a starker, more mysterious sound that is less easily defined (or parodied), and which rewards repeated listening. Part of the credit is due to a heck of a support team: producers Lanois and Eno inspire the band to stretch out and experiment, Lillywhite comes back to remix several tunes, and a talented young engineer named Flood captures it all on tape.

Rattle and Hum, 1988 [1.5 stars]

Alas, it was one step forward and two steps back. U2 followed the unprecedented commercial success of *The Joshua Tree* with this mix of new material and live tracks that aspire to pay tribute to American roots music but wind up amplifying all the worst traits of *The Unforgettable Fire*. It's awkward, pretentious, ponderous—a real mess. But maybe the band had to get this out of its system before it got where it was going next.

Achtung Baby, 1991 [4 stars]

The group's masterpiece, and the introduction of U2, Mach Three. Under the increasingly powerful spell of Eno, that unparalleled artistic instigator, the band finally abandons all lingering hints of its old chest-thumping and flag-waving in favor of giving a great big postmodern raspberry. But while Bono's live posturing and the whiz-bang technical assault of the subsequent Zoo TV tour were absolutely lousy with irony, the music itself is never cold or alienating. In fact, "One" is probably the most heartfelt and moving song the band has ever recorded.

Overall, *Achtung Baby* stands as a disc that is both resonant of its time and absolutely timeless—the perfect soundtrack for slipping on the virtual reality helmet and flipping through 300 channels of satellite TV while waiting for the ecstasy to kick in.

Zooropa, 1993 [3.5 stars]

Recorded in the midst of the Zoo TV tour, these 10 songs don't have quite the same impact but they do continue the playful experimentation of *Achtung Baby*. Bono in particular has blossomed under Eno's tutelage, just as David Bowie and David Byrne did before him. In keeping with his new stage persona of a Vegas-style Satan, he adopts a darker, more sinister tone on "Daddy's Gonna Pay for Your Crashed Car," "Some Days Are Better Than Others" and the title track, while on other tunes, he successfully tackles Tony Bennett-style crooning ("Babyface") and a Smokey Robinson falsetto ("Lemon").

Bono also sits out for two songs, allowing the band to prove that its identity extends beyond its photogenic frontman. Johnny Cash sings on the wonderfully apocalyptic "The Wanderer," and The Edge does his best Lou Reed imitation on "Numb." This is far from U2's most consistent collection. But you know what they say about consistency.

Pop, 1997 [2 stars]

Have you sensed a pattern here yet? U2 seems to run in cycles of one great breakthrough album, followed by a few strong discs with various refinements, followed by a real stinker. This is another stinker.

Eno isn't around this time—Flood and trip-hopper Howie B. are at the helm—and the disc has a harsh digital sheen that contributes to its incorrect dismissal by some as a "techno" record. The band talked a lot about experimenting with electronic dance music, and they actually made a fairly interesting ambient album in 1995, working with Eno under the name Passengers. But *Pop* might have been better if U2 actually did go techno. Instead, we get tired dinosaur rock.

"Mofo" is a plodding and inferior rewrite of "One"; the chiming guitar break in "Discotheque" reaches back to *Boy*, and "Last Night on Earth" is just U2 circa *The Joshua Tree* tarted up with some electronics. Lyrically, Bono is still "Lookin' for to fill that God-shaped hole," but he wrongly thinks he's going to find what he's looking for in the tired cataloguing of pop-culture icons ("The Playboy Mansion") as well as some lame synthesizers and tired drum patterns. The band seems to be running on empty.

All That You Can't Leave Behind, 2000 [3 stars]

It's hard to say exactly where this effort fits in. It's a departure from *Pop*, to be sure, but as fans and critics have noted, it's a return to an "older" U2 sound—the sound of the second incarnation, more or less. It's an album that anyone who likes the band will find hard to resist, even if it's unlikely to rank as anyone's all-time favorite.

There's no heavy lifting or serious artistic ambition here. "There's nothing you can throw at me that I haven't already heard/I'm just trying to find a decent melody/A song that I can sing in my own company," Bono sings in "Stuck in a Moment You Can't Get out Of," and that pretty much sums things up. The band does deliver a batch of fine melodies— "Beautiful Day," "Wild Honey," "Peace On Earth," "New York"— but there's nothing as potent or memorable as "One," "Even Better than the Real Thing," or "With or Without You."

Are Bono, The Edge, Mullen, and Clayton still capable of making another artistic leap forward a la *Achtung Baby* or *The Joshua Tree*? We'll have to wait and see where the band is going next. Right now, it has given us an apt summation of where it's been, and the perfect fodder for an onstage celebration of all that is U2.

U2

Boy

U2: Aiming for Number 1
Boo Browning
***The Washington Post*, February 27, 1981**

Ambition, in its incubation stage, is often characterized by the afflicted party's willingness to make a fool of himself. Judging from their debut album, *Boy*, the members of U2 have contracted an acute case.

U2 mixes early Pink Floyd/King Crimson guitar vagaries with lots of images concerning rain and shadows and oceans, after the fashion of Jim Morrison; they eschew the ragged punk beat that brought fame and disfavor to their fellow Irishmen, the Boomtown Rats, and adopt nicknames like "The Edge" and "Bono Vox" in the time-honored tradition of rockers from the Beatles to the Sex Pistols. The result, though billed as "unique," is predictably confused.

But the determination with which this band flaunts its symptoms of ambition is mildly infectious. With *Boy*, for example, they have attempted to create a kind of concept album about the pitfalls of post-puberty. While this is not an original idea—indeed, it can be argued that the whole of rock rests on just such a precarious promontory—U2 (ages 18 to 20) boasts the special advantage of having had few other experiences to clutter up the theme.

To U2, the creation of literary hooks (in lieu of musical ones), consisting largely of the word "trees," seems a novel device, although to others it sounds like a dream Joyce Kilmer might have after overindulging in garlic. Similarly, the band offers unabashed metaphors about the ocean splashing "the soul of my shoes" ("The Ocean") and strings of brave non-sequiturs such as the following (from "Shadows and Tall Trees"):

(Out there)
Do you feel in me, anything redeeming,
Anything worthwhile feeling
Is life like a tightrope, hanging on my ceiling.

This kind of sloppy sentimentalism would make Janis Ian queasy; and U2 tends to spice it up with a lot of heartfelt moaning.

But the sheer exuberance that redeems these 11 songs is admirably fresh. Perhaps the restraint and experience that come with age may yet lend U2 an identity all its own. They already have the necessary chutzpah.

U2 Takes the Fifth
Jon Pareles
***The Village Voice*, March 11, 1981**

I worry about U2. With sound commercial advice, these 18, 19, and 20 year olds could turn into an absolutely awful band. They've already got the makings. The acclaim: as Ireland's best new rockers, although none of them is over 20 years old, they could easily go the way of former titleists like the Boomtown Rats, the Undertones, or Horslips. The musical limitations: U2's repertoire consists of long, loud songs, all but one of them in the key of either D or E, none of whose arrangements would exist without lots of reverb. Most of all, the pretensions: U2's lyrics scan like first-person Kansas or de-Gilbraned Moody Blues, with symbols on the order of "a tightrope" and "the ocean." I fully expect *Boy*, U2's debut, to be their best album. And yet, on first hearing, I thought *Boy* eclipsed anything else in Britain's existentialist (hardly psychedelic) revival, and since then I've grown inordinately fond of it. Their set last Saturday at the Ritz was even better than the album. For neurological, psychological, and maybe even sentimental reasons, U2's got me right now.

Neurology first; without it, the rest wouldn't matter. U2 happens to be a great drone band in the Velvets/Byrds/Who line (but without as many foreground distractions), and a good drone bypasses the rational faculties. Granddaddy minimalist composer La Monte Young, who claims that "each harmonically related interval creates its own feeling," which is intensified as the interval is sustained or repeated, recently performed his *The Well-Tuned Piano,* a four-piece that uses resonant tremolo chords sustained for up to half an hour. U2's Ritz show gave me a similar buzz, only louder (more kinetic, too; drummer Larry Mullen, like the Stone's Charlie Watts, can wallop one lick forever and keep it suspenseful). Young could have planned U2's set: a clump of songs in E, a break in which lead singer Bono Hewson addressed the crowd, a clump of songs in D, another break, a clump in E, exit, first encore in D, exit, second encore—the same song that opened the set—in E. In other words, three long drones and two reprises. The song order is different on *Boy*, so I won't try to guess whether U2 deliberately grouped the songs for maximum drone live.

Within their drones, U2 favors a specific interval, the perfect fifth (music theory note: the fifth is a stable interval, but a hollow-sounding one, because we're used to hearing it filled with the major or minor third that turns it into a chord). Guitarist "The Edge" Evans is obsessed with the interval: given the chance, he strums fifths, not chords, as in "Stories for Boys." When a lead seems called for, he tends to play fifth and upper harmonics that could almost be overtones of the bass line. Like the Feelies' guitarist, he'd rather reinforce the drone than solo on it. Meanwhile, Bono's vocal lines often include leaps of a fifth, and when they don't, the bass lines do.

The feeling the open fifth creates—a clear, empty, where's-the-rest-of-me anticipation—meshes exactly [with] U2's lyrics. Their "I" is a hyper-sensitive adolescent boy on the terrifying cusp of adulthood, his feelings out of control, who can't decided whether he should face the outside world or run for his life. Every song takes place in a void fraught with allegory—everyteen's mental landscape—where each step calls for an existential decision. Sometimes the boy seems to understand exactly what's happening to him ("My body grows and grows/It's frightening, you know") and sometimes he's hopelessly overwrought ("Are the leaves on the trees just a living disguise?"). U2 don't reflect on "Growing Up" like Springsteen—they're in it so deep they can't imagine anything else. And the reason it gets me is that I think they mean every word: clever ones, goofy ones, insights, clinkers. The emotions are as cheap and universal as Goffin-King's teen fantasies, but I lived 'em, and you probably did too.

I hesitate to suggest that any pro rock group is innocent, particularly when they've been homeland heroes for a year, but U2 sure act that way. *Boy* shows they don't quite trust their drone instincts, as they allow producer Steve Lillywhite to add entangling glockenspiel hooks. And for all the noise they make, U2's stage presence fits their rhetoric. They move like flotsam in their own music, taking two steps back or sideways for every tentative one forward; when Bono sings, his face looks like an astronaut's distorted by high G-forces. In his second speech to the audience, Bono asked humbly that they give back some "energy," and concluded, "This is a very important night for U2." When they outgrow adolescence, every moment won't seem so important; after a few years on the circuit U2 are likely to become cynical, careerist, or—worse—more self-absorbed. I worry about them looking back on *Boy* with embarrassment, and trying to repudiate it or exploit it. Was there ever a sequel to *Peter Pan?*

U2

War

U2's Inspired War
Mark Peel
***Stereo Review*, August 1983**

Last year was to have been the year for the Irish band U2 to make its mark in the States. The group had even planned to have its own float in New York City's St. Patrick's Day parade. But the presence of leaders of the Irish Republican Army threatened to turn the event into a pro-IRA demonstration; joining it could have been seen as tacit approval of the IRA's terrorism. Instead, U2 returned to Ireland and began work on its first political album after two critically acclaimed but socially noncommittal releases.

War is the inspired result. It is an album of brutal power and aching emotion: everything about it is harsh, jagged, and unyielding, from the muffled bashing of the drums to the impassioned vocals and shattered guitar chords to the gloomy piano that wanders through the beat like a survivor picking through the rubble of a bombed-out city. Lead vocalist Bono's cracking, boyish timbre gives an added intensity to the band's blunt, unguarded playing. There's so much passion and honesty in this music, it's unsettling.

War is one of the finest fruits of new wave rock, but it's new wave in sensibility rather than instrumentation. There are no fancy synthesizer effects here, just the stark sound of the quartet—Bono on vocals and guitar; The Edge on guitars, piano, and vocals; Adam Clayton an bass; and Larry Mullen, Jr. on drums—augmented occasionally by a violin, a trumpet, or a back-up vocal. Just as important as what is in these songs is what isn't in them. U2 spares us the platitudes and snap judgments that pass for "political consciousness" in much of American rock and instead wrestles with the tragic folly of killing in the name of an ideal: "Angry words won't stop the fight/Two wrongs won't make it right." And, while recognizing the futility of war, U2 also recognizes its awful human toll in terms of the death of the spirit as well as the flesh: "A new heart is what I need/Oh God, make it bleed."

U2 doesn't pretend to have the answers to human conflicts—the band doesn't even take sides. What *War* does instead is to convey, in violent sounds and terrifying images, a picture of war's reality that may disturb even us Americans, accustomed as we are to watching the devastation in places like Ulster or Beirut on TV while we calmly eat our dinners. For a people so saturated with reality, yet so safely removed from it, *War* is more than a shock—it's a devastating reproach.

U2

Under A Blood Red Sky

Under A Blood Red Sky
Bob Christgau
***Creem*, April 1983**

They broke AOR rather than pop for the honorable reason that they get across on sound rather than songs, and this live "mini-LP" (34:28 of music listing at $5.99) should turn all but the diehards around. Only one of the two new titles would make a best-of, but the two-from-album-one, one-from-album-two, three-from-album-three oldies selection is the perfect introduction. And although I was right to warn that this was an arena-rock band in disguise, I never figured they'd turn into a great arena-rock band. A-

U2

The Unforgettable Fire

The Unforgettable Fire
Bill Wolfe
***ROCK!* magazine, January 1984**

The Unforgettable Fire is an album full of noble sentiment and subdued passion. Unfortunately, it's sabotaged by vague expression, lackluster melodies, under-utilization of the band's strong suit (The Edge's careening guitar work) and overproduction (courtesy of Brian Eno and Daniel Lanois). Unlike last year's *War*, the melodies are hard to grasp, and the various instruments often blend into a blurry wall of sound.

Fire does have moments of power and grace, most notably on the single, "Pride (In the Name of Love)." The Edge's strident guitar, Larry Mullen's muscular drumming, and Bono's soaring vocals make this tribute to Martin Luther King, Jr. a U2 classic. And U2's new "mature" approach works well on "Bad" and the title track; moody, mid-tempo songs that build to stunning climaxes. "Indian Summer Sky" is also potent and dramatic, as is the prayer-like "MLK," which closes the album. However, songs like "Elvis Presley and America" and "A Sort of Homecoming" simply meander, saying nothing musically or lyrically.

The Unforgettable Fire is clearly a transition album: the next album will determine whether the Irish quartet will continue to pursue this moodier, less aggressive sound or return to their stormy, guitar-driven style. U2 may have wanted to show people they were capable of change, but they were more compelling before.

The Joshua Tree

Love and Friendship, and You're All Invited
Bill Flanagan
***Musician*, April 1987**

Bono is the best folksinger going right now; *The Joshua Tree* proves it. In 1987 the local folk music is rock 'n' roll, so rather than simply play an acoustic guitar, Bono is accompanied by bass, drums, and electric guitar. Rock 'n' roll bands have usually found their fire in tension and competition: instruments daring each other to *top this*, individuals matching talent, and egos, yet how remarkable to find a great rock 'n' roll band born of musical cooperation and unselfishness.

Adam Clayton, Larry Mullen and The Edge play like one person—the web of sound on *The Joshua Tree* gives equal weight to rhythm, melody and harmony, to top, middle, and bottom. Just like an acoustic guitar. Much of the time the three players hold down a steady throb, and let Bono's voice add the tension and dynamics. It's less minimalism than subtlety—if Bono goes from a whisper to a wail, there's no need to start pounding and cascading behind him. And when the whole band does cut loose—as they do on "Exit"—it hits twice as hard.

This is the group's second collaboration with Daniel Lanois and Brian Eno, and their sound is very much a continuation of 1984's *The Unforgettable Fire*; the same misty moodiness, the pings and pangs of Edge's guitar over sheets of drone chords. The prototypical U2 song may turn out to be 1984's "Bad," which contained—as many of these songs do—both passion and gentleness, and was constructed as these are over (what sound like) triggered drums and a blanket of ringing eighth notes. In the two and a half years since *The Unforgettable Fire* so many groups have copied U2 that a stylistic departure seemed likely this time, yet *The Joshua Tree* is more a refinement. Like Dylan and the Stones, U2 has found a musical base that can contain all sorts of songs; rather than abandon it, they are moving further inside the sound, examining its possibilities.

U2 has always proposed a world vision, and their experiences working for Amnesty International have only expanded their ability to connect the dots between different cultures, to find common ground. A lot of songs on *The Joshua Tree* could be loosely called "political" or "religious" but that would miss the point, just as reading U2's lyrics can distract one from the points made by Bono's voice. What is important is the sense of dignity and potency—that the world is a beautiful place, and the greatest injustice is not to cause another pain, but to deprive another of that beauty.

There's a wonderful moment here, on a song called "Trip Through Your Wires," when Bono takes a raggedy harmonica solo. As a mouth organist this guy is never going to threaten Lee Oskar or Toots Thielemans, yet he blows his harp with such joy and abandon that it's hard not to be caught up in his enthusiasm. Then Edge comes in to take a guitar break. Almost any other guitarist would respond to the messy harmonica with something melodic and restrained—for the good purpose of returning the song to musical order and for the nasty purpose of showing up the sloppy harp player. But Edge follows Bono's solo with a thrashing, primitive bent-string frenzy. It's got nothing to do with good musicianship, and everything to do with love and friendship. It's a moment when real happiness jumps out of the grooves and into the room. And while it contains no evidence of planning or conscious decision, those back-to-back solos are a small example of U2's "You, too" philosophy: one guy jumping around by himself is a clown—two guys jumping around together is a movement.

Sure they get too ambitious, and sometimes that looks a little silly. But U2 offers two choices—stand on the side and snicker, or climb down and join in the game. How much invitation do you need?

U2

Rattle and Hum

Elvis Is Alive!?
Tom Carson
***The Village Voice*, November 15, 1988**

By almost any rock and roll fan's standards, U2's *Rattle and Hum* (Island) is an awful record. But the chasm between what it thinks it is and the half-baked, overweening reality doesn't sound attributable to pretension so much as to monumental know-nothingness. The aural companion to the just-out U2 movie, in one of its capacities this double-LP preserves the stadium artifacts of a band already over convinced of its importance in rock history (alternate title: *It Takes a Nation of Millions to Give Us Our Due*). The interpolated new studio material, unconsciously but patently reeking of pampered callowness indulging a new crush, documents the fledgling results of the same band's astonishment that in said history other people, chiefly black and often even non-Irish, preceded them.

In a bid for legitimacy, or something even more annoying, *Rattle and Hum* is decked out like one of the Christmas trees it'll soon be under with borrowed greatness. There are allusions to, songs by or about, or snippets from, among others, Billie Holiday, the Beatles, Jimi Hendrix, Bob Dylan, and B.B. King, two of whom also appear here as sidemen. Given the ambience, however, you often aren't left any too clear as to just whose mantle is being conferred on whom.

The record's an embarrassment; and yet, undoubtedly, neither the band nor its fans will be aware of any reason to act embarrassed. As you might expect in dealing with superstars who've only gotten around to wondering who Elvis was somewhere around the half-dozen LP mark, this band and its audience alike have never found much point in measuring U2 by rock and roll standards.

I ought to make it clear that I'm not talking about music. U2 aren't especially good players, but nearly all the bands I love have been as bad or worse. The question is sensibility. Even punks who manifestly did not know how to play let you know they knew how to listen, but U2 have never given the impression that they spent their youth turned on by records or obsessed with records, or even noticing records particularly—or humming much. Their belated discovery of roots rock might be touching if not for its insular self-congratulation. Apparently, it hasn't dawned on them that other young rockers caught the Memphis train before they did. But the fact that they've only just now become fans, and not noticeably savvy ones at that, leaves you with no choice but to glumly recognize that they aren't primitives but bumpkins.

It isn't even as if they acquit themselves entirely dishonorably. "When Love Comes to 'Town"—Bono's almost disarmingly incongruous attempt at emulating Sam and Dave, and the cut to which B.B. lends the cachet of his voice and guitar—would probably, given a less overeager lead vocal, sound adequate as the fourth or fifth single off the next Robert Cray album. "Angel of Harlem," their Billie Holiday tribute, is maybe less adequate, starting with the confusing fact that this celebration of jazz, written about a blues singer, kicks off by malapropizing the organ intro to "Like a Rolling Stone."

Such gawking enthusiasm is in a tradition: it's basically *the* rite of passage for British Isles bands to wax wonderstruck upon first crossing the pond. But U2's predecessors have generally been canny enough to put a skew on the New World myth by making up about half of it from scratch (the Stones' solution) or, at the very least, satirically underlining their own credulity (the Clash). The most incisive *Rattle and Hum* gets on this topic, in the limp (Mississippi Delta, Route 66, so on) heartland catalogue "Heartland," is the comment "Heaven knows this is a heartland." Oh, for God's sake, Bono: so does *USA Today*.

While these gaucheries at least sound earnest, what they share with the in-concert scenery-chewing is a lack that sticks out like a giveaway third eye from rock's highest-up advocates of so-called Christian values: humility. Look, guys. It's *presumptuous* to cast yourselves as the Dr. Livingstones of the American musicological soul after you've given what sounds like three spins each to one K-Tel and one Folkways compilation album. But in all fairness, the band's latest infatuation makes for at least equal dopiness when applied retroactively to their own oeuvre. "I Still Haven't Found What I'm looking For" is done here as gospel call-and-response, with the New Voices of Freedom choir. That may sound plausible—U2's style up to now could be described as perfecting the difficult art of call without response, so adding the latter can only help, right? Instead, you're left with the impression that these guys don't understand even their own songs very well. It doesn't work, not only structurally—on most lines, the New Voices have to rush the tempo to get the repetition in—but thematically: the emphasis Bono's lyrics put on the singular pronoun, which was disturbing enough *last* year, doesn't exactly lend itself to community-sing fervor.

No less misconceived and corny—their corniness is what makes them presumptuous—are the two staking-our-claim live covers. *Rattle and Hum's* first word's are Bono's onstage announcement, "This is a song Charles Manson stole from the Beatles. Now we're stealing it back." Then the band launches into a "Helter Skelter" that sounds unformed, and/or uninformed, even to those of us who always felt that Poppa Chuck was pretty much welcome to the whole *White Album*. The other homage-as-rodomontade, "All Along the Watchtower" includes the rap: "All I have is a red guitar/Three chords and the truth/All I have is a red guitar/The rest is up to you." Three chords and the *truth?* What are we supposed to do, hold his coat?

This tone undermines even the U2 hit you'd have thought least assailable. On the live "Pride (In the Name of Love)," you can't avoid noticing that the before-the-parens titular virtue Bono's praising—getting turned on by, really—doesn't sound much like the pride implied by "I am somebody." Rather, it begins to blur into something suspiciously closer to what Bono's ostensible subject Dr. King would call a sin, and we culture critics label plain, old hubris.

Still, such egregiousness isn't likely to make much [of a] dent in U2's audience, not going by my sense of them anyway. Just as they don't seem to relate to the records primarily as music, they don't judge Bono as a star (which means he's immune from being considered an asshole). To most U2 fans, the band fills a need for belief that's a logical if depressing outgrowth of rock's usefulness in filling the need for questioning and kicks. To them, that may even make U2's lack of affinity with more down-to-earth uses of the band's chosen form a plus.

I don't have any desire to mock the need, however mockable I find the priggish, thin-skinned egoist and the three dullards who owe it their career. But as I tried to account for U2's popularity in more familiar ways (nothing new under the sun, and all that), I did hit on one satisfyingly unlikely parallel. Aren't U2 kind of like the Doors? It's not only that they're as big a pain in the ass. There just aren't that many other rock bands who've excited a comparable devotion in the mass audience while seeming so fundamentally unattuned and/or indifferent to rock and roll for it's own sake. The Doors too, as Christgau mentioned way back when, lost whatever salience they had once Jim Morrison discovered he liked rock for the music; as U2 well may also, unless they come up with better R&B than this. It's not even a contradiction that the '60's dorks promoted an adventurousness that seemed liberating, but turned regressive in its reduction of all mystery to mystique, while their'80 s counterparts promote a passion that seems liberating, but turns regressive in its reduction of all commitment to faith. It's just the turn of the wheel. That was in another country, and besides, Nico is dead.

U2

Achtung, Baby

U2 Is Back out on Edge with Bracing Baby
Roger Catlin
***The Hartford Courant*, November 19, 1991**

Achtung *plays on trashy, dark, sexy, industrial. Achtung babies, U2's latest has a new, unforgettable fire.*

It's been 4-1/2 years since the last studio album from U2, the fiery Irish rock band that dominated the end of the '80s with their strident anthems of rebellion and redemption.

Much of what they achieved seemed threatened by their very success, which spawned a typically overblown stadium tour and its subsequent documentation on self-important film and recorded versions. There seemed to be way too many comparisons to the Beatles, most of them coming from the band itself.

The years away from the public eye seemed to solve their overexposure problem. But there was very little exciting, frankly, about the music that slowly came forth. A version of "Night and Day" on the AIDS benefit album *Red, Hot + Blue* seemed all stage smoke and little substance. The score for a London musical of *A Clockwork Orange* by guitarist The Edge seemed indulgent and unlistenable.

Even the first single from their much-delayed *Achtung Baby* album, with its troubling title, was cause for worry. The nearly structureless "The Fly" was a common, house-music variety, it turned out. It had a beat, a shimmering guitar, and a soulful refrain, but none of it seemed to hang together particularly well or remain memorable. Rather, it sounded like a desperate stab at sounding like English chart upstarts Jesus Jones and EMF.

It's a pleasure and a relief to report that on the entire *Achtung Baby*, finally out in stores today, "The Fly" makes perfect sense and sounds better within the context of the whole album, a bracing, exciting change of pace for U2 that heralds a new chapter for the still very important band.

Brian Eno, who helped produce, wrote in *Rolling Stone* that during the one-year recording process, the bywords were: "trashy, throwaway, dark, sexy, and industrial (all good)" while "earnest, polite, sweet, righteous, rockist, and linear" were considered all bad. "It was good if a song took you on a journey or made you think your hi-fi was broken, bad if it reminded you of recording studios or U2," Eno wrote.

By doing away with expectations to either sound like itself or be righteous, which was long its code, U2 has opened itself up to a world of new and sonically updated music.

The band's aim—from the metallic arpeggio that begins the album to the raw, stark sound of Bono on the vocals—is to challenge their legions of fans. Although the band retains the usually pristine and atmospheric production of Daniel Lanois, the sound absolutely crackles with a revitalized, post-industrial buzz, with experimental vocals, generally big drum sounds, and startling electric guitar riffs slicing through the stormy din. At the core of the tunes are The Edge's melodic, ringing chords and Bono's impassioned vocals, making it all unmistakable U2.

Early word on the album was that a dance beat played a more prominent role. And while that might be somewhat true, it never seems done in an obvious or pandering way. The second single, "Mysterious Ways" seems to better meld dance and rock.

No longer spokesmen for the saving of the world (the song "Tryin' to Throw Your Arms Around the World" is about promiscuity), nor lecturers on the history of American popular music, U2 uses the dozen songs on *Achtung Baby* to focus—much more personally—on the painful comings and goings in a relationship. It may be seen as a song cycle on faithfulness in couples or faith itself on a grander scale, if one can cut through the dense lyrics, which are often as abstract and surprising as the sound.

"You're the real thing," Bono sings on the second song, quickly amending it, "You're better than the real thing."

The stream-of-consciousness "Who's Gonna Ride Your Wild Horses" seems compiled of two different songs; nevertheless, they sound terrific together, and make up one of the album's great anthems.

At times Bono seems to directly access the band's bold new direction. "I'm ready, ready for what's next," he declares on the frantic album-opening "Zoo Station." "Time is a train, makes the future the past. Leaves you standing in the station, your face pressed up against the glass."

And to those with faces pressed to the glass, he inquires, on the next track: "Did I disappoint you?"

As rock 'n' roll continues to shatter into different directions, into post-punk, metal, industrial, alternative, mainstream, and pop, U2 uses the strength of its standing to combine approaches and lead a unified group of rock fans into the next decade, on a train speeding forward.

U2

U2 Achtung, Baby
Parke Putterbaugh
***Stereo Review*, February 1992**

Performance: U Who?
Recording: Poor

No, your stereo isn't broken, nor did the record company accidentally slip the long-awaited CD version of Lou Reed's *Metal Machine Music* (with bonus tracks!) into the wrong jewel box. That distorted noise crackling out of your speakers is U2's five-years-in-the-making new album, the perplexingly titled *Achtung Baby*. In its murky experimentalism and casually desperate attempts at plumbing for the unexpected, this is the sound of a band on the run. While some might laud it's daring, I say that it's simply not very good.

The first minutes of the opener, "Zoo Station" will have you on the phone to the hi-fi repair shop. The Edge executes snaky, slalom-run guitar riffs and is answered by hyperdistorted bass splats; Bono's heavily treated voice makes him sound like he's shouting through a cardboard paper-towel tube. It's hard to decipher what he's singing—or to want to make the effort. This is U2 reflected off a funhouse mirror, playing around with sounds and disfiguring songs out of a reckless desire to deconstruct their music. While oblique strategies and spontaneous creation might serve some artists well, it makes U2 sound indifferent at best and incompetent at worst.

Moments of *The Joshua Tree*-style yearning peep through the surreal scrim, as in "Tryin' to Throw Your Arms Around the World," but they are faint, secondhand echoes drowned out by the clamorous context. That the band may be pushing toward something new and worthwhile is suggested by the R&B-inflected chants and kinetic rhythm guitar of "Mysterious Ways" and "Even Better than the Real Thing," but for the most part *Achtung Baby* is a bomb that misses its target from a band whose sense of itself has been ruptured by a suffocating fame. Let's hope it's a temporary condition.

Zooropa

Zooropa
Steve Simels
***Stereo Review*, October 1993**

Performance: Offhand
Recording: Okay

Zooropa is not great U2, but it may be the most important thing they've done in ages, albeit for extra-musical reasons. Recorded between March and May of 1993, what it recalls most (not stylistically, of course) is the Rolling Stones' *December's Children*, or any other sixties record thrown together by a band on the run. Which is to say it's a revolutionary anachronism in music-biz terms—an album made and sold for no other reason than to document what's on the band's collective mind this very moment.

True, that turns out to be not much. The songs here are the sketchiest of fragments, essentially excuses for the band and conceptual accomplice Brian Eno to overlay the usual trendy noises in accordance with the usual critical theories. To be fair, though, it sometimes works. "Babyface," for example, comes off appealingly as half soul-plaint, half children's tune, while the uncharacteristically witty "Some Days Are Better than Others" almost passes for *U2 a la Chinoise*.

Still, about the best you can say for this music is that it conspicuously lacks the histrionic gestures amid moral posturing that in the past have made the band alternately inspiring and annoying. But then the music isn't really the point here. What's cool about *Zooropa* is that it's a calculated affront to current industry practice, to the system by which bands make albums conforming to demographic studies and marketing plans rather than their own musical vision. And what will be really interesting is if some other comparably successful group responds to the albums implicit challenge. Hey—it could happen.

U2

Pop

Millennial Dancing
Nicholas Jennings
***Maclean's*, March 24, 1997**

U2 fills the spiritual vacuum with techno music.

An instant assault on the senses, U2's latest album kicks off with unsettling groans, ominous grinding, and riveting jackhammer beats. From the disquieting sounds of "Discotheque," *Pop* then careens into the rhythmic vise-grip of "Do You Feel Loved," which, despite its dreamy, falsetto vocals, is hardly soothing either. But nothing prepares the listener for what awaits them on the album's third track. Played at breakneck speed, with clattering metallic noises and wailing electronic effects, "Mofo" is U2 at its most radical and disturbing. "Lookin' for a sound that's gonna drown out the world," Bono moans over the thundering backdrop. He needn't worry; he's already found it.

Louder and edgier than anything the Irish band has produced to date, *Pop*—particularly its first three songs—suggests that the four members of U2 have been spending time at all-night warehouse raves, drawing from the cutting-edge, hypnotic dance sounds of techno, trance, and trip-hop music. But *Pop* is more than just some aging rockers' attempt to keep up with musical trends. With its twin concerns for things spiritual and superficial, the album seems perfectly suited to the twilight years of the 20th century.

"Miami" is superficial in the extreme, reveling in the "print shirts and southern accents/cigars and big hair" of America's kitsch capital. Similarly, "The Playboy Mansion," a fantasy about gaining entry into Hugh Hefner's pleasure palace, delights in itemizing the brand names of pop culture. These amount to the best songs on the album, displaying a fun-loving decadence that U2 first revealed on *Achtung Baby* and later explored on its elaborate Zoo TV tour.

Several numbers on *Pop* also deal with a crisis in faith, as if there cannot be decadence without penance. On "If God Will Send His Angels," a weary-sounding Bono wonders whether God would answer his phone calls if he could. And on "Wake up Dead Man," he speculates that although Jesus is undoubtedly "looking out for us, " he is probably far too busy to actually help. Both songs pick up where Joan Osborne's "One of Us" left off, attempting to fill the spiritual vacuum of the times by bringing God back down to earth.

But ultimately, it is the sonic onslaught that gives *Pop* its punch. Like David Bowie, whose influence can be heard on the album, U2 is proving itself adept at synthesizing the sounds of the dance underground for a more mainstream audience. The experiment may not sit well with fans of the group's soaring, guitar-driven rock anthems—such classics as "Pride (In the Name of Love)" and "With or Without You"—but for lovers of adventurous, groove-oriented dance music it will go down just fine. In its constant quest to redefine itself, U2 has succeeded in coming up with a brave sound for the new millennium.

U2

Pop
Charles Taylor
Salon.com (www.salon.com), March 13, 1997

"I want to be the song, be the song that you hear in your head," Bono sings on "Discotheque," the opening track of U2's new album, *Pop*, and that's the band's furious ambition in a nutshell. It would be enough for most bands to want their new record to take over the charts. U2 wants *Pop* to take over the moment, to exist at the center of pop consciousness, the way *Thriller* or *Murmur* did. It's impossible to imagine a record like *Pop* being attempted by any musicians who didn't think of themselves as rock stars, who didn't have complete faith in their ability to realize their huge ambition. Its impact depends on our being able to hear a familiar group talking to us in an unfamiliar way.

U2 is still preoccupied with salvation and redemption, though now the lyrics make room for irony and ambiguity, humor and doubt. The pretension is gone from Bono's voice. But the meaning of *Pop* is inseparable from its sound. U2 hasn't abandoned guitar rock, as the buzz on the album would have you believe. But Bono wasn't kidding when he told *Spin* that U2 is "trying to make a kind of music that doesn't exist yet." Putting themselves in the hands of producer Flood and the British ambient DJ Howie B., they've made an album that suggests how the new electronic dance music might break with a mass audience. I think that in a few years their embrace of electronic music may feel something like Neil Young's embrace of punk, and to some older fans it may be just as alienating.

How could U2 not be attracted to dance music? Dance is the most messianic of all pop music, aiming at transcendence through the relentlessness of the beat, abandonment of the self in ecstatic communion. If *Achtung Baby* and *Zooropa* were frontal assaults, a band toying with a new style, *Pop* is a total immersion, encrusted with rhythm tracks and electronica, razor-blade guitars, and pure fuzz-toned noise, like the doodads that cover every available space of Latino religious art.

U2 has joined its infatuation with the new dance music to end-of-the-millennium hopes and fears that bring out its naturally apocalyptic sense of drama. What they've heard in house and ambient and techno is the ticky, nervous rush of urban life and the exciting uncertainties of a world making connections via technology. Roving over a large landscape encompassing Europe and America, *Pop* is U2's attempt to keep a step ahead, an album that aims to sound like the day after tomorrow. If skepticism creeps in about the state of things, so does a conviction about the necessity (and the thrill) of living in the moment. "She feels the ground is giving way," Bono sings about the young woman who's the subject of "Last Night on Earth," "but she thinks we're better off that way." He even manages to take a detail another singer would use against her—her love of tabloids—and turn it into an image that quotes one of the Beatles' loveliest songs: "She's at the bus stop with the *News of the World* and the *Sun*, sun, here it comes." As befits an album named *Pop*, U2 is both acknowledging the discontents of a disposable culture and rushing headfirst into its pleasures.

They don't pretend adults are immune to those pleasures. "Miami" moves like the sleek, elliptical marriage of an action movie and a tourist brochure. Elsewhere, Bono asks, "Have I got the gifts to get me through the gates of that mansion?" Which is exactly the sort of question you'd expect him to ask, except that it comes in a song called "The Playboy Mansion." The song happily draws a mustache on the longing for salvation of numbers like "Still Haven't Found What I'm Looking For." In that number, Bono was Jesus in the desert. Here, he's Jesus in the Ritz.

Opening with The Edge playing a sort of corrupted blues riff (the blues reduced to a series of electronic blips), "The Playboy Mansion" proceeds through a list of temptations—Big Macs, Cokes, lotto tickets, talk shows that function like confessionals—to break a modern pilgrim's will. There's a dry wit to the number but nothing is clear-cut, and the beautiful gospel chorus that brings it to a close confuses things even further. If capitalism can sound so good, who could ask for anything more?

Pop is U2's attempt to "take this tangle of a conversation" (as Bono sings on "Do You Feel Loved") and get at the beauty of the way the threads twist around each other. It's not so experimental that it loses sight of its desire to be a huge global hit, but it wouldn't be so thrilling if it did. U2 is trying to sum up what rock 'n' roll feels like at this moment, when the grumblings that electronica isn't rock 'n' roll are starting to echo the same things that were said about disco, punk, rap. On *Pop*, U2 moves like kings of the dance floor throwing down flashy moves and a challenge: Open your ears or get left in the dust.

U2

Best of 1980–1990

U2: *The Best of 1980–1990*
Vic Garbarini
***Playboy*, February 1999**

Slightly annoying but lovable, U2 is the musical equivalent of a frisky sheepdog who jumps up and licks your face. The first retrospective in U2's 20-year history, *The Best of 1980–1990,* comes in two formats. The single-disc edition covers the hits through *Rattle and Hum*, and the double-disc adds 15 B-sides and rarities. In the Reagan years, the recordings were erratic. U2 could be bombastic, but it had heart and spirit. The studio versions of the early productions included here are drenched in reverb. Drums drown out guitars. The best renditions of early hits such as "Sunday Bloody Sunday" and "I Will Follow"—the songs that broke the band in America—appear on the live EP *Under a Blood Red Sky*. Producer Brian Eno's cerebral touch made U2's albums more adventurous and focused. *Wide Awake in America* was U2's eighties masterpiece. The music was spectacular, the lyrics dealt more maturely with spiritual crises and hopes, and Bono had learned to "shout without raising his voice." The three songs included are faultless, but any fan should have the whole album. *Rattle and Hum*, its flawed roots album, is over-represented.

All That You Can't Leave Behind

U2 Comes Back from the Future

J.D. Considine

***The Baltimore Sun*, October 29, 2000**

The Irish rockers return to something resembling their past.

On its last album of new material, 1997's *Pop*, U2 threw its past away and lunged for the future. Sensing a shift in the zeitgeist, the four lads from Dublin declared that rock was dead and insisted they were going to ride the mirror ball of electronica into the next millennium.

Well, everybody makes mistakes.

Now that they're actually in that new millennium, rock and roll doesn't seem quite so outmoded. At least, that's what the group suggests with its new album, *All That You Can't Leave Behind*, arriving in stores today.

It isn't just that the band has abandoned the synthesized sheen and looped rhythms of *Pop* and moved back to the guitar-driven sound of its youth; if its lyrics are to be believed, U2 has seen the future and decided it doesn't belong there.

As Bono sings on "Kite," he's "The last of the rock stars/When hip-hop drove the big cars."

So instead of continuing to update its sound, as the band has done since its breakthrough 1987 album *The Joshua Tree*, this new album marks a sort of sonic consolidation. Instead of dance beats, there's a mild retread of the fuzz-guitar funk rock that fueled "Mysterious Ways." In place of bold new sounds, we get new arranging tricks, like the vintage Chamberlain providing the synthesized string sounds on "Kite."

For those who winced at the band's blind pursuit of cool in recent years, it's probably a relief that U2 stopped before it got to Limp Bizkit. But that doesn't mean *All That You Can't Leave Behind* is a return to the glory days. For all its strummed guitars and passionately thumping drums, the album never touches on the sonic heroism that made its early efforts so uplifting.

All That You Can't Leave Behind simmers more than it soars, preferring crooned vocals and softly chiming guitars to fist-pumping fury of such oldies as "I Will Follow" or "Sunday Bloody Sunday." That doesn't necessarily mean all's quiet on the U2 front, as "Elevation," "Beautiful Day," and even the semi-acoustic "Wild Honey" all build a pretty good head of steam rhythmically. But even at its most insistent, this isn't an album that begs to be blared from windows.

Blame Bono for much of the music's diffidence. Where once his lyrics wrestled with issues and abstractions, suddenly they've turned personal and self-doubting. "I hit an iceberg in my life," he sings in "New York," and then casts himself as a lesser character in *Titanic*: "You lose your balance, you lose your wife/In the queue for the lifeboat," he croons.

It isn't just the lack of heroism that makes the lyric so surprising; it's the naked admission of failure implicit in his metaphor. Even though the lyric assures us that our hero is "still afloat," there's no missing the fact that he sees New York not as a new home, but as an escape. Rather than face the issue head-on, he opts for distance and reflection—and the music mirrors that avoidance of conflict.

To their credit, the lads are more than capable of pulling interesting music from such anomie. No matter that Bono jokes in "Stuck in a Moment You Can't Get out Of" that he's "just trying to find a decent melody"—the gently insistent groove and gorgeous, gospel-inflected keyboards behind him make the tune memorable. The song's slow-paced, sweetly harmonized chorus is one of the album's highlights.

Still, it's hard to be happy with occasional cleverness when dealing with a band that was once routinely brilliant. Sure, there's a certain kick to the way "Beautiful Day" builds from the heartbeat thump of its slyly insistent verse to the roaring guitars and triumphant vocals of the chorus. But there's no denying that the song itself is appallingly trite, urging listeners to forget their petty personal troubles and tune in to the beauty of nature.

Been reading the greeting cards again, Bono?

There are moments when it would almost be easier to appreciate the album if you weren't burdened with an ability to understand English. "Elevation," for example, is wonderfully eloquent on a musical level, playing off the rubbery thump of Adam Clayton's bass and the rasping pulse of The Edge's wah-wah guitar. But the lyric is built around rhymes so obvious and nonsensical ("A mole, digging in a hole/Digging up my soul...") you'd think Bono had overdosed on Dr. Seuss. Except Dr. Seuss generally reads better than that.

Then again, this is a man who thinks that lines such as "The only baggage you can bring/Is all that you can't leave behind" constitute deep thoughts. So maybe it's better just to focus on the music, and take this album as a reminder that while U2 is no longer at the top of its game, it still plays pretty well.

U2

Is This Desire?
Ann Powers
***Spin* magazine, November 2000**

On *All That You Can't Leave Behind*, U2 finally find what they're looking for.

Throwing your hands up in the air can be an act of faith. Stick 'em up—there's no resisting the way life constantly robs you of control. But open those arms wider, and defeat becomes elation. "Stretch out your hands toward the sanctuary," the psalmist instructed pilgrims seeking the Promised Land. Don't be surprised when submission turns to strength.

U2 know plenty about spiritual abandon. From their early work as flag-waving Christians soldiers through the ecstatic desert wanderings of the mid '80s, to the fall to dirty earth that started in 1991 with *Achtung Baby*, the Irishmen specialized in the plunge, riding rock's gravitational pull to states of unchecked emotion. With a force that sometimes seemed ridiculous, each album was a dunk in the river, and loving the band meant giving in—not to God but to the problematic idea of meaningful rock.

Yet U2 have never explored their fetish for surrender with such relaxed eloquence as on *All That You Can't Leave Behind* (Interscope). Nor has the band ever worried less about proving its genius. After *Pop*, 1997's uncomfortable tiptoe into techno, they've realized that the rash pursuit of the moment works only for Madonna. Self-respect demands U2 ignore Kid Rock and eliminate the need for Creed.

Fact is, even after Bono stuffed piety down his vinyl pants, people continued to use rock as a source of spirit raising. U2 light the unfashionable fire better than anybody else, and with age have become more adept at contemplation. Bono's preaching now has an air of weathered serenity. The Edge rarely careens around as if his guitar is a flame-thrower, instead stressing sharp finger work. Brian Eno and Daniel Lanois, back as producers (with Steve Lillywhite and others helping), use effects—churchy organ, backward violin, whale sounds—but keep the colors between the lines. The songs are still full of deep thoughts, but now they come from a quieter place.

Call it the happy aftermath of a midlife crisis. U2 is relaxing, reasserting some beliefs critics love to shove back in their face—most importantly, that uplifting art is not necessarily dumb. The album's opening one-two-three punch irresistibly makes this point. "Beautiful Day" is a hip-shakingly messianic exhortation of faith found through adversity, while "Stuck in a Moment" takes hope higher in a gospel arrangement that fulfills the Harlem dreams the band's been chasing since *Rattle and Hum*. Then comes "Elevation," a flat-out sex song seductively posed in an electronica bed. But it's really about love as salvation, with Edge showing his mysterious ways, the rhythm section fluffing its funky feathers, and Bono testifying like he's dreaming of Aretha and feeling like a natural man.

A dip in energy would be understandable after this rush, but U2, being U2, wanna take you higher, as "Walk On" and "Kite" return to the desert of *The Joshua Tree*. Piano, strings, and background voices expand to fill Lanois and Eno's cathedral-size mixes, and Bono's proclamations swell along with the sound. Every sentence is a proverb of wind and water, but the band offers its inspiration in a modest way, so it doesn't grate.

After these peaks, the record detours into eddies U2 have explored before. The mellow "In a Little While" turns "Satellite of Love" into an Al Green song, with Bono using his new and at times bothersome soul shout, and the real interest coming in the interplay between Clayton's fuzz-touched bass and Edge's velvety guitar. "Wild Honey" nods at the Beach Boys, and several songs revisit the darker musings of *Pop*, letting the album drift a bit toward inertia. This detour leads nowhere, especially on the embarrassing "New York," a (hopefully) final bid by Bono to inhabit Frank Sinatra's moldering persona.

But the delicate coda, "Grace," puts us back on solid, sacred ground. The song is a parable about a woman saintly enough to be a Lars von Trier heroine. Such an exercise in virtue will put off sophisticates—I mean, where are the supermodels? But as Edge and Clayton spool a slow dance, sparked by tiny cloudbursts from Eno's keyboards, celebrating faith, hope, and love doesn't seem that bad. In fact, it's exactly what U2, giving in to itself, is meant to do.

U2

CHAPTER

10

ON THE SCREEN

It is not coincidental that U2 and MTV came to be at around the same time. U2 have always been a startlingly visual band, from early performance videos to the elaborate shoots that found them dressing like the Village People and in dresses.

U2 have long wanted to join Howard Stern as the kings of all media, or perhaps the Prime Ministers of all media owing to the way they go about it. Their concerts do not air on Pay Per View. They opt for broadcast networks, the better to reach everyone. Not everyone can get a ticket to see U2 live? Fine, they'll make a film of the concert that adds so much that even people who saw the concert will want to see the film.

Beyond all this, as much musical innovation as the group constantly exhibits, they also display a long streak of visual innovation. Little wonder that two of their Grammy awards are for their long-form videos. Some of their longest-standing artistic relationships have been with visual artists. Anton Corbijn is their de facto official photographer. Their music graced films by Wim Wenders for many years. They helped launch the career of film director Phil Joanou.

U2's visual streak brought them to the outlandish stage sets that informed their concerts through the '90s; it gave them license to use the startling, touching projection of September 11th victims' names during the '00s. It made Bono's wrap-around sunglasses a trademark in which even the Pope wanted to trade.

When MTV cablecast the Buggle's "Video Killed the Radio Star," they closed one door—the door that allowed 300-pound Leslie West to become a rock icon of sorts—but they opened another for bands that were willing to allow their musical vision to extend into a visual element. For U2, being young and pretty from the beginning proved a mighty asset in this context. Seeing something beyond the music kept them going.

U2: Rattle and Ho-Hum

Armond White
***Film Comment*, November 1988**

Phil Joanou thought about the proposition. Are concert films the new form of musical? Then he surmised, "Well, if they're a new form, Martin Scorsese already invented it. Instead of breaking into song, his characters break into fights. Scorsese's a master of musical movement. His films are all musicals, *New York, New York*; *Raging Bull.* Check out the pool hall fight to "Please, Mr. Postman" in *Mean Streets*."

Rattle and Hum, Joanou's U2 concert film, proves his boyish enthusiasm when it shows him asking the group sycophantic questions just as Scorsese asked the Band in *The Last Waltz*. U2's immense popularity catches Joanou in a bind. This is his second feature ("The first time I've done something representative of where I'm not a hired gun") but he can't simply present U2 putting on a show. He has to apotheosize them according to the scale of their success.

"Music videos have opened up people's sense of what they'll accept visually. They would have rejected black-and-white before MTV," Joanou says, explaining his film's exalted visual style. "Kodak had to specially print an extra batch of black-and-white stock because there wasn't enough in storage. And Paramount agreed to print the film on black-and-white, which is rare—not even *Under the Cherry Moon* was printed on black-and-white. I was lucky. The band let me see my vision through and put their money behind it."

Joanou's visual drama distracts from the vagueness of U2's socially conscious rock with stark hyperbole. And just as David Byrne's big suit trapped a white man in a black man's jazz form ("*Stop Making Sense* was technically the best executed concert film," Joanou says), U2 hardly measures up to Joanou's tailoring. He inflates what drummer Larry Mullen calls "a musical journey" into a rather awed odyssey of working-class Irish lads turned gods. The film shows U2 trying on mythological guises: a Beatles song, Dylan tunes, a snatch of the Stones, some sampled Hendrix, a stop at a Harlem church, a session with B.B. King, and a visit to Graceland, where Mullen absolves the film career of Elvis Presley.

All this bucking for legendary status takes the place of a lucid, satisfying show. Instead of offering a new perception of the rock concert experience as the Smiths' Rank album does, or that can be sensed from the lively idiosyncratic representation Alex Cox found for The Pogues in *Straight to Hell* and Alan Rudolph found for Willie Nelson and Kris Kristofferson in *Songwriter*, Joanou polishes the concert tropes in order to preserve U2 as an institution. No concert film has shown more care or concentrated imagination. It's not Joanou's fault his subject is the world's most pompous rock band.

U2 Hits the Road in *Rattle and Hum*

Janet Maslin
***The New York Times*, November 4, 1988**

As a whole new generation of filmmakers cuts its teeth on rock video, the hardest thing about filming concert documentaries may be insuring that they don't look better than they should. Flashy, high-style concert footage is by now rock's most numbing cliché, and it has a way of destroying any grit or authenticity that exists in the music itself.

Luckily, this isn't much of a liability for U2: *Rattle and Hum*, even though its director, Phil Joanou, made an earlier feature (*Three O'Clock High*) that invested a schoolyard fight between a nice kid and a bully with the visual importance of a moon launch. This time, Mr. Joanou devises a sinuous black-and-white style that superbly showcases the simplicity and directness of the group's performing style, and he has the good sense to stay with it. The temptation to make the film showier is apparent here and there, especially when it bursts into color to capture the excitement of a big U2 stadium appearance. Instead of heightening the film's energy, this episode nearly dispels the remarkable intimacy that Mr. Joanou's gliding black-and-white footage has been able to establish. Indeed, the best parts of U2: *Rattle and Hum*, which opens today at Loews Astor Plaza and other theaters, underscore the difference between concert effects designed to please fans at a great distance and cinematic effects that work at very close range. U2 is one of those rare bands capable of casting their full spell on either scale.

If anything, the camera might have lingered longer in close-up on the musicians as they play, since they are at their best when the camera's intensity matches their own. U2's concert performances here, filmed during their American tour last year, are for the most part thrilling, all the more so for the complete absence of posturing in the band's onstage manner. Instead of acting out the songs that he performs, the singer Bono makes himself a supple, unselfconscious extension of the music itself, and the film captures this beautifully. The band's musicianship also remains astonishingly tight and focused, even in stadium surroundings.

The film captures much more of U2's personality onstage than it does elsewhere, though it includes a number of extracurricular vignettes. The best of these send the band members to Harlem, where they record a spine-tingling version of "I Still Haven't Found What I'm Looking For" with a gospel choir; another sends them to Sun Studios in Memphis to record several songs beneath the likeness of Elvis Presley. The film is on shakier ground when it sends the musicians, like so many tourists, on a visit to Elvis Presley's Graceland, or even when Mr. Joanou sits the musicians down and attempts to ask them questions. U2's music speaks much better than this for itself.

U2's U-Turn (excerpt)

Robert Hilburn
***Los Angeles Times*, March 1, 1992**

The band's ambitious Rattle and Hum *film and double album rattled many fans, critics, and even the four Irish idealists themselves. On the eve of their U.S. tour, they talk about how they got back on the high road.*

The surprise still shows on U2 drummer Larry Mullen's face as he recalls his reaction after picking up a copy of *Rolling Stone* magazine's recent critics' poll and seeing that his band had been picked as "comeback of the year."

"I couldn't believe it," the young man with classic, James Dean good looks says, sitting in a chair during a break in a video shoot on a sound stage at suburban Pinewood Studios, where many of the James Bond movies were shot.

On the surface, it's easy to understand the drummer's surprise over anyone even suggesting that the heralded new U2 album, *Achtung Baby*, represented a comeback.

Why?

The Irish quartet has been one of rock's most popular and acclaimed groups for years—the most popular and acclaimed since the estimated 14 million worldwide sales of 1987's Grammy-winning album *The Joshua Tree*, an inspiring series of songs about spiritual quest.

On its last tour of the United States in 1988, U2 packed stadiums and generated reviews that compared the group to the Beatles, The Who, and other landmark bands of the '60s. Certainly, critics were divided over *Rattle and Hum*, a 1989 concert film and soundtrack album, but the double album sold about 7.5 million copies around the world.

After a three-year break, the band roared back late last year with *Achtung Baby*, which entered the U.S. album charts at No. 1 and has already sold more than 6 million copies. This weekend, U2 begins its first U.S. tour since 1988, and tickets for tonight's Miami show sold out in 12 minutes. The group will play the Los Angeles Sports Arena on April 12–13 and the San Diego Sports Arena on April 15, and there's talk of a Southern California stadium show later in the year.

Yet the "comeback" line—even if it was meant a touch playfully—struck a nerve in Mullen and probably in some of the group's most demanding fans.

"You know," he says earnestly as the rest of the group stands nearby, watching a playback of the video scene that has just been shot, "there was some truth in it. We had some serious problems when we got back to Dublin after *Rattle and Hum.*

"A lot of our fans were confused by the movie and they started asking what we were all about and where we were headed—and that's good because we needed to sit down ourselves and think about those questions.

"There were times (since *The Joshua Tree*) where priorities got confused. There were times when you weren't sure what you were meant to be doing. Are you a musician? A rock star?"

Those are questions faced by every band that enjoys massive success in pop and learns that the old cliché about the pressures of fame are all too real. But the questions were particularly delicate for U2 because this was an idealistic band that had seen so many earlier groups succumb to lifestyle excesses or artistic complacency. As with Bruce Springsteen in the '70s, there was an unwritten pledge by U2 in the '80s to be tougher than the rest.

After a few months of individual soul searching in 1990, the band headed to a Berlin recording studio for some tense weeks to deal with the question of its future.

"We had to start from scratch in a way…get in touch with ourselves musically," Mullen continues. "If we didn't come up with the right answers, it could have all been over because I think we all care enough about U2 to end it before we just make a joke of it. Everything was on the line. We didn't want *Rattle and Hum* to become our *Let It Be.*"

It's a sobering parallel: *Let It Be*, the 1970 documentary about a Beatles recording session that telegraphed the friction that would eventually cause the band to dissolve, and *Rattle and Hum*, the 1989 U2 tour film.

The tension in the latter case was not between the band members—who, by all accounts, still maintain the closeness that has characterized the group since it was formed during their school days in Dublin. The strain was on the group's image.

Some critics saw the U2 actions during the *Rattle and Hum* project, including writing a song with Bob Dylan and performing with B.B. King, as an egomaniacal attempt to demonstrate that U2 is what many other critics had been calling it for years: the legitimate heir of the '60s rock tradition. Some longtime fans saw the relatively big-budget movie as pretentious—a sign that U2 had lost touch with its audience and its rock ideals.

Though they stand by the film, the band members acknowledge some misjudgments in letting what was conceived as a small-scale project grow into a wide-screen spectacular that opened in nearly 1,500 theaters and was backed by a suffocatingly massive Hollywood film ad campaign.

"It was just the sheer quantity of the promotion that turned people off," guitarist Edge (Dave Evans) says. "There is something in rock about discovering a band…about it being your own personal band and when its picture and name is on every billboard across the whole nation and on television every 15 minutes, it's a different thing. It's like peanut butter or a product. The whole thing was out of scale."

Paul McGuinness, the group's Dublin-based manager, takes the blame for the extensive campaign.

"I never realized what an enormous thing a movie campaign could be," he says. "From my experience in the record business, I always believed that if all the visual elements of a campaign were tasteful and good-looking, nothing could go wrong.

"But I wasn't prepared for the difference in the size of the movie campaign and the average record campaign...how all across America for a couple of weeks, you couldn't turn on your TV without getting U2 in your face. That's not the way records are marketed. It's much more subtle and I think a lot of the band's old fans found it distasteful. The aftermath I think, quite honestly, was that no one wanted to hear about U2 for a while."

Marc Porter, a 22-year-old Englishman, was among the fans turned off.

"My friends hated *Rattle and Hum* because it was U2 trying to be Michael Jackson or something," he said two days before the Pinewood video shoot, while waiting on London's famed Carnaby Street to watch the band shoot some other scenes for the video.

"It was like they were more interested in being stars than in making music. You see it happen to so many bands, but I never thought it'd happen to U2. They were writing about real issues about the heart and the soul, and suddenly they were in Hollywood like (expletive) Warren Beatty or Richard Gere. I even threw away my old U2 T-shirts."

Even an early evening rain couldn't dampen the enthusiasm of the fans who were waiting outside the Zoo, a Gap-like clothing store on the street that was the heart of the Mod fashion scene in the '60s.

When Bono, the group's charismatic lead singer, arrived at the store with Mullen, Edge, and bassist Adam Clayton, Porter unbuttoned his bulky jacket to reveal his new T-shirt with homemade lettering.

It was an update of the title of U2' s first hit single: "I Will Still Follow."

The idea at the Zoo was for U2 to perform "Even Better than the Real Thing," a song from *Achtung Baby*, in the store window while the audience watched through the glass. The glass between the band and the audience was designed to underscore the song's theme about how fantasies and something untouchable become even more intoxicating than the actual experience.

As the camera began rolling, the song was played over a sound system in the street and the fans swayed to the swirling instrumental textures. In the store window, Bono—dressed in a shiny leather outfit and wearing dark glasses in a teasing poke at rock star clichés—moved with many of the twisting and turning gestures that have become his trademark on stage.

As the record played on, he began pressing against the glass, as if trying to make contact with the girls who were reaching up for him. During the instrumental break, he noticed a woman's jacket on a sale-rack hanger and grabbed it. The jacket was much too small, but he put it on and began strutting around the floor.

A member of the video crew seemed puzzled by this ad-lib, but the fans on the street outside whooped it up. They're not used to seeing U2 in such a playful mood.

During the early years, the group struggled to find itself thematically in a series of deeply introspective songs that explored spiritual and political issues. While not doctrinaire, the lyrics were based on the group's acknowledged Christian perspective. The group had built such a following by the time of its *Joshua Tree* album that it was widely regarded as the most important rock group in the world.

Rattle and Hum, which was a mix of live versions of old songs and new songs, reflected in places the pressures of all that attention and stardom—as the band dealt with questions of whether rock, in an age where the music was often viewed as simply entertainment, still had the power to move audiences and affect social change as it did in the '60s.

Even before the film, however, some critics and fans found the group too "self-important." In one sarcastic review of *Rattle and Hum*," a critic referred to U2' s lead singer as "God…err Bono."

But Dave Marsh, the outspoken New York critic, defended the group with a telling appraisal of the contemporary rock scene. Writing about the critical backlash to *Rattle and Hum*, he said: "It is as if living in a mediocre period, people believe it's the obligation of a young band to live down to those standards."

By the end of the group's 1989 world tour, there were so many pressures on the band that Bono stunned a New Year's Eve audience in Dublin by declaring at the end of the concert that it was time for U2 to go away. Some interpreted the remark as a sign the band was going to break up. Bono didn't mean it that way, he explains now. But the irony was, there was considerable uncertainty about the future of the band in the weeks and months afterward.

If the *Rattle and Hum* backlash represented the early signs of a possible public crisis facing the band, the band's struggle for identity and direction in the early months of 1990 represented a private crisis. Bono pauses when asked about the strain of *The Joshua Tree* and *Rattle and Hum* periods.

"There was a reason we opened *Rattle and Hum* with (the Beatles' frenzied) 'Helter Skelter.' That's the way our lives felt sometimes," he says, almost with a sigh. "There were times on that tour when things could have unraveled. Even on *Joshua Tree*, heads left people's bodies (laughs) and not just the four members of the band, but some of the people around us.

"It's hard to talk about that and the reasons behind the songs on the album without sounding like a guest on one of those (confessional) TV shows, but there were definitely times when the fire you are playing with starts to play with you and it can destroy you before you even know it's there. But there is a thing we have that makes us strong. You can call it faith, you can call it lots of things, but it helps pull you through."

A video aide enters the room and tells Bono he's needed on the set.

The young Irishman, however, wants to first go back to an earlier question about the reason for so much tension and doubt on the album.

"Basically, for the first half of the '80s there was a slight ostrich element about us and that was good. We were on a spiritual sojourn and we discovered a lot of good stuff that keeps you strong and opens your eyes a bit," he says.

"But there was a point then where you have to actually walk into the real world and it kind of went a bit wrong. I had a few bad experiences, really bad experiences, and some of that is what you hear in the album. If the first chapter of U2 was innocence, this one is about innocence lost."

Achtung Baby Video Recording Reviews

Marianne Meyer
***Video Magazine*, February 1993**

Nowadays, it seems every rock band with a single college-radio hit gets the toss-some-clips-together-with-hand-held-camera-and-interviews long-form video treatment. So what can genuine superstars like U2, probably one of the best studio and live bands of the day, do to separate themselves from the pack?

As befits the band's latest touring persona, in which earnestly P.C. lead singer Bono gyrates in leather pants and dark shades, these videos exult in excess. Like last summer's multimedia U2 concerts, many of these clips are pricey, state-of-the-art assaults that use sampled visuals, frenetic pacing, and news-room-style text to bombastic effect. Without knowing the band's real penchant for committed, intelligent songcraft, one might dismiss it all as superficial indulgence. Even the compelling ballad "One" appears here not once or twice, but in three different versions, including a sepia-toned edition featuring the quartet in drag.

Bono has a charismatic camera presence—just watch him smolder in the simplest, Phil Joanou-directed "One"—and his lizardly rock-god act is a send-up, of sorts. This eventually comes out in the interview segments, though stylistically they're akin to fawning MTV rockumentary bits. Still, by collecting U2's recent videos in all their obscure variations, and offering a commercial-free retrospective of the band's extraordinary recent output, this video compilation rises above the standard to engage even non-fans.

U2

U2's Home Video *Stop Sellafield*: Good Music and a Message

Steve Morse
***The Boston Globe*, March 5, 1993**

Never say that Irish rockers U2 don't follow through on a commitment. In continuing their anti-nuke crusade, the band has just released a new home video, *Stop Sellafield: The Concert,* taken from a show last year to protest the Sellafield nuclear plant in northwest England, just 60 miles from the Irish coast.

"I just resent that an installation in another country can mess up a body of water that belongs to both countries—and that emissions can reach Ireland," U2 guitarist The Edge says in documentary footage added to concert shots of U2, Public Enemy, Kraftwerk (a rare peak at this fabled German synth band), and Big Audio Dynamite.

You may remember the wire service photos last year showing U2 dressed up in protective flak jackets before staging a public protest at Sellafield, a site that pours a reported 2,000 gallons of radioactive waste into the Irish Sea each day. Explaining their protest, U2 singer Bono says, "My first duty in a rock 'n' roll band is not to be boring. I don't mean to go on and on about it, but this cause is really important." The Sellafield site has also been notorious for radioactive leaks, prompting Bono to add, "There's a real threat of this being another Chernobyl."

There are accompanying interviews of Irish fishermen worried about contamination, as well as families of plant workers who've had a high incidence of cancer. It's [a] heavily one-sided presentation, but a gut-wrenching portrait emerges.

The performances also stand out. U2 does several songs, including "The Fly" and "Even Better than the Real Thing," with the same light show they brought to the United States last year. Public Enemy does the aggressive "Can't Truss It," while Kraftwerk (with strobe-lit robots hanging on a back wall) and Big Audio Dynamite also shine. The proceeds from the video go to Greenpeace.

U2

U2 on the Tube: The Rock Superstars Conquer Prime Time

Bill Flanagan
***TV Guide*, April 26, 1997**

Irish rock group U2 is the biggest band in the world—a position it has held virtually unchallenged since the release of *The Joshua Tree* 10 years ago. That's not enough for U2. They're now intent on taking over your TV set.

The band's ambitious three-part television project, *Zoo TV*, is currently airing on MTV, and they will perform live on the music channel's "Video Music Awards" next fall. They sold tickets on VH1 for an upcoming stadium tour before making them available at the box office. They're launching that tour with an ABC special, "U2: A Year in Pop," which will document the making of their new album. *Pop*, and includes tour rehearsals and footage from the first concert in Las Vegas on April 25. U2's music and image will be used widely to promote the network's May sweeps programming, and the band has recorded the theme song for the new ABC series *Gun*.

Clearly this is a group that, unlike Pearl Jam and other rack purists, is not afraid to plunge into the hurly-burly of the marketplace. "In white rock music, there's this idea that the music is sacred and the lucre is filthy," says U2's singer, Bono, taking a break from rehearsals in Dublin. "In the hip-hop community it's very different. They're not afraid of commerce or technology. Meanwhile, all the middle-class white rock acts are holding onto this brown-rice idea of what music is, which was their parents' idea in the '60s. We're not afraid to take on the mainstream. We can't be bought."

On its last campaign, the 1992–93 Zoo TV Tour, U2 took a television station on the road, performing in front of walls of video screens that flashed images pulled down by satellite dishes. Bono would stand before stadium crowds with a microphone in one hand and a remote-control clicker in the other, flipping through the channels. In their grander moments, U2's members dream about someday trying to launch a cable or satellite network of their own. They figure if they don't do it, some other band will.

After all, rock 'n' roll and television are like a pair of misfit twins. The two giant forces of popular culture grew up together in the '60s and have coexisted uneasily side by side. Finally, in the '80s, MTV reconciled them, updating TV's visual vocabulary while drawing rock toward the values of Madison Avenue. By the '90s, the merger was complete: Rock 'n' roll provided the soundtracks for sitcoms, cop shows, and the commercials in between.

Yet for all the growing pains and sibling rivalries, the biggest rock stars have always been those who have known how to use TV to their advantage. Think of the Beatles with Ed Sullivan or Elvis's '68 comeback special. Imagine how different the careers of Michael Jackson and Madonna would have been without videos.

U2 has a history of engaging TV on its own terms. Its members are famous for the tight control they exert over any product with their names on it. But the plan to culminate the ABC special with footage shot the previous evening will obviously limit U2's ability to refine the material. The group is resigned to the situation, according to guitarist Edge. "It won't be a fully produced, 16-camera Hollywood affair" he says. "We're trying to capture the excitement rather than represent the show itself. You can't squash a stadium into a TV screen and hope for it to be powerful. It's never going to be. TV is good at the close-up view. Television scale is a small place, a small area. It's good at amplifying and magnifying."

Edge serves as the levelheaded counterweight to the impetuous Bono—he plays Spock to Bono's Kirk. The pair met in high school in Dublin in the late '70s, when Edge was still called Dave Evans and Bono was Paul Hewson. Together with schoolmates Larry Mullen and Adam Clayton they formed a band, playing their own songs because they did not know their instruments well enough to learn covers. Out of their determination, loyalty to each other, and talent, U2 created music that won over first Dublin, then Ireland, then got the band a British record deal. In their younger days, the boys were as judgmental as any punk rockers. Evangelical Christians with a leftist social conscience, they combined the self-righteousness of the born-again with the finger-pointing of the protest singer. In their personal lives the band members retain their faith and idealism, and as they have matured, they have become more tolerant of others and tougher on themselves.

"I think in the '80s we were like a lot of people who achieved great success," says Bono. "We were sort of rabbits in the headlights. Looking back on it, I think it made us a bit precious. When you're younger, your idea of who the bad guys are is often quite simplistic. When you get to 30 you start to see that your own demons are more of a threat than any outside force. You turn on your own hypocrisy. You question your values rather than the guy across the road with the straight haircut."

And if that guy is watching TV rather than checking out the latest CD, well, U2 will take its music to his living room.

"That's the whole energy of rock 'n' roll," says Bono. "It's about connection and communication. It's about stirring up the mainstream. What I'm trying to organize [with ABC] at the moment is I want Edge to do the weather."

Watch out, Spencer Christian.

CHAPTER

11

AMONG PEERS

Musicians can be a contentious and an arrogant lot, who often don't have a lot of respect for their peers. Stories of headliners' various means of torture and humiliation for opening acts have become legend in pop music.

The kind of passion U2 inspires is not uncommon among fans. However, that they also inspire a similar awe among their peers is remarkable. Musicians sing the praises of U2 as U2 often sings the praises of others. Hit musicians count themselves among the band's biggest fans—in one story, Axl Rose travels all the way to Italy to meet them.

I once observed Bono pull up in a limousine and get besieged by a crowd of people hoping to catch a glimpse of him. Where many other stars would enter a venue through the rear stage door, Bono seemed that night to enjoy, to get energized by, the adulation. He signed papers, body parts, CDs, books, and posed for paparazzi and fans.

Once inside the invitation-only, industry-only event, Bono was the most photographed person there, mobbed by his peers almost as much as by the fans. Everyone wanted a piece of him, and he seemed to have more than enough to go around.

U2 seems to abide by the code of behavior, "If you can't say something nice, say nothing." Even in jest, U2's remarks about other musicians are apt to be kind, or at least charitable. As a result, criticisms and condemnations of the band by their peers, in comparison, sometimes sound like sour grapes.

Do You Know This Man?

Dermott Hayes
***Select*, June 1993**

Do you know this man? Compulsive artist or egotistical fraud? From his Dublin beginnings to the global pillage of Zoo TV, 40 friends and enemies tell the Secret Life of Bono.

Sinead O'Connor: was recording the theme song for a movie soundtrack by The Edge when she first met Bono. Her vitriolic and oft-quoted attacks on U2 in the early days are said to have dismayed Bono.

"The first time I met him he gave me an Ella Fitzgerald album and I love Ella Fitzgerald. I don't really know him. I think he's a good songwriter and he's a great singer. He's a little boy."

Paul Byrne: former In Tua Nua songwriter and drummer. One of the first songs In Tua Nua recorded was written by a 14-year-old Sinead O'Connor after Byrne heard her sing at his sister's wedding. Bono was a friend of Steve Wickham (of In Tua Nua and later, the Waterboys) who played electric violin on U2's *War* LP.

"It was Bono who instigated the Mother Records deal. He told Steve [Wickham] he was setting up a label. We called a meeting in a little cottage by the sea near Howth where we rehearsed. He said he wanted to call the label Mother and to use a little old granny in a wheelchair as a logo, just like in *The Man from U.N.C.L.E.* It was very wacky. He really is quite wacky, but he very quickly passed it on to Adam, the business brain in the label. Then the single was made and sat there for three months when they realized there was no 'record label' to take it any further. I never found him that serious…he was always a real joker. If he was meeting the whole band he was always into having a bit of fun and making wisecracks."

Terry O'Neill: a legend in the Irish music business. At 18 he "sold" management of Thin Lizzy for £150 so the band could get better equipment and have a stab at recording. Later a music publicist for Hothouse Flowers, the Pogues, and Mother Records, he lost the latter job after a bitter falling out with U2 drummer Larry Mullen, Jr.

"I booked U2 into McGonagles lots of times in the early days, but the incident that always sticks in my mind was a couple of years later. They were just becoming a success abroad. I had a house in Harold's Cross and I was looking out the window one day and could have sworn I saw Bono running by the window. Then I saw him run by again in the opposite direction. So just as I went out the door, he runs in through the garden gate and I says, 'Bono.' And he says, 'Terry, I didn't expect to find you here. I'm looking for someone completely different.' I said, 'There's no such thing as a coincidence.'"

Kate Hyman: vice president A&R International, Imago Records and her husband, Phil Joanou: *Rattle and Hum* director, explain their sudden decision to fly to Las Vegas and get married in the Graceland Chapel on March 19, 1992.

KH: "What inspired us was...well, Bono was singing and in between songs he said, 'Let's go to Vegas and get married for a while.' And he should be careful what he says because there are some impressionable people in the audience, and we're two of them and we did it."

PJ: "We were not even sitting together at the time either. In fact, the subliminal advertising from the concerts is not on the screens, it comes from Bono—it's not like 'Your Mother is a Whore' or whatever."

Barry Devlin: former Horslips bassist, producer of early U2 singles, director of several U2 videos, scriptwriter, filmmaker, and friend.

"They are a band who are very careful and sparing about how they put out the thing they call U2. There are two entirely separate entities—there's the four guys and the way they are and what they do, and then there's this monster which is called U2. Nobody knows how that thing functions better than they do, *nobody*, and they're very careful about what they do with it. They take advice, but very sparingly. Nobody gets to go, 'Well, I know what

U2 is, so I'm going to tell you...' *They* know what U2 is. You can't fault them, in a way. Whatever you make of it, it is an extraordinary and unique thing...

"Yes, they document everything they do on video. They also have the good grace to can about 90 percent of it...But aside from the visual thing, this is the ticket that America has been waiting for. The last tour, people wanted Bono to save the world, but this tour is much more demanding, they want him to save the American recording industry."

Barbara Skydel: executive vice president, Premier Talent Agency, on her first meeting with U2 in 1980.

"We went out to dinner that night in Pete's Tavern near Greenwich Village. At one point I had to leave and Bono and Larry jumped up and said, 'Oh, we'll find you a taxi'—they didn't want me to walk out alone. We went out and they were running down the street. We ran for about a block and they hailed a taxi for me and they said, 'Do you remember the restaurant we came out of, do you know how to get back?' They had actually forgotten and they wouldn't have known where to go..."

Frank Barselona: president of Premier Talent, the world's biggest rock agency, on the first show he ever booked for U2 in America.

"The group comes in and I see them for the first time. And the only applause is from 100 people—the rest of the audience is either hostile or silent. And I go, 'Oh my God, I've made a major blunder.' But the group starts and there's no panic in their demeanor—as far as they're concerned those 2,200 people were their audience. And after that first number there's the stalwart 100 people and the rest do either nothing or boo.

"It was the most incredible way to have seen U2 for the first time, because it wasn't a pre-sold audience, it was an audience that was hostile, that they had to win and turn around. It was the most incredible thing, because with every song a little bit more of the audience would start listening and getting involved. So as the show developed you would see this wave from that 100 all the way back. About 60 or 70 percent of the audience were now listening, because once they got about 70 percent then they were loud enough and everyone else said, 'Oh, hold it, what are we missing?' Then they got everybody, and from that point on it was a triumph—I think they got three or four encores, they probably could have done more, but they probably didn't have any. It was just so exciting, I was choked."

Fachtna O'Ceallaigh: a reporter on Dublin's *Evening Press* when he began a music management career with Clannad, and later discovering the Boomtown Rats. He helped out Bananarama before becoming general manager of Mother Records. He was fired when he described U2's role in Mother as "precious and meddling." He went on to manage Sinead O'Connor, and now manages the West London raga crew Dread Broadcasting Federation.

"Like almost all pop stars, Bono—Plastique Oh No!—carefully picks and chooses his 'issues.' He has, for example, shamelessly turned a blind eye for years to the continuing existence of British-controlled and -funded death squads murdering his fellow countrymen and women. And when he has spoken about the war in Ireland, he has invariably mouthed the words of the oppressor against the oppressed. Like many others, he appears ashamed to be Irish. Musically he is the lard-arsed, pompous godfather of constipated white rock. I would recommend a strong laxative and early retirement."

Charlie Rafferty: former singer with The Real Wild West, now manages infamous Soho drinker The Coach and Horses, Jeffrey Barnard's local.

"I was at one of their earliest gigs in St. Brigid's hall in Finglas and they were supported by the Virgin Prunes. I remember Adam, Larry, and The Edge were the backing band for the Prunes. But by the time I met Bono he was a post-punk Cliff Richard. It was during the whole Mother debacle. We had this two-hour meeting with him in the Factory. He promised the sun, the moon, and the stars. He made me feel spiritually enriched. He kept saying, 'I'll see if I can get this done and that done.' And I stopped him and said, 'Hang on a minute, you own the fucking company.'"

Anton Corbijn: photographer and man often credited as U2's "image-maker" for work on their videos and record sleeves.

"If it wasn't for that famous quote, 'Elvis is alive and he's bleedin' Irish,' the notion of Bono the singer would nearly have gone past me. No disrespect, it's just that he means so much more to me.

"This fellow Taurus has been in front of my camera more than anyone else, either in a Trabant, behind a cactus, or in a dress, and he still argues. How brilliant!

"Always analyzing and constructively criticizing my work, he helped me grow in many ways—and I am not just talking about bank accounts.

"In my pidgin English, Bono means good egg. He is my big brother and I love him."

Eamon McCann: prime mover and student agitator in the Northern Ireland civil rights movement. Co-founded the People's Democracy Party with Bernadette Devlin. Rock columnist McCann and Terry O'Neill once wrote a film script for U2. He MC'd the recent four-day San Francisco Festival of Celtic Arts and Music because they mistook him for B.P. Fallon.

"I can genuinely say from the first time I met him he was a star. He was a great performer but one of the few who learned his trade as he went along. He obviously studied how to be a rock 'n' roll star. I remember after the book (*The Unforgettable Fire*) and *The Joshua Tree*, and all that palaver, I was sitting in a pub in Dublin with him and people were taking no notice of him. The kids in the street used to laugh at him. Instead of being awestruck, they'd just laugh and jeer, 'Jaysus, it's Bono.' And he handled all that well. He's very likeable, even if some of his opinions and ideas are a bit wild.

"He couldn't sing well, he couldn't hold notes, but he sang as if he was singing brilliantly. In the early days, in the Gaiety Green Centre, he was the Eddie the Eagle of rock 'n' roll—but unlike Eddie, Bono got better."

Dave Fanning: DJ who gave U2 their first radio exposure while he and producer Ian Wilson were working on Dublin pirate stations. When Wilson and Fanning were later recruited for national radio's 2FM pop station, Fanning invited U2 to air their debut single and ask listeners to nominate the A- and B-sides. He is still a close friend.

"I was in Bono's house a year ago and he showed me the gazebo down the end of the garden and said, 'I'm painting down there.' And I said, 'What color?' God, I really blew that.

"He is very committed, very sincere, and very honest. Many people lost U2 when they went looking for their musical roots, but I thought that was great. Anyone who can appear on the cover of *Vogue* and keep their rock cred intact must be good. He used to waffle a lot, but he was a quotable person.

"I loved the growing up in public. Things they did like waving the white flags were embarrassing. Now he's less eager. Bono has mellowed and matured, so a lot of that stuff about him is redundant now. When they did that last show in The Point on New Year's Eve in 1989/90 he said they were going to go away and dream it all up again—and they did it."

Gavin Friday: Island artist, former Virgin Prunes frontman and Bono's best friend.

"He lived at the other end of the road, Number 10 Cedarwood Road. I lived in the cul-de-sac; there was an almost subliminal divide in the road—Protestants at one end and Catholics at the other. Bono was an interesting diversion because his mother was a Protestant and his da's a Catholic.

"I was shy and retiring apart from my clothes. I was into Marc Bolan and had an earring and I used to walk up the road past Bono and his gang, with Marc Bolan and Bowie albums under my arm. He approached me one day; he was wearing white jeans and a T-shirt and platforms. He had suddenly decided I was an interesting person to talk to. I was immediately suspicious. I was right, he just wanted to borrow my records. I got them all back with jam on them and lyric sheets missing.

"Bono had an old reel-to-reel and couldn't afford cassettes, so he borrowed records and recorded them on this reel-to-reel that belonged to his father. We all had a lot in common. We hated football. We hated sitting around the green drinking cider. So we all hung out together in Lypton Village, our gang, sitting around in each other's living rooms. We all painted and fantasized and plotted about becoming famous and changing the world. We gave each other names: Bono was called Bono Vox of O'Connell Street after the hearing aid shop down there; and I was called Gavin, because of my square-shaped head and Wavin pips, and Friday because I was able to get on with anyone.

"Bono is totally misunderstood. I find it hard to talk about him because we're like brothers. I know by the smell of him what mood he's in. He's probably one of the funniest guys I know. He's a fucking lunatic. He's all those things and those characters in Zoo TV, and they make sense to me.

"He's a performer, an entertainer, an artist. We formed bands at 15. We're not normal."

Jackie Hayden: of *Hot Press.* He was marketing manager with CBS (Ireland), which co-hosted a talent contest with the *Evening Press* in Limerick. U2 won, and first prize was a chance to record a single. Jackie numbered the first 10,000 limited editions by hand.

"There are two Bonos I know. Bono One is the marketing/media-created saint with all the problems of the world on his shoulders and some of the answers in his heart. The other Bono knows that Bono One is not to be taken too seriously and is normal enough to steal your drinks at any time necessity or poverty or the true rock 'n' roll spirit demands it."

Bill Graham: writer and veteran rock journalist, one of U2's early champions who introduced them to their manager Paul McGuinness. Graham wrote the text for 1989's *U2, The Early Days: Another Time, Another Place.*

"When I went to Ethiopia five or six years ago, Concern (*Irish Third World charity*) said, 'We can take care of you when you get there, but you'll have to find the cost of the flight yourself. At the time it was something like £800, so we started asking around to see if anyone would sponsor the trip. We went to Principle Management and two days before the flight I had a long chat with Bono and he said, 'Go ahead.' When I got back I met Paul McGuinness and he said, 'Where did you get the tan?' And I said, 'Ethiopia, of course.' But he knew nothing about it, and it was then that I realized Bono had just paid for the ticket out of his own pocket.

"People who know him better always felt he was a funnier, more humorous person than has been portrayed. People who know him will know his instinctiveness and attentiveness and hyper alertness. The whole nature of U2 not using stage shows before means it exaggerated the emotive personality of the character at the front. The Zoo TV technology helps him because it allows him to show other aspects of his character."

Phillip King: singer, producer, and director of *Bringing It All Back Home* and *Rocky World*, a documentary on Daniel Lanois.

"The first time I met him we (Scullion) were recording 'White Side of Night' in Windmill Lane ('80/'81) and Larry and Bono came into the Green Room with a copy of the new video, and they showed it to us and we had a perfunctory conversation. Years later I worked with him when we were making *Bringing It All Back Home.* I've always found Bono very engaging and interested in finding out things. It's a testament to the man that he's always inquisitive and interested. And if he has a lack of knowledge on a subject he won't be arrogant and pretend he knows about it. He'll call somebody and ask them.

"But they do move on. Three years after *Bringing It All Back Home* we were standing on a bridge in Montreal doing an interview and he's talking about making industrial rock music with Daniel Lanois in a freezing studio in Berlin. His inquisitiveness is the key, it's what keeps him going. There is great drive and tremendous energy in Bono."

The Edge: on Bono in *Musician*, March 1992.

"Maybe over our career our ability to create music that shows the full range of the personalities of Bono and the other members of the band was very poor—but that's the truth. That guy is totally different to the way most people think of him. He's far funnier, takes himself far less seriously than most people think. He's wild, you know, he's not reserved, none of the clichés that spring to mind when you think of people's perception of him."

Keith Walker: of Power of Dreams.

"Our album had just come out and people were asking us about 'I Don't Want to Go to Texas,' which was about them seeking their roots in America with B.B. King. So on the night of our first gig in the SFX (in Dublin), Bono sent us a bunch of flowers, a big chocolate cake, Smarties, a B.B. King record, and some condoms. He thought it was really cool to do things like that, God help him. We sent him back a Dinosaur Jr. album and some of our own condoms. I think he's Mr. Cool now, he's really happening with his shades and all."

Dave Pennefather: general manager, MCA Ireland and Mother Records.

"A few years ago when I had just started with MCA, the Damned came to play in the Top Hat in Dun Laoghaire. It was really stuffed and the lads from the band spotted Bono at a table in the corner. So they said they'd really like to say hello to him and could I set that up? I said I'd give it a go, and I went across and introduced myself and explained why I was there. He listened patiently and then he said, 'No.' I nearly died. I was faced with going back to the Damned and telling them what had happened. Then Bono said, 'I'll go over to their table and say hello. If they're visitors in my town then I should go up and say hello to them.' It doesn't sum the man up by any means, but it was a lovely attitude."

Chris Blackwell: music director of Island Records.

"The first time I saw U2 was at a small club in South London: it must have been of their earliest shows in Britain. I thought they were absolutely great. Everything seemed to be right: the singer brilliantly held the audience, the guitarist had a real streak of originality, and the rhythm section kept the whole show together. I guess it's easy to say in retrospect that U2 were destined to become one of the world's greatest bands but, that evening, you had a real sense of their future."

Niall Shortall: U2 sound engineer in the early days who was dropped by the band. Has since toured with many Irish bands, most recently the Saw Doctors. Runs a studio maintenance company.

"I hold no grudges against anyone in the band and I occasionally see them around. The book (Eamon Dunphy's *Unforgettable Fire*) was a real shock and what it said about me was completely untrue. We didn't part on bad terms—our working relationship just changed.

"Bono was extremely devoted to his band and his religion at the time. He was careful not to break his own rules regarding sex, drugs, and rock 'n' roll before marriage. We were typical roadies, devoted to sex, drugs, and rock 'n' roll. Adam began to lean our way until the band decided he should go theirs. I was a bit of a tearaway and I said the wrong things, but I don't regret it. If I'd been as devoted to them as they were to themselves I might be with them still."

Hugo McGuinness: friend and band photographer in the early days. Photographed the cover of the band's debut album, *Boy*.

"The band were playing in Dandelion Market on a Saturday afternoon and the place was always under one foot of water. Suddenly the PA went 'bang' and everything fused. Then this guy walked in screaming and shouting at Eric, their roadie. He lifted up a cable from an amp, ran a lighter under it, stuck it in his mouth, and bit the cable, exposing the wires. He plugged those directly into the amp and everything worked again. 'Who was that?' I said to Bono. 'That's Paul and he's our manager,' says Bono. 'Now you know why every band should have one.'

"I remember they were always playing jokes on each other. One night we were in the Yacht, a bar in Sutton (North Dublin suburb) and everyone was talking about this really important showcase that was coming up. The problem was Bono had been called for jury duty. Someone told him the only way he could get out of it was if he had a criminal record or he said he was homosexual. Bono was in a dilemma for days."

Neil Storey: publicist and former head of Island Records' press. Remembers Bono as one of the only major artists with whom he has never developed an enduring friendship.

"I don't think Bono's any different from you or me, apart from the fact that he fronts a rock 'n' roll band. The real guy is warm, loving, caring, sharing, and one of the funniest guys I've ever met. He's a great mimic and a master of the one-liner and a great host. There's a very private side to him and that's when you discover the warmth and the caring, sharing human being.

"They knew what they wanted from day one although the trappings were never that important. When *October* came out it went straight to Number One and I drew the short straw to present them with the gold discs. They were playing in the Lyceum supported by the Bunnymen, as far as I can remember, and I went down to present these things. But Bono was more interested in getting something to eat with Ali, who had just arrived in town. And I have this memory of him disappearing down the Strand with Ali and leaving me holding the gold discs. For some bizarre reason Bono has always been portrayed as a really serious person. He's very serious about what he does, but he's always portrayed as this serious person. Like with the current thing they have going (Zoo TV), they have to explain that it's a joke. It's either not a very good joke or something has been lost. It is inconceivable you should have to explain a parody to anyone."

Shane O'Neill: lead singer with the Blue Angels and former lead singer with Blue in Heaven.

"The Edge heard a tape of ours and he was impressed enough to offer us a support slot in Galway. This would have been around 1982. Then he offered to produce a demo for us down in Windmill Lane. Bono came to one of these sessions and spent some time with The Edge discussing guitar sounds—we were in awe because they had names for individual guitar sounds. He told us our music was 'highway music.'

"Another thing about it all was just how much in control they were. There was always a feeling of 'drive' about them. We were really impressed that they took time out from such a heavy schedule to spend it with us. We were just before the Mother thing started, which was kind of a pity, but the demo helped us get signed in London."

Simon Carmody: drinking partner and singer with the Golden Horde, former Mother signing.

"There's a thing that's overlooked about Bono—he's a good man to drink with. He'll drink you fucking dry. With Bono it's champers all the way.

"I'll never forget one night, there was myself, Bono, Cuddy, Bowyer, and Dolan, all the lads, and we were having a bit of a session. And I put my hand in my pocket to get a round in, when Bono grabbed my arm and he said, 'Put your money away, it's no good here.' And he pulled out £15 and slammed it on the bar, and he said, 'Right lads, we're not leaving here 'til that's gone.' And we didn't. We fell out of the place and it was early houses, the lot.

"And that's the kinda fella Bono is..."

Wayne Sheehy: former drummer with Cactus World News. More recently the drummer with Hinterland and the Sun Gods, and has just finished a tour of Japan with Ronnie Wood. Bono produced Cactus World News's *The Bridge* EP.

"We were in Windmill Lane II (St. Stephen's Green) and Bono had just got this really old green Humber. He was producing *The Bridge* EP for us, and every time we got a mix done we all piled in the car and drove round and around the Green listening to a cassette. At one stage the police followed us, but we waved and they must have recognized him.

"On one of the tracks, we were just sort of jamming—it was 'Frontiers'—and Bono got into Hiawatha mode and stripped down to his keks and wrapped himself in loo paper. He stood at the desk and finished the mix that way."

Jimmy Iovine: long-time U2 collaborator, produced *Under a Blood Red Sky* and parts of *Rattle and Hum*.

"In my old neighborhood, the jazz guys used to have a tag for something that was true and original. It was 'The Shit.' This was the ultimate tribute in Brooklyn, where we were bred to presume that most people were the opposite of The Shit, and that was Full of Shit. Bono is The Shit. After years spent working with such artists as John Lennon, Patti Smith, and

Bruce Springsteen, I have learned one important thing: the pain required to make a truly great record is almost unbearable because the journey sometimes leads to some very dark places. Most people are only willing to make that journey once or twice before they start taking shortcuts through Malibu. But Bono, Larry, Adam, and Edge don't seem to be intimidated by the darkness. As a matter of fact, they often seem to take a perverse enjoyment in it. Bono, in particular, seemed to be having the most fun when I was on the verge of suicide. And out of that willingness to not only be at risk, but also find humor in it, comes some of the most amazing and death-defying tightrope walking I have ever seen."

U2

The Joshua Tree

Bruce Hornsby
***Playboy*, August 1987**

Without question, Bruce Hornsby (with his band, the Range) is rock's rookie of the year—he's got the Best New Artist Grammy to prove it. Currently working on his second LP, he commented on another group making serious music—U2. Here's Bruce's word on *The Joshua Tree*."

"I've liked U2 ever since I saw the band in 1983. On *The Unforgettable Fire*, U2 started expanding, with more variety in sound and production.

The Joshua Tree continues in that direction, from the beautiful church-organ opening—a lot of U2 songs have a certain spiritual quality—to the use of harmonica, acoustic guitar, percussion, and, on "One Tree Hill," even strings. The folk influences seem a bit more pronounced on "Running to Stand Still."

"U2 retains its intensity, especially in Bono's vocals and The Edge's rhythmic guitar playing. Bono's range of vocal nuance and emotion on "With or Without You" just could make it my favorite song—I know it's the hit, but it really is the one that gets me the most. The lyrics are evocative and express a lot of feelings. I also love "I Still Haven't Found What I'm Looking For." These guys do a lot of things that other pop musicians can learn from."

U2

The Ground Beneath My Feet

Salman Rushdie
***The Nation*, July 9, 2001**

In the summer of 1986, I was traveling in Nicaragua, working on the book of reportage that was published six months later as *The Jaguar Smile*. It was the seventh anniversary of the Sandinista revolution, and the war against the U.S.-backed contra forces was intensifying almost daily. I was accompanied by my interpreter, Margarita, an improbably glamorous and high-spirited blonde with more than a passing resemblance to Jayne Mansfield. Our days were filled with evidence of hardship and struggle: the scarcity of produce in the markets of Managua, the bomb crater on a country road where a school bus had been blown up by a contra mine. One morning, however, Margarita seemed unusually excited. "Bono's coming!" she cried, bright-eyed as any fan, and then added, without any change in vocal inflection or dulling of ocular glitter, "Tell me: who is Bono?"

In a way, the question was as vivid a demonstration of her country's beleaguered isolation as anything I heard or saw in the frontline villages, the destitute Atlantic Coast bayous, or the quake-ravaged city streets. In July 1986, the release of U2's monster album *The Joshua Tree* was still eight months away, but they were already, after all, the masters of *War*. Who was Bono? He was the fellow who sang, "I can't believe the news today, I can't close my eyes and make it go away." And Nicaragua was one of the places where the news had become unbelievable, and you couldn't shut your eyes to it, and so of course he was there.

I didn't meet Bono in Nicaragua, but he did read *The Jaguar Smile*. Five years later, when I was involved in some difficulties of my own, my friend the composer Michael Berkeley asked if I wanted to go to a U2 *Achtung Baby* gig, with its hanging psychedelic Trabants. In those days it was hard for me to go most places, but I said yes and was touched by the enthusiasm with which the request was greeted by U2's people. And so there I was at Earl's Court, standing in the shadows, listening.

Backstage, after the show, I was shown into a mobile home full of sandwiches and children. There were no groupies at U2 gigs; just crèches. Bono came in and was instantly festooned with daughters. My memory of that first chat is that I wanted to talk about music and he was keen to talk politics—Nicaragua, an upcoming protest against unsafe nuclear waste disposal at Sellafield in northern England, his support for me and my work. We didn't spend long together, but we both enjoyed it. Bono was less taken with Michael Berkeley, however. Years afterward he told me he'd felt condescended to by the classical composer. My own view is that there was a misunderstanding—Michael isn't a condescending man, but a high culture/low culture rift had opened, and that was that.

Two years later, when the giant *Zooropa* tour arrived at Wembley Stadium, Bono called to ask if I'd like to come out on stage. U2 wanted to make a gesture of solidarity, and this was the biggest one they could think of. When I told my then-14-year-old son about the plan, he said, "Just don't sing, Dad. If you sing, I'll have to kill myself." There was no question of my being allowed to sing—U2 aren't stupid people—but I did go out there and feel, for a moment, what it's like to have 80,000 fans cheering you on. The audience at the average book reading is a little smaller. Girls tend not to climb onto their boyfriends' shoulders during them, and stage-diving is discouraged. Even at the very best book readings, there are only one or two supermodels dancing by the mixing desk. Anton Corbijn took a photograph that day for which he persuaded Bono and me to exchange glasses. There I am looking godlike in Bono's wraparound Fly shades, while he peers benignly over my uncool literary specs. There could be no more graphic expression of the difference between our two worlds.

It was inevitable that both U2 and I would be criticized in Britain in bringing these two worlds together. They have been accused of trying to acquire some borrowed intellectual "cred," and I of course am supposedly star-struck. None of this matters very much. I've been crossing frontiers all my life—physical, social, intellectual, artistic borderlines—and I spotted, in Bono and Edge, whom I've come to know better than the others so far, an equal hunger for the new, for whatever nourishes. I think, too, that the band's involvement in religion—as inescapable a subject in Ireland as it is in India—gave us, when we first met, a subject and an enemy (fanaticism) in common.

An association with U2 is good for one's anecdote stock. Some of these anecdotes are risibly apocryphal: A couple of years ago, for example, a front-page Irish press report confidently announced that I had been living in "the folly"—the guest house with a spectacular view of Killiney Bay that stands in the garden of Bono's Dublin home—for four whole years! Apparently I arrived and departed at dead of night in a helicopter that landed on the beach below the house. Other stories that sound apocryphal are unfortunately true. It is true, for example, that I once danced—or, to be precise, pogoed—with Van Morrison in Bono's living room. It is also true that in the small hours of the following morning I was treated to the rough end of the great man's tongue. (Van Morrison has been known to get a little grumpy toward the end of a long evening. It's possible that my pogoing wasn't up to his exacting standards.)

Over the years U2 and I discussed collaborating on various projects. Bono mentioned an idea he had for a stage musical, but my imagination failed to spark. There was another long Dublin night (a bottle of Jameson's was involved) during which the film director Neil Jordan, Bono, and I conspired to make a film of my novel *Haroun and the Sea of Stories*. To my great regret this never came to anything either.

Then, in 1999, I published my novel *The Ground Beneath Her Feet*, in which the Orpheus myth winds through a story set in the world of rock music. Orpheus is the defining myth for singers and writers—for the Greeks, he was the greatest singer as well as the greatest poet—and it was my Orphic tale that finally made possible the collaboration we'd been kicking around.

It happened, like many good things, without being planned. I sent Bono and U2's manager, Paul McGuinness, pre-publication copies of the novel in typescript, hoping they would tell me if the thing worked or not. Bono said afterward that he had been very worried on my behalf, believing that I had taken on an impossible task, and that he began reading the book in the spirit of a "policeman"—that is, to save me from my mistakes. Fortunately, the novel passed the test. Deep inside it is the lyric of what Bono called the novel's "title track," a sad elegy written by the novel's main male character about the woman he loved, who has been swallowed up in an earthquake: a contemporary Orpheus' lament for his lost Eurydice.

Bono called me. "I've written this melody for your words, and I think it might be one of the best things I've done." I was astonished. One of the novel's principal images is that of the permeable frontier between the world of the imagination and the one we inhabit, and here was an imaginary song crossing that frontier. I went to McGuinness's place near Dublin to hear it. Bono took me away from everyone else and played the demo CD to me in his car. Only when he was sure that I liked it—and I liked it right away—did we go back indoors and play it for the assembled company.

There wasn't much after that that one would properly call "collaboration." There was a long afternoon when Daniel Lanois, who was producing the song, brought his guitar and sat down with me to work out the lyrical structure. And there was the Day of the Lost Words, when I was called urgently by a woman from Principle Management, which looks after U2. "They're in the studio and they can't find the lyrics. Could you fax them over?" Otherwise, silence, until the song was ready.

I wasn't expecting it to happen, but I'm proud of it. It's called "The Ground Beneath Her Feet." For U2, too, it was a departure. They haven't often used anyone's lyrics but their own, and they don't usually start with the lyrics; typically, the words come at the very end. But somehow it all worked out. I suggested facetiously that they might consider renaming the band U2+1, or, even better, Me2, but I think they'd heard all those gags before.

There was a long al fresco lunch in Killiney at which the film director Wim Wenders startlingly announced that artists must no longer use irony. Plain speaking, he argued, was necessary now: communication should be direct, and anything that might create confusion should be eschewed. Irony, in the rock world, has acquired a special meaning. The multimedia self-consciousness of U2's *Achtung Baby-Zooropa* phase, which simultaneously embraced and debunked the mythology and gobbledygook of rock stardom, capitalism, and power, and of which Bono's white-faced, gold-lame-suited, red-velvet-horned MacPhisto incarnation was the emblem, is what Wenders was criticizing. Characteristically, U2 responded by taking this approach even further, pushing it further than it would bear, in the less-well-received PopMart tour. After that, it seems, they took Wenders's advice. The new album, and the Elevation tour, is the spare, impressive result.

There was a lot riding on this album, this tour. If things hadn't gone well it might have been the end of U2. They certainly discussed that possibility, and the album was much delayed as they agonized over it. Extracurricular activities, mainly Bono's, also slowed them down, but since these included getting David Trimble and John Hume to shake hands on a public stage and reducing Jesse Helms—Jesse Helms!— to tears, winning his support for the campaign against Third World debt, it's hard to argue that these were self-indulgent irrelevances. At any event, *All That You Can't Leave Behind* turned out to be a strong album, a renewal of creative force and, as Bono put it, there's a lot of good will flowing toward the band right now.

I've seen them three times this year: in the "secret" pre-tour gig in London's little Astoria Theatre and then twice in America, in San Diego and Anaheim. They've come down out of the giant stadiums to play arena-sized venues that seem tiny after the gigantism of their recent past. The act has been stripped bare; essentially, it's just the four of them out there, playing their instruments and singing their songs. For a person of my age, who remembers when rock music was always like this, the show feels simultaneously nostalgic and innovative. In the age of choreographed, instrumentless little-boy and little-girl bands (yes, I know the Supremes didn't play guitars, but they were the Supremes!) it's exhilarating to watch a great, grown-up quartet do the fine, simple things so well. Direct communication, as Wim Wenders said. It works.

And they're playing my song.

U2 Q & A

Billy Corgan
***Live!* magazine, May 1997**

I guess I was destined to meet U2 the moment I heard their song "New Year's Day." It was 1983, I was 16, and it was unlike anything I'd ever heard: fierce, political, passionate, sexy. They quickly became the most important band in the world to me. Since then, I have followed their every move with fascination, sometimes with clucking disdain, but always ascribing revelations to their rock 'n' roll choices. I assigned to them the weight of not only saving the world but saving music as well, because they understood the spot where the heart, the soul, and the political man all crisscrossed into a fireball. The ever-enigmatic Bono only fed my curiosity to meet them, so when I was offered the chance to interview them, it seemed a natural. In a way, I knew them and they me.

I would first speak with the band via video teleconference. In my best robe, I called up some of my idols. They chatted easily and responded openly to my questions. At one point, a man appeared in my hotel room with two bottles of Guinness stout, compliments of Bono, The Edge, Adam, and Larry. Cute. Then a pizza arrived. Then a belly dancer, who introduced herself as a dancer with "mysterious ways." Then the bagpipes arrived. They were initiating me.

Fast forward a couple of weeks. I fly to Dublin to interview Bono in person. In my 24 hours there, we do not sleep. We watch the sunrise, listening to U2's new album, *Pop*. We talk and talk and talk, and what I perceive at first to be pretension is easily replaced by astute integrity and insatiable curiosity. My preconceptions, built from years of flag waving, melt away until it is just one man who stands for so much.

When I first heard *Pop*, it sounded like a greatest-hits album—every era of U2 represented and spit back out in one giant remix. I thought they were crazy. Where was the next step beyond *Zooropa*? But as I dug deeper and scratched beneath the glamour of pop writing, out came the voice I recognized so well. You know it, you've heard it...the U2 thing, like heaven.

Billy Corgan: Once again, you surprised me with the new record. I was expecting a technological leap forward, but it's more of a classic-song record. Every time I think I know what you're gonna do, you do the opposite, so I shouldn't be surprised. What was the thinking going into making* Pop*?

Bono: As usual, we talk an awful lot for the first nine months. The last three months are a flurry of activity when we're trying to write the songs and record them. We kind of knew what we wanted to do: write some great songs, but have it sound like something we've never done before, and we wanted to incorporate a lot of interesting music we'd been listening to. As we got into it, we discovered some of those ideas just were not gonna work, and we were heading down the road of creating an album that was hopelessly diverse. What we managed to do was turn that weakness into kind of a strength. We were surprised when we finally put the record together that it hung together at all for a start. When you finish a song, like "Wake up Dead Man," and then you consider something like "Mofo"—I mean, we were really biting our nails for a while about how the whole thing hung together.

Well, I think in its diversity it does come together as a whole. It's like listening to your record collection.

Bono: Yeah, it does seem that there shouldn't be any one tribe anymore to rock 'n' roll. As I've been telling people, in my house I'm listening to the Sex Pistols next to Chic next to the Beastie Boys next to the Smashing Pumpkins next to opera, and all in the same hour. We're just trying to distill all the influences. It's being true to what you hear. I think I was sort of fed up with the rock stance as well. We thought, let's take all the references that we didn't grow up with, like KC & the Sunshine Band or Donna Summer. Just allow all these pop references.

What kind of pressure do you feel to top yourself when you make a record?

Bono: Not wanting to top yourself is part of it, for sure, as well as wanting to. In a way, I think it would be the end of our group if we didn't make a record we believed in. We've broken our band up so many times internally. When we started working with Brian Eno early on, in a way we had to break up and start over. We did it again with

Achtung Baby. We had to shoot U2 in the head before anyone else did. It's just about asking some very simple questions: Why do you want to be in a band, and what do you want to do with it? Are our four interests served? Because there's no other reason at this point for us to make a record. It gets down to corny old words like self-respect.

Larry: Self-respect...and PolyGram.

Bono: That's true. There's always the record deal.

Adam: I think there is a process of recommitment for each record, though. I think when we do get back together there is that initial month or two of dreaming up the kind of record you want to make. Then the history of the band comes into play, and you get fired up and inspired. You kind of follow your lead singer into the sunset.

Bono: When we're making the records, it always feels a bit like we're drowning, and you do wonder if there's an easier way. But we seem to need some chaos to bring us together.

I've always paid close attention to what you've said in public and how people perceived you. When you first started, there was a kind of save-the-world feel about the underlying messages. How do you feel now about your relationship to the world on a social level?

Bono: I don't think anything has changed for us, but we have caught onto a few things, which is that you can make it very easy for your cartoonists if you're not careful. What happens, and I think it's quite sad, is that in some political and social respects, rock 'n' roll is being gagged because of some opportunists. At a certain point, it looks like you are marketing idealism. People started to imagine we were doing this because it was good for an image. We decided if people think that, we should walk away from it. So we did our very best, and enjoyed it I might add, to completely f—k that up, because we believe the spirit of the band and the music are what's important, not the clothes. There was a kind of righteousness that was thrust upon us, and that is dangerous for a band. But we're talking about images here. The reality of where we stand has not changed.

There was a point where people started accusing me of, in essence, using my anger and childhood pain as a marketing ploy. I know what you're talking about, because it comes from such an earnest place, but when you cast it out into the world, it gets knocked around, and what comes back to you is often something very, very different.

> *Bono*: The crucial point is, how do you work in the very commercial world of making and selling records? I think commercialism can affect you two ways. One, your opposition to it can actually take all your energy. I think that happened to some of the bands that came up around your time. I remember an interview with Kurt Cobain. He said early on, "We're never playing arenas; we're a punk band and we play clubs." The interviewer said, "But you're playing arenas now," and Kurt had the nerve and the balls to say, "I changed my mind." I think it can take up a lot of your energy. The other one is, if you just embrace that whole commercial world, then I think it takes you over. So you have to find a balance. You seem to have done very well in that regard.

Well, I think we decided along the way that it was about people and it was about music, and at some point, selling records and being a successful band is the best avenue for people to hear your music. When we start out, all we want is for people to hear the music. It seems disingenuous to decide who shall and who shall not listen to your music. I remember being 16 years old in suburban America and hearing one of your songs on the radio. It was so different from anything I ever heard. If "Sunday Bloody Sunday" wasn't on the radio, I wouldn't have known about you. There was no other avenue. It's different today because you have MTV, so the access is greater, but it strikes me that there's always gonna be that kid. People don't sit around and wonder who's on the charts. Sometimes it has to be directly in front of their face for them to say, 'Wow, this is really poignant.' As far as I'm concerned, I want everybody to listen. I don't care how old they are or where they come from.

> *Bono*: But it's also fun, I think, watching your favorite band try to stay up on the board. I do think it's a spectator sport. They're watching you, how you deal with it, and the momentum is something you can have fun with.

Okay, so tell me about the tour.

Bono: The first thing we decided was that we were going to be true to the concept of the Zoo TV tour, which is that stadiums are the big prize, they're the big challenge, they're in a sense where rock 'n' roll—

Edge: Falls apart or comes together.

Adam: So we decided to put all our efforts into making those big venues into something we can be proud of—not go in halfheartedly and do a stripped-down little rock 'n' roll show on a small stage in a vast arena, but actually try to fill the stadium. Try and have it make sense.

Bono: [Arenas] can be the most awful places on earth, but they can be turned into a great scene with the right people and the right music. Also, we always thought our music didn't have a roof on its head anyway, and we enjoy playing outdoors. You can go to clubs and be 15 feet from the lead singer and feel a million miles away from him. It's not about physical proximity. Anyway, these are all our excuses for why we don't want to back down.

I don't think you have to justify. But I can tell you from my end it gets weird, because you reach a point where the inertia of the whole thing takes you to bigger venues and you really can't go back.

Bono: Yeah. The Rolling Stones were a great club act. Their music really suited the clubs. But we played the clubs years ago, and I'm not sure we were ever that good in them. I mean, we enjoyed them, but there is an extraordinary thing that can happen when you've got 50,000 people agreeing on one thing for a moment. 'Cause they're probably not gonna agree on a lot of things—and you wouldn't want them to. But for that moment...

Edge: Maybe that sounds corny, but I have had some of the most extraordinary moments in the last 10 years shared with people I don't know…this personal music put out on these huge PA systems. It's an odd thing.

I've found that the atmosphere of performing live is kind of dismal now. I don't know what it is, but I'd be curious to ask you a year from now what you feel, having gone up against that.

Bono: Well, we actually found ourselves on the Zoo TV tour very much out of step with what was happening. Maybe it's that we're coming out of Ireland, where we're on the fringe of Europe. We're the cousin of what's happening in the U.K., but we're also very aware of what's happening in America. So we're never really part of anything other than simply what we choose to be interested in at any one time. With Zoo TV, when we arrived in the States, the two movements that seemed to be in full flight were grunge and hip-hop. Zoo TV was so different and in some ways flying in the face of both those ideas. We were paddling our own canoe, and I think this time it's gonna be the same. I don't think there are very many other artists who are doing what we're doing with *Pop*. That's why some of the bands that are trying to break down those barriers are quite interesting to us. Like Beck. And like the Beastie Boys. Who would've thought when they released their first single all those years ago that they would at this point be kind of holding the flag for what you might call white and black ideas?

I don't think black music and white music are as foreign to the generation that's now getting into music, as they grow up with those things side by side. I think ultimately it will just melt together.

Bono: That'll be an amazing moment, when the music gets completely mixed up again.

There's one last area I want to touch on. As we become more of a technological society, the connections between people erode. What are your feelings about that future?

Bono: A friend of ours who we hadn't seen in many years came back to town for a wedding. He was in the corner the whole night, and we were trying to figure out why. He just said, "Look, I'm not used to dealing with people in their bodies." I realized that there are people who really are living in cyberspace, and you do kind of have mixed feelings about that. I would say one thing, though, and it's hard for me not to get into my whole theory here on technology and bore your arse off, but what I saw with hip-hop people was how 16- and 17-year-olds were getting in touch with the music from their ancestors through technology. That made me feel very positive about technology. Because they're using it with great joy and glee and often very quickly making records that are very true to where they've come from.

It takes the pretension out of music making.

Bono: [On the other hand,] as we approach a world where everything is more digitized, it makes the analog moments more special. In a way, that freedom of information, that ability to duplicate everything endlessly, ultimately devalues itself, and it's the human moments, the live performances that are gonna mean so much more.

I'm wondering if we're headed in the opposite direction. I'm wondering if we may reach a stage where the digital possibility creates a standard that we humans cannot live up to.

Bono: I think what's happening is that we're creating technologies that, really, we have no use for. Technologies are so far ahead of where we're at that in some ways they render themselves redundant before they're even in the marketplace. A great example of that is the CD-ROM, where you have on a single CD an endless number of mixes of one song. Well, the truth is, people don't want that. They want to hear the best you have to offer, and I don't think music has gotten that much better since the days of four-track recordings. So it's still the same. It's about ideas. It's about hearing in the most pure medium possible what the person who created the work intended. It's really about the song that you've written.

U2

U2 at Madison Square Garden

Moby
Official Moby website (www.moby.com), October 24, 2001

U2
10/24/2001, New York City

The I.R.A seems to have laid down their weapons. I'm not quite sure what the exact situation is, but I'm hopeful that this is an actual breakthrough and even a potential end to the horrifying violence of the struggle.

Good luck to the people of Northern Ireland. It would be amazing to see a peaceful resolution to the problems.

And in similar news, I went to see U2 again tonight. Boy, are they good in concert.

Wowee. They're just amazing. Melodic and powerful. I wish there were more musicians who:

a - Write great songs
b - Are nice people
c - Have a strong social conscience
d - Play all their hits in concert...

In a part of the U2 show they listed some of the people who were killed in the terrorist attacks (they couldn't list all 6,000, 'cos that would've taken hours).

Seeing the names of some of the people who were killed in the terrorist attacks made me sad but it also made me angry. The victims were individuals. Innocent individuals. The terrorists are wrong. It needs to be said a million times, the terrorists are wrong.

Killing innocent people is a profound wrong, and we can't forget that.

I know that sounds simple, but we can't forget that one basic fact: killing innocent people is wrong.

Ok, so the U2 show was great. "Sunday Bloody Sunday" had a particular and almost uncanny resonance given the terrorist attacks on the U.S. and Bono is a New Yorker (as well as an Irishman), so it seemed as if the show had special meaning for him.

And now it's 2 A.M. and that means it's time to go into my studio and try to get some work done.

Goodnight,

Moby

CHAPTER

12

THE BUSINESS OF U2

U2 own everything they do. They own the publishing; they own the masters. This largely has to do with their "fifth member," manager Paul McGuinness. In person, McGuinness looks like a former boxer. He has an incredibly quick wit and an even quicker protective instinct about "his boys."

His background in film and music, the position of power he had built over the past twenty-five years, along with this quickness has made McGuinness one of the most feared negotiators in pop music. Generally, what McGuinness wants, McGuinness gets. This helps keep U2 on top.

Paul McGuinness is a shrewd businessman. He knows that the royal road to wealth in any business involving intellectual property is to own that property and lease it out to the highest bidder. This savvy—being at the right place at the right time, and *creating the context* of the right time and place—has made McGuinness and the band members some of the wealthiest men on the planet.

Between McGuinness and the group, they have built up quite a little musical empire, with offices in Dublin and New York. Yet, McGuinness remains accessible. As the old song says, people are constantly calling him up for favors. And fortunately for the band, McGuinness more often than not has to say no. It is a combination that breeds a level of respect that few in the music business earn and enjoy.

McGuinness on the "Principle" of U2 Management

Thom Duffy
***Billboard*, November 16, 1991**

When U2's new album, *Achtung Baby*, arrives worldwide from Island Records Nov. 19, it will mark a new career milestone for a band that, since 1978, has risen from the pubs of Dublin to the stadiums of America.

One of the constants throughout U2's rise has been its management by Paul McGuinness, whose Dublin-based firm, Principle Management, has worked with no other client. As U2 has grown into one of the most popular bands in the world, Principle Management has grown apace. Ellen Darst heads McGuinness's New York office. Activities from marketing to merchandising have been handled in-house.

Days before the release of *Achtung Baby*, during a visit to New York, McGuinness spoke with *Billboard* about his role in bringing U2's art to the pop marketplace and his views on trends in the industry.

Billboard: How do you see your role?

> *McGuinness*: It's been changing all the time. I've been managing U2 for 14 years so we know each other pretty well. Really what makes the process fascinating for me is that they are such good artists and are still developing and progressing and challenging the art form in which they operate. It is an industry as well and the way in which the art integrates with a very complicated commercial business, that's my responsibility.

BB: This is the first U2 album since Island's sale to PolyGram.

> *PM*: In many ways, it makes it all simpler because, in the past, Island was licensed to a great variety of licensees around the world. Some of them are still in place. BMG distributes Island still in most European countries. But with only two major deals, with BMG and PolyGram, it's really a lot simpler...it is a different time for Island, that's true. As it happens, we had, in fact, become our own organization [at Principle Management]. An awful lot of the creative work, the design, the film production, and a lot of the marketing thrust came from us anyway over the years. The album package was entirely generated in Dublin.

BB: The cover art of* Achtung Baby *is a striking collection of images. How does the artwork help market the album?

PM: The retailing environment has changed enormously since the last time we were out. The implications of the smaller [album] packages are enormous. Going into one of the new mall-type stores in America...the opportunity for display has almost disappeared. So you really have to think very creatively about how to get visual imagery in front of people. One of the programs we're running at retail is to distribute these images as posters. Another thing I'm very interested in is the growth of free [weekly] newspapers in America. We're distributing a very large number of posters through those publications. Getting that imagery onto people's bedroom walls is what we're trying to do.

BB: Beyond plans for the album's launch, what future marketing strategies do you foresee?

PM: I have been talking to a lot of EPK people—in the electronic press kit business. I think that television is comparatively under-exploited by our business. The way in which the movie industry markets through television is very interesting. I'm just exploring ways in which we can learn from that.

BB: What contrast do you see between the music business and other fields of entertainment?

PM: Compared to other parts of the entertainment industry where art and commerce have to interact, the chances of getting your original creative intention onto a CD are excellent compared to the chances of getting a creative idea onto the screen in a movie or television. There is still something very pure about a record by comparison and I think that's a reason people are still fascinated by rock 'n' roll and the people who make it.

BB: Does the aggressive, industrial edge of this album reflect what's happening around U2 in rock today?

PM: I try to avoid interpreting them. I produce the opportunities for their art to enter the world but I don't interpret it...but this record is most unusual. It's not the dance album that we were rumored to be making, but this is 1991 and dance is a heavy influence on everyone's music, and rock 'n' roll is always a creature of the time in which it is made. It's a very simple record; the primary colors of rock 'n' roll. Virtually every instrument on the album was played by the four members of the band. In that respect, it's going to be a fascinating album to perform live.

BB: What are U2's tour plans?

PM: We're going to do something a little unusual with the tour, which will start in the U.S. in March with a tour of one-night stands, about 30 cities over seven or eight weeks. We'll do arenas but only play each city one night, partly to get to as many as we can [but also to] reintroduce the American public to the concept of the hard ticket, which has almost been forgotten. Perhaps we'll come back later in the year and play larger venues. I know the concert business is down, but frankly there hasn't been much very exciting or new talent touring over the last year.

BB: What is the extent of your current contract with Island?

PM: There are two more records after this one and I must say that the relationship with Island, and the new relationship with PolyGram, is excellent. I recently went around to all nine of the PolyGram branches [in the U.S.] with Rick Dobbis, Chris Blackwell, and Andy Allen from Island and presented the album and met people and I was very impressed.

BB: How do you view the recent publicity about superstar deals and the future of such deals?

PM: I think it's a lot of exaggeration. It's become a very macho thing—my deal's bigger than your deal. I don't think it's very dignified to have that kind of business done in public anyway...we are—U2 represented by me—in the rights-owning business. We own our songs, the recordings as well as the songs. In each case, they are licensed for a finite period of time...it's quite clear that, in the future, a number of different physical sound carriers will be augmented by different kinds of transmission [of music to consumers] and the way in which income arrives to rights owners will change.

BB: You are anticipating the day of digital delivery of music directly to consumers.

PM: I'm not looking forward to it because I'm in show business and I always try to remind people that the thing we sell is not the number of times the consumer dials up that track. The thing we sell is that moment on Saturday morning when that fan has to have that recording and walks into a store and walks out with it. The further we get away from that, the less opportunity there is for the magic and mystery and excitement of show business.

U2

Paul McGuinness: How the Fifth Man Turned Empire Builder

Paul Gorman
***Music Business International*, October 1997**

Suited and booted like an Irish country squire, Paul McGuinness strides through Prague's Strahov Stadium as if he owns the place. And for tonight at least he very nearly does.

It's August 14, 1997, date 31 on the yearlong PopMart world tour. Secreted around the vast stadium are the 450 [members of the] road crew, sound, and production staff and all manner of other functionaries required to put this show on the road. Out front are 60,000-plus Czech youths and up on stage U2 themselves are going through their paces with the aid of a 30-meter-high golden arch and four-meter stuffed olive.

At the pinnacle of this organization stands McGuinness, U2' s manager and mentor for the best part of two decades.

It has not been a happy 12 months for the 46-year-old. The band delivered their latest album too late to meet its anticipated pre-Christmas 1996 release date. It finally emerged to a lukewarm reaction. Then the tour—by any standards a record-breaker with the band scoring a $115m guarantee from a consortium of promoters—began badly, plagued by technical problems and bad publicity.

All that's forgotten tonight, however. McGuinness is in his element. His band is playing—and they have finally hit their stride.

That McGuinness is the fifth member of the act is indisputable. He receives credit as such on U2 releases, and as manager he also shares a fifth of the record royalties earned from the 76m or so albums they have sold in their career. After every show he sits in with the four members and studio wizard/DJ Howie B for a "debriefing" session where they discuss the night's set and ideas for future shows. It is obvious that their relationship extends beyond the boundaries that can exist between a band and a manager 10 years their senior. While Bono philosophizes about the psychology of performance, McGuinness chips in with anecdotes and advice.

McGuinness's indivisibility from his charges is not the only characteristic that marks him out among the upper echelon of rock managers. Since the mid-eighties he has placed himself and the band at the centre of a sprawling business empire. He handles the broad sweep of the band's affairs, while the nuts and bolts of such maneuvers as the business planning of the PopMart tour and 1993's contract renegotiation with Island—netting the band a 25-percent royalty rate and $10m advance per album—are largely handled by accountant Ossie Kilkenny.

They are a formidable team. For example, in 1986 when Island was in need of finance, they invested $5m in the label in exchange for a 10-percent stake in the company and reversion of their masters at the end of their contract. When PolyGram bought the label six years later, they were able to cash in that stake for $30m and receive an option to buy shares in the major [label] in the future at the same price as they were at the time of the takeover.

And they are undoubtedly wealthy—although quite how wealthy remains unclear. McGuinness declares, somewhat disingenuously, that he does not know how much he is worth. When in 1995 Irish magazine *Business & Finance* estimated the band's earnings at more than $300m, McGuinness ripped out the article, scribbled "bollocks" on it, and sent it back to the magazine.

At the operation's heart is Principle Management. U2 and McGuinness together also act as the nexus for a complicated series of business interests which extend from record labels to music publishing companies, a merchandising wing, tour and recording facilities, film studios, investment in *Riverdance*, and extensive property interests.

In business terms, U2 long since stopped being merely a rock band. These days it is almost a mini-conglomerate. But McGuinness says there is no grand scheme. "We improvise to a certain extent. The band have always been aware that we exist in a commercial world and, in order to maximize the creative possibilities of being a big rock band, you have to pay attention to the business," he says.

The ad hoc nature of their expansion could, in part, account for the less than startling headway made by some of these ventures. Mother Records, for example, was started as a "philanthropic" exercise in the mid-eighties, becoming a joint venture with PolyGram five years ago. Only now is it bearing fruit with U.K. acts Audioweb and the Longpigs. Meanwhile, merchandiser Ultra Violet was unveiled as a venture with Winterland, but this partnership swiftly disintegrated.

On the other hand, publisher McGuinness Whelan handles the copyrights for composer Bill Whelan, whose *Riverdance* show has been an international smash, while the spin-off album has sold 1m copies.

Whatever the success rate, such diversity has granted McGuinness and U2 an unusual degree of self-sufficiency. "The aim is to be sufficiently independent of the commercial process to do what you want creatively," McGuinness adds. "We have always been able to do that." Such independence has also allowed the manager and band to make some bold business moves and to shun convention when they see fit, be it with attacks on the social deductions imposed by European rights societies on live performance royalties, or their support of Island Records refusal to pay U.S. retailers "price and positioning" dollars for the current album.

This maverick spirit has informed the entire PopMart tour. Long before it kicked off in Las Vegas in April, McGuinness and Kilkenny were ruffling feathers by cutting out agents and demanding that potential promoters pitch for the tour. In the event the TNA consortium, fronted by Michael Cohl, won the contract with a package containing a $115m guarantee. The result was that U2 were almost guaranteed a profit before they had sold a single ticket.

"At the end of the day, Paul's job is to do the best for his band, in terms of maintaining stature and making money," says Cohl, who first encountered McGuinness in the early eighties. "That is the key to his success. He is very bright and knows what is good for U2."

That McGuinness and Kilkenny should formulate a business plan for PopMart whose ambition matches the sheer creative scale of the tour is not unusual in a relationship in which both sides appear to feed off each other. So how did a former film technician achieve such success?

Kilkenny, who first met McGuinness in 1978 when he was managing a Celtic rock combo called Spud, says his colleague's ability to see the big picture sets him apart. "Paul is a globalist," he says. "There is nobody in the European business who understands the U.S. industry better, for example. He also understands that it is the manager's job to deliver the band's artistic vision, and nobody does it better."

McGuinness himself credits his Irish roots as a major factor. Although born at a German military base while his father was serving in the British armed forces, he has lived in Ireland since the age of 10 and believes that this has helped open doors around the world. "One of the best things about being Irish is, because we're neither English nor American, nobody is intimidated by us," he says.

This emphasis on Irishness is one of the qualities that first struck Chas de Whalley, a former CBS A&R manager, when McGuinness walked into his office in London's Soho Square in 1979. "He came in one day with a variety of tapes ranging from an Irish milk marketing board TV jingle to a country rock singer-songwriter. All were too parochial. The last thing he played was a rough demo by a punk band he managed who he insisted I should come and see."

De Whalley did just that—and went on to record two singles with U2 for release by CBS in Ireland. The next year McGuinness sought a bigger deal that would enable the band to relocate to London, but no label would put up the necessary cash. The deal he ultimately struck with Island Records (including an advance well below £50,000) meant that the band had no choice but to remain in Dublin. In retrospect this proved to be a blessing in disguise—not least because in Ireland, songwriter and composer royalties are tax-free.

McGuinness himself claims that his metamorphosis from traditional rock 'n' roll manager into music business entrepreneur was in part provoked by his unwillingness to lose valued workmates. "I wanted to hold on to my staff," he says. "It's not good enough to say at the end of a particular U2 campaign, "I'll see you in nine months time and we'll do it again.'"

He admits feeling responsible for staff members such as Keryn Kaplin, who runs Principle's New York office, and her Dublin counterpart Sheila

Roche, and proudly points out that their predecessors Ellen Darst and Anne Louise Kelly only left Principle to concentrate on their personal lives rather than join other companies.

In tandem with this nurturing of a core team has been the construction of an impressive global network of relationships that span labels, the media, promoters, and many others. "People we knew at one record company have often reappeared at another one," says McGuinness, citing Columbia Records group senior VP [of] A&R Tim Devine, who he first met 17 years ago when Devine was U2's first product manager at Warner in the U.S. Now Devine is working on signing Principle Management client Sinead O'Connor.

McGuinness can also claim a hand in the foundation of the red-hot Interscope label, after he pointed entrepreneur Ted Field in the direction of former U2 producer Jimmy Iovine. And his relationship with Universal Music Group chairman and CEO Doug Morris stretches back to the time of U2's U.S. distribution deal through Atlantic. Years later this friendship bore fruit when Morris entered Atlantic into a joint venture with McGuinness to form roots label Celtic Heartbeat. This joint venture has now followed Morris to Universal.

"Paul is a very smart, intelligent, and hard working guy," says Morris. "I have always found him to be very honorable and I'm really delighted that we're getting the chance to work together again."

Such networking has in turn built considerable expertise within the 25-strong Principle Management organization, which operates offices in London and New York, not least because McGuinness has always insisted on a hands-on approach to every market, unwilling to leave the tasks of marketing, promotion, and sales to the record company alone. "Through the eighties and into the nineties we as an organization had to go into markets and find out how they operated with the intention of making U2's records succeed," he says, pointing out that even after PolyGram's acquisition of Island there were outstanding licenses with Festival in Australia, BMG in most of Europe, Sonet in Scandinavia, and Ricordi in Italy.

Island U.S. executive VP Hooman Majd says this accumulation of knowledge has become an important weapon in McGuinness's arsenal. "He knows his markets and is probably the most hardworking and professional manager I have come across," he says. "The thing about Paul is he's not a quitter—he's very driven, committed and passionate."

Kilkenny says this is a factor which has served the act well. "For a band in their mid-thirties they are the only surviving act of the seventies and the only relevant act from the eighties," he says. "How is it that they are able to continue attracting 16-and 17-year-old fans? Because Paul has developed an environment in which they flourish."

McGuinness makes a point about the majors being "supposedly homogeneous." The 47-year-old makes no bones about his disappointment with *Pop's* undistinguished performance in the States, laying the blame squarely with Island U.S.

With 6m sales worldwide since release in the early spring, *Pop* is fast approaching the 7m sales of experimental predecessor *Zooropa* but is dwarfed by the more mainstream albums whose success it was supposed to replicate, particularly *The Joshua Tree* (15m units). Indeed, at the end of last year McGuinness told MBI that any U2 album that does not sell 10m units is "disappointing."

Five months after *Pop's* release, McGuinness stresses it is performing well in Europe—with the exception of Germany—and Japan. But, he says, "The U.S. is a disappointment. We made the assumption that (recent single) "Staring at the Sun" was going to be a Top 40 hit but it wasn't. U.S. radio is so research-driven at the moment, but the research response hoped for by Island's promotional people did not occur until about 16 weeks in. Unfortunately they took their foot off the pedal at around 13 weeks and lost the opportunity to cross over."

Island's Majd disputes this charge. "It would be foolish to say there isn't disappointment with *Pop's* sales levels," he says. "But I deny vehemently that this has been due to Island. "Staring at the Sun" got as much exposure as possible, including incredible coverage on MTV, but it failed to strike a chord. Over time I believe that the album will grow, particularly when the band returns to the U.S. this autumn and the next single comes out."

Some might say that Island's strategy of refusing to follow the now traditional practice of paying for "price and position" at retail may have backfired, but McGuinness blames a more basic factor—the health of a U.S. label which has undergone top-level management changes. "The U.S. company was stronger a couple of years ago," he says. "Record companies go through cycles and I'm sure Island will be hot again but it certainly isn't at the moment."

Another problem, blame for which lies this time squarely with the band, was the delay in *Pop's* delivery, originally scheduled for last autumn. "This is a creative process and it just took longer than expected," says McGuinness. "By preparing an autumn release, the plan was to have two or three singles out and known before we started performing.

"It was too much of a rush in the spring and has taken a little while to recover. I and the band would have preferred to have more time, but we take responsibility for that. We're grown-ups."

When PopMart ends next spring, McGuinness promises to take time off before planning a strategic foray into his first love: the film business—a move which could be allied to reports that he and Kilkenny are preparing another franchise bid for an Irish television channel.

"We would like to become more involved in the financing, development, and production of films," confirms McGuinness, who originally started his professional career as assistant to film director John Boorman. "There's an unstoppable trend towards more movie production in Europe, and the economic climate has improved dramatically."

He already has the wherewithal, including a major interest in the Ardmore Film Studios shared with Kilkenny, as well as an impressive range of contacts built by U2 soundtrack work on such films as *Batman Forever, Mission Impossible*, and *Goldeneye*.

For now McGuinness has to take care of the more immediate business of ensuring that both *Pop* and PopMart match previous U2 endeavors. A re-recording of the album track "Please" will be the next single, and McGuinness is putting his faith in a Howie B production "which gives us a shot at crossing over into the Top 40 in the U.S." The sound which has evolved via Howie B's live mixing on tour also raises the prospect of a live album, though of more immediate concern is the potential sales boost offered by a television special planned around the November 14 show in Miami. The aim is to involve a combination of broadcasters—MTV, Showtime, and PBS have all been mentioned.

McGuinness has strong views on the relationship between television and the music business, particularly when it comes to advertising campaigns. "Most artists' contracts describe TV marketing as exceptional and unusual," he notes. "If a record company decides to go on TV they don't have to get the artist's permission, but can pay for half the cost out of the artist's royalty. We're having this discussion with PolyGram, who take a hard line on applying the contract. Something's got to give."

This crusading attitude is never far from the surface with McGuinness and U2. "We're not particularly looking for fights," he protests. "But if you're not proactive, if you just sit in the office and wait for the record company to seek the path of least resistance, then I think you have a less successful career and a less interesting business."

As rights societies, U.S. retailers, film companies, Island/PolyGram executives, and tour promoters can attest, Paul McGuinness never chooses to "just sit in his office." This modus operandi looks set to continue as his interests spread and he considers a fully-fledged entry into the movie business.

But whatever the coming months hold there is one certainty: on many nights until spring 1998, McGuinness will assume a prime position in front of a stage in a stadium somewhere in the world and, for two-and-a-half hours, forget his grand schemes as he marvels at the sensory assault concocted by his four closest business partners.

Paul McGuinness

1951: Born June 16 in Germany.

1969: Studies at Trinity College, Dublin.

1973: Drops out to work on director John Boorman's *Zardoz* at Ardmore Film Studios.

1978: Starts to manage U2.

1979: CBS Ireland releases first two U2 singles.

1980: Island Records signs U2. *Boy* sells 2.5m.

1982: Establishes Principle Management.

1983: Launches McGuinness Whelan Publishing, *War* sells 7m, *Under a Blood Red Sky* [sells] 7.5m.

1984: Launches Mother label, *Unforgettable Fire* sells 6.5m.

1985: *Wide Awake in America* sells 2m.

1987: *The Joshua Tree* sells 15m, Acquires Texas-based Upfront Staging.

1988: *Rattle and Hum* movie falters. Album sells 9.5m.

1989: McGuinness and Ossie Kilkenny launch London video post-production house and acquire Ardmore Film Studios with Irish Development Agency.

1991: *Achtung Baby* sells 10m.

1992: Band embarks on ambitious Zoo TV tour.

1993: *Zooropa* sells 7m, Launches campaign against European rights societies.

1994: Launches merchandising joint venture Ultra Violet, Invests in *Riverdance*.

1995: Launches Celtic Heartbeat with Atlantic Records.

1996: Promoters pitch for 100-date U2 tour, *Pop* delayed, Bono and Edge open Clarence Hotel in Dublin.

1997: *Pop* released—sales currently at 6m. PopMart tour is a record-breaker

PopMart: The Tour overcomes initial hitches to reap record returns

U2's refusal to involve corporate sponsorship in their gargantuan world tours was but one of a number of knotty problems facing McGuinness and his team when they came to draw up plans for the 100-date PopMart excursion.

Not only does the tour involve the logistical nightmare of taking 250 people, 16 buses, and 75 articulated trucks (not to mention the world's largest LED screen, a 100-foot-tall golden arch, and a 12-foot stuffed olive complete with a 100-foot cocktail stick) around the world, but the manager, the band, and accountant Ossie Kilkenny were also unwilling to go the traditional route and use booking agents as middlemen.

"Under previous working arrangements the show was a separate transaction and we weren't really sure of our profit until we got to the end of the tour," says McGuinness. "We were simply not prepared to do that again. "This time we sought bids based on the paradigm of 100 dates with

5m tickets sold at an average price of $45. We got five very competitive bids including some from the major talent agencies who clearly see this is the only way tours like this can be funded. An enterprise of this size cannot be underwritten by the performer, which is the tradition."

The process provoked complaints from within some quarters of the live industry—complaints McGuinness dismisses as "lot of moaning and whining." Michael Cohl's TNA consortium was ultimately chosen: "We believed they knew the business better than the other candidates and were able to make a more competitive bid financially," says McGuinness.

The deal is based around a guarantee to the band of $115m to cover costs and take them to the first stage of profit. Although McGuinness declines to comment in detail, it is understood that U2 received an advance in the region of $15m and are also paid a substantial fee per date. Once 4m tickets have been sold, TNA is set to recoup and profits are to be shared. Under normal circumstances the promoter would be expected to receive 10 percent of profits.

PopMart is currently on target to achieve the minimum 4m sales, with 3m-plus under its belt before the return to the U.S. and then on to Asia and Australia. This summer Performance magazine reported PopMart as the biggest grossing tour of 1997, with a take of nearly $56m from just 29 shows.

Although the tour cancelled some U.S. dates due to poor advance ticket sales—such as a second show at Philadelphia's Franklin Field June 7—it has still grossed more than the Zoo TV tour, which boasted U.S. receipts of $67m. Overall PopMart is expected to bring in around $400m.

This has not stopped the flow of negative stories, particularly in the U.K. press. "A lot of what was written was completely untrue," claims McGuinness. "In the U.S. we were at least able to point to the real figures, which are a matter of public record." he adds.

The bad press also centered on ticket prices which ranged from $37.50 to $52.50 in the U.S. and $35 to $55 in Europe, but McGuinness points out that, since there is a theoretical worldwide average of $45, ticket prices fall as low as $20 in emerging markets such as eastern Europe and South America.

The Business Network

The impetus behind U2, their manager and their accountant investing in a range of ancillary businesses came in the form of the Republic of Ireland taxman, according to Paul McGuinness.

"We found ourselves paying a lot of tax instead of supporting new business, " he recalls." I would be reluctant to call it a strategy but it is more fun to develop new things than give the money to the government."

There have been many new things in many different spheres over the years. Not all are run or owned along the same lines, and they form a complex business empire—McGuinness alone is listed as having 19 company directorships. Not surprisingly, perhaps, given the involvement of so shrewd an accountant as Ossie Kilkenny, the value of most of these crisscrossing operations is hard to ascertain from the accounts lodged in Ireland's Companies House.

Management: the establishment of McGuinness's core business, Principle Management, dates back to 1982. Today the company employs 20 people in Dublin and five at the New York offices of Principle, Inc. The roster now extends to PJ Harvey, new singer Laszlo Bane, and Sinead O'Connor.

Publishing: in 1983 McGuinness launched publisher McGuinness Whelan with composer Bill Whelan. This reaped its reward in 1994, when Barbara Galavan—who handles U2's publishing affairs through the Mother Music company they set up in the late eighties—picked up on *Riverdance*, an Irish folk dance piece Whelan had written as intermission music for the Eurovision Song Contest.

Subsequently released as a single on U2's fledgling indie label, Son, it spent 20 weeks at the top of the Irish charts and reached number 11 in the U.K. Whelan then developed it into a full musical, backed by McGuinness and Irish broadcaster RTE, which broke U.K. and U.S. box office records.

Record labels: McGuinness and company operates two labels. Mother Records was set up in 1984 to release one-off singles by breaking Irish acts. In 1993 the label became a joint venture with PolyGram and relocated to London. Early signings, including singer Lena Fiagbe and veteran poet/rapper Gil Scott Heron, stiffed, although young alternative acts Audioweb and the Longpigs are now making some noise. More successful projects have included the disco soundtrack to indie movie *Priscilla Queen of the Desert* and last year's *Mission: Impossible* (2.5m units sold).

Celtic Heartbeat was launched as an Irish roots music label by McGuinness, Galavan, and Clannad's manager Dave Kavanagh in a joint venture with Atlantic Records U.S. in 1995. The label's 12 releases have so far sold 2m units worldwide, with *Riverdance* accounting for more than half. McGuinness says that the switch of partners from Atlantic to Universal will herald a burst of new releases this autumn.

Facilities: in 1987 when *The Joshua Tree* tour was traveling the U.S., McGuinness and U2 bought Texas-based staging company Upfront. This continues to supply steel frameworks for U2 and other acts with giant stage shows.

Media: at the end of the eighties, McGuinness and accountant Ossie Kilkenny launched an Irish TV franchise bid, which was unsuccessful but necessitated, with the Irish Development Agency, the acquisition of Ardmore film studios. These have subsequently benefited from government tax breaks and housed a number of high-profile movie projects.

McGuinness and Kilkenny also own digital video post-production house The Mill in London, recently merged with film director Ridley Scott's FX co, the owner of Shepperton Studios, and advertising company RSA.

Merchandising: in 1994 the manager and U2 launched Ultra Violet, a merchandising company run as a joint venture with Winterland. When Winterland withdrew last year, it was renamed Deluxe, licensing T-shirts and other products in Europe to PolyGram's merchandising division.

Accountancy: Ossie Kilkenny has been involved with McGuinness since 1978. Though he is not involved in every aspect of U2's business—he acts as U2's accountant but not Principle's—he is almost as central to the operation as the manager. OJ Kilkenny's clients also include Oasis, Van Morrison, Bryan Adams, Chris de Burgh, Bjork, Morrissey, and Sinead O'Connor. In addition to his stake in Planet Hollywood in London, Kilkenny is also understood to have a 50-percent share of the Dublin branch of the theme restaurant.

Property: McGuinness and Kilkenny have operated extensive property interests through a number of companies including Leisure Corp, which was set up to develop leisure centers in Ireland and has also opened six in Germany. They also owned Dublin's Galleria Centre, sold in 1995.

U2

Iovine Learns U2's All About El-E-Va-Tion to a New Demographic

Wayne Friedman
***Advertising Age*, March 25, 2002**

U2 has been one band looking for elevation.

The band, around since the'80s, wanted to attract a new audience—a 12-to-18-year-old audience—for its latest release, *All That You Can't Leave Behind* and build sales from that demographic to make the album a hit.

Enter Jimmy Iovine, chairman of Interscope Records and producer of earlier U2 albums. Mr. Iovine had one clear idea how to achieve the goal: make believe U2 was a new band—with absolutely no history.

"It was one of the rare times that you could actually feel a marketing plan in the record business," Mr. Iovine says.

U2 and Interscope had to do it differently—specifically, have a long-term plan—vs. the quick hits of other musical releases. "We realized that this was an 18-month plan," says Steve Berman, Interscope's senior executive of marketing and sales. "The key was how Jimmy set the tone for marketing."

That tone included a number of high-profile TV performances—including halftime at last month's Super Bowl, the National Basketball Association All-Star Game, "The Tonight Show with Jay Leno" and "Late Show with David Letterman."

Perhaps the key was Viacom's MTV. Not only would there be videos—four different ones—but U2 would do special appearances, such as a rooftop concert, a la the Beatles, during MTV's "Total Request Live."

Mr. Iovine "had a lot do with the band trying to shed their credibility fears," says Paul Kremen, head of brand marketing for Interscope. "It is harder to take a band that's been around as long as U2 and make them relevant to 12-to-18-year-olds."

To target teens further, U2 also got involved with another Viacom unit, Paramount Pictures, by including the band's third single, "Elevation," in the soundtrack of the summer 2001 movie *Tomb Raider.*

All efforts helped U2 sell a sizable 4 million records in the U.S. and 11 million worldwide. The band released four singles with the new album—"Beautiful Day," "Elevation," "Stuck in a Moment You Can't Get Out Of" and "Walk On." Last month it won four Grammys as well.

U2 Grammy Awards

2001 – 44th Annual Grammy Awards

Record of the Year .... *Walk On*

Best Pop Performance
by a Duo or Group with Vocal .... *Stuck in a Moment You Can't Get Out Of*

Best Rock Performance by a
Duo or Group with Vocal .... *Elevation*

Best Rock Album.. *All That You Can't Leave Behind*

2000 – 43rd Annual Grammy Awards

Record of the Year .... *Beautiful Day*

Song of the Year .... *Beautiful Day*

Best Rock Performance by a
Duo or Group with Vocal .... *Beautiful Day*

1994 – 37th Annual Grammy Awards

Best Music Video, Long Form .... *Zoo TV- Live from Sydney*

1993 – 36th Annual Grammy Awards

Best Alternative Music Album .... *Zooropa*

1992 – 35th Annual Grammy Awards

Best Rock Performance
by a Duo or Group with Vocal .... *Achtung Baby*

1988 – 31st Annual Grammy Awards

Best Performance Music Video .... *Where the Streets Have No Name*

Best Rock Performance by a
Duo or Group with Vocal .... *Desire*

1987 – 30th Annual Grammy Awards

Album of the Year... *The Joshua Tree*

Best Rock Performance by a
Duo or Group with Vocal .... *The Joshua Tree*

Index

DEMCO